OXFORD TEXTS IN APPLIED AND ENGINEERING MATHEMATICS

OXFORD TEXTS IN APPLIED AND ENGINEERING MATHEMATICS

Titles marked with an asterisk (*) appeared in the Oxford Applied Mathematics and Computing Science Series, which has been folded into, and is continued by, the current series.

ion to Parallel Computing

W. P. Petersen

Seminar for Applied Mathematics
Department of Mathematics, ETHZ, Zurich
wpp@math.ethz.ch

P. Arbenz

Institute for Scientific Computing
Department Informatik, ETHZ, Zurich
arbenz@inf.ethz.ch

OXFORD
UNIVERSITY PRESS

OXFORD
UNIVERSITY PRESS

Great Clarendon Street, Oxford OX2 6DP

Oxford University Press is a department of the University of Oxford.
It furthers the University's objective of excellence in research, scholarship,
and education by publishing worldwide in

Oxford New York

Auckland Bangkok Buenos Aires Cape Town Chennai
Dar es Salaam Delhi Hong Kong Istanbul Karachi Kolkata
Kuala Lumpur Madrid Melbourne Mexico City Mumbai Nairobi
São Paulo Shanghai Taipei Tokyo Toronto

Oxford is a registered trade mark of Oxford University Press
in the UK and in certain other countries

Published in the United States
by Oxford University Press Inc., New York

© Oxford University Press 2004

The moral rights of the author have been asserted
Database right Oxford University Press (maker)

First published 2004

A catalogue record for this title is available from the British Library

Library of Congress Cataloging in Publication Data

(Data available)

ISBN 0 19 851576 6 (hbk)
0 19 851577 4 (pbk)

10 9 8 7 6 5 4 3 2 1

Typeset by Newgen Imaging Systems (P) Ltd., Chennai, India
Printed in Great Britain
on acid-free paper by
Biddles Ltd. www.biddles.co.uk

PREFACE

The contents of this book are a distillation of many projects which have subsequently become the material for a course on parallel computing given for several years at the Swiss Federal Institute of Technology in Zürich. Students in this course have typically been in their third or fourth year, or graduate students, and have come from computer science, physics, mathematics, chemistry, and programs for computational science and engineering. Student contributions, whether large or small, critical or encouraging, have helped crystallize our thinking in a quickly changing area. It is, alas, a subject which overlaps with all scientific and engineering disciplines. Hence, the problem is not a paucity of material but rather the distillation of an overflowing cornucopia. One of the students' most often voiced complaints has been organizational and of information overload. It is thus the point of this book to attempt some organization within a quickly changing interdisciplinary topic. In all cases, we will focus our energies on floating point calculations for science and engineering applications.

Our own thinking has evolved as well: A quarter of a century of experience in supercomputing has been sobering. One source of amusement as well as amazement to us has been that the power of 1980s supercomputers has been brought in abundance to PCs and Macs. Who would have guessed that vector processing computers can now be easily hauled about in students' backpacks? Furthermore, the early 1990s dismissive sobriquets about *dinosaurs* lead us to chuckle that the most elegant of creatures, birds, are those ancients' successors. Just as those early 1990s contemptuous dismissals of magnetic storage media must now be held up to the fact that 2 GB disk drives are now 1 in. in diameter and mounted in PC-cards. Thus, we have to proceed with what exists now and hope that these ideas will have some relevance tomorrow.

For the past three years, the tip-top of the famous *Top 500* supercomputers [142] has been the Yokohama *Earth Simulator*. This project's success is no secret at all: combining a well-designed network with very powerful vector processor nodes, the NEC and climate modeling scientists knew what they were doing. Here are some basic facts why this formula works.

1. Modern computer architectures run internal clocks with cycles less than a nanosecond. This defines the time scale of floating point calculations.
2. For a processor to get a datum within a *node*, which sees a coherent memory image but on a different processor's memory, typically requires a delay of order 1 μs. Note that this is 1000 or more clock cycles.
3. For a *node* to get a datum which is on a different *node* by using message passing takes more than 100 or more μs.

Thus we have the following not particularly profound observations: if the data are local to a processor, they may be used very quickly; if the data are on a tightly coupled *node* of processors, there should be roughly a thousand or more data items to amortize the delay of fetching them from other processors' memories; and finally, if the data must be fetched from other nodes, there should be a 100 times more than that if we expect to write-off the delay in getting them. So it is that NEC and Cray have moved toward strong nodes, with even stronger processors on these nodes. They have to expect that programs will have blocked or segmented data structures. As we will clearly see, getting data from memory to the CPU is the problem of high speed computing, not only for NEC and Cray machines, but even more so for the modern machines with hierarchical memory. It is almost as if floating point operations take insignificant time, while data access is everything. This is hard to swallow: The classical books go on in depth about how to minimize floating point operations, but a floating point operation (*flop*) count is only an indirect measure of an algorithm's efficiency. A lower flop count only approximately reflects that fewer data are accessed. Therefore, the best algorithms are those which encourage data locality. One cannot expect a summation of elements in an array to be efficient when each element is on a separate node.

This is why we have organized the book in the following manner. Basically, we start from the lowest level and work up.

1. Chapter 1 contains a discussion of memory and data dependencies. When one result is written into a memory location subsequently used/modified by an independent process, who updates what and when becomes a matter of considerable importance.
2. Chapter 2 provides some theoretical background for the applications and examples used in the remainder of the book.
3. Chapter 3 discusses instruction level parallelism, particularly vectorization. Processor architecture is important here, so the discussion is often close to the hardware. We take close looks at the Intel Pentium III, Pentium 4, and Apple/Motorola G-4 chips.
4. Chapter 4 concerns shared memory parallelism. This mode assumes that data are local to nodes or at least part of a coherent memory image shared by processors. OpenMP will be the model for handling this paradigm.
5. Chapter 5 is at the next higher level and considers message passing. Our model will be the message passing interface, MPI, and variants and tools built on this system.

Finally, a very important decision was made to use explicit examples to show how all these pieces work. We feel that one learns by examples and by proceeding from the specific to the general. Our choices of examples are mostly basic and familiar: linear algebra (direct solvers for dense matrices, iterative solvers for large sparse matrices), Fast Fourier Transform, and Monte Carlo simulations. We hope, however, that some less familiar topics we have included will be edifying. For example, how does one do large problems, or high dimensional ones? It is also not enough to show program snippets. How does one compile these things? How does one specify how many processors are to be used? Where are the libraries? Here, again, we rely on examples.

W. P. Petersen and P. Arbenz

ACKNOWLEDGMENTS

Our debt to our students, assistants, system administrators, and colleagues is awesome. Former assistants have made significant contributions and include Oscar Chinellato, Dr Roman Geus, and Dr Andrea Scascighini—particularly for their contributions to the exercises. The help of our system gurus cannot be over-stated. George Sigut (our Beowulf machine), Bruno Loepfe (our Cray cluster), and Tonko Racic (our HP9000 cluster) have been cheerful, encouraging, and at every turn extremely competent. Other contributors who have read parts of an always changing manuscript and who tried to keep us on track have been Prof. Michael Mascagni and Dr Michael Vollmer. Intel Corporation's Dr Vollmer did so much to provide technical material, examples, advice, as well as trying hard to keep us out of trouble by reading portions of an evolving text, that a "thank you" hardly seems enough. Other helpful contributors were Adrian Burri, Mario Rütti, Dr Olivier Byrde of Cray Research and ETH, and Dr Bruce Greer of Intel. Despite their valiant efforts, doubtless errors still remain for which only the authors are to blame. We are also sincerely thankful for the support and encouragement of Professors Walter Gander, Gaston Gonnet, Martin Gutknecht, Rolf Jeltsch, and Christoph Schwab. Having colleagues like them helps make many things worthwhile. Finally, we would like to thank Alison Jones, Kate Pullen, Anita Petrie, and the staff of Oxford University Press for their patience and hard work.

CONTENTS

LIST OF FIGURES

LIST OF TABLES

1

BASIC ISSUES

No physical quantity can continue to change exponentially forever.
Your job is delaying forever.

G. E. Moore (2003)

1.1 Memory

Since first proposed by Gordon Moore (an Intel founder) in 1965, his *law* [107] that the number of transistors on microprocessors doubles roughly every one to two years has proven remarkably astute. Its corollary, that central processing unit (CPU) performance would also double every two years or so has also remained prescient. Figure 1.1 shows Intel microprocessor data on the number of transistors beginning with the 4004 in 1972. Figure 1.2 indicates that when one includes multi-processor machines and algorithmic development, computer performance is actually better than Moore's 2-year performance doubling time estimate. Alas, however, in recent years there has developed a disagreeable mismatch between CPU and memory performance: CPUs now outperform memory systems by orders of magnitude according to some reckoning [71]. This is not completely accurate, of course: it is mostly a matter of cost. In the 1980s and 1990s, Cray Research Y-MP series machines had well balanced CPU to memory performance. Likewise, NEC (Nippon Electric Corp.), using CMOS (see glossary, Appendix F) and direct memory access, has well balanced CPU/Memory performance. ECL (see glossary, Appendix F) and CMOS static random access memory (SRAM) systems were and remain expensive and like their CPU counterparts have to be carefully kept cool. Worse, because they have to be cooled, close packing is difficult and such systems tend to have small storage per volume. Almost any personal computer (PC) these days has a much larger memory than supercomputer memory systems of the 1980s or early 1990s. In consequence, nearly all memory systems these days are hierarchical, frequently with multiple levels of cache. Figure 1.3 shows the diverging trends between CPUs and memory performance. Dynamic random access memory (DRAM) in some variety has become standard for bulk memory. There are many projects and ideas about how to close this performance gap, for example, the IRAM [78] and RDRAM projects [85]. We are confident that this disparity between CPU and memory access performance will eventually be tightened, but in the meantime, we must deal with the world as it is. Anyone who has recently purchased memory for a PC knows how inexpensive

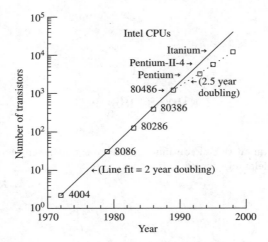

FIG. 1.1. *Intel microprocessor transistor populations since 1972.*

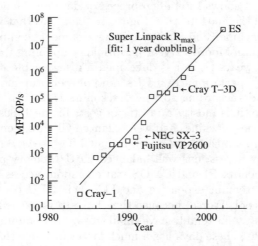

FIG. 1.2. *Linpack benchmark optimal performance tests. Only some of the fastest machines are indicated: Cray-1 (1984) had 1 CPU; Fujitsu VP2600 (1990) had 1 CPU; NEC SX-3 (1991) had 4 CPUS; Cray T-3D (1996) had 2148 DEC α processors; and the last, ES (2002), is the Yokohama NEC Earth Simulator with 5120 vector processors. These data were gleaned from various years of the famous dense linear equations benchmark [37].*

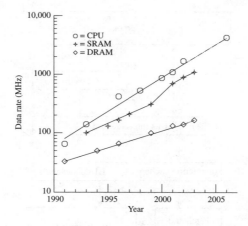

FIG. 1.3. *Memory versus CPU performance: Samsung data [85]. Dynamic RAM (DRAM) is commonly used for bulk memory, while static RAM (SRAM) is more common for caches. Line extensions beyond 2003 for CPU performance are via Moore's law.*

DRAM has become and how large it permits one to expand their system. Economics in part drives this gap juggernaut and diverting it will likely not occur suddenly. However, it is interesting that the cost of microprocessor fabrication has also grown exponentially in recent years, with some evidence of manufacturing costs also doubling in roughly 2 years [52] (and related articles referenced therein). Hence, it seems our first task in programming high performance computers is to understand memory access. Computer architectural design almost always assumes a basic principle—that of **locality of reference**. Here it is:

> **The safest assumption about the next data to be used is that they are the same or nearby the last used.**

Most benchmark studies have shown that 90 percent of the computing time is spent in about 10 percent of the code. Whereas the locality assumption is usually accurate regarding instructions, it is less reliable for other data. Nevertheless, it is hard to imagine another strategy which could be easily implemented. Hence, most machines use **cache** memory hierarchies whose underlying assumption is that of data locality. Non-local memory access, in particular, in cases of non-unit but fixed stride, are often handled with pre-fetch strategies—both in hardware and software. In Figure 1.4, we show a more/less generic machine with two levels of cache. As one moves up in cache levels, the larger the cache becomes, the higher the level of associativity (see Table 1.1 and Figure 1.5), and the lower the cache access bandwidth. Additional levels are possible and often used, for example, L3 cache in Table 1.1.

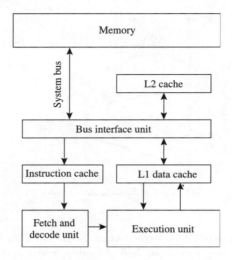

FIG. 1.4. *Generic machine with cache memory.*

Table 1.1 *Cache structures for Intel Pentium III, 4, and Motorola G-4.*

Pentium III memory access data			
Channel:	M ↔ L2	L2 ↔ L1	L1 ↔ Reg.
Width	64-bit	64-bit	64-bit
Size	256 kB (L2)	8 kB (L1)	8·16 B (SIMD)
Clocking	133 MHz	275 MHz	550 MHz
Bandwidth	1.06 GB/s	2.2 GB/s	4.4 GB/s
Pentium 4 memory access data			
Channel:	M ↔ L2	L2 ↔ L1	L1 ↔ Reg.
Width	64-bit	256-bit	256-bit
Size	256 kB (L2)	8 kB (L1)	8·16 B (SIMD)
Clocking	533 MHz	3.06 GHz	3.06 GHz
Bandwidth	4.3 GB/s	98 GB/s	98 GB/s

Power Mac G-4 memory access data				
Channel:	M ↔ L3	L3 ↔ L2	L2 ↔ L1	L1 ↔ Reg.
Width	64-bit	256-bit	256-bit	128-bit
Size	2 MB	256 kB	32 kB	32·16 B (SIMD)
Clocking	250 MHz	1.25 GHz	1.25 GHz	1.25 GHz
Bandwidth	2 GB/s	40 GB/s	40 GB/s	20.0 GB/s

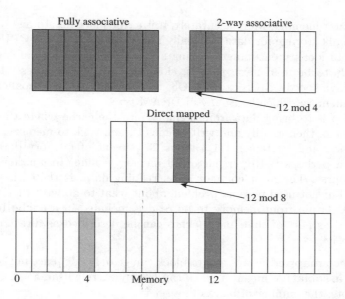

FIG. 1.5. *Caches and associativity. These very simplified examples have caches with 8 blocks: a fully associative (same as 8-way set associative in this case), a 2-way set associative cache with 4 sets, and a direct mapped cache (same as 1-way associative in this 8 block example). Note that block 4 in memory also maps to the same sets in each indicated cache design having 8 blocks.*

1.2 Memory systems

In Figure 3.4 depicting the Cray SV-1 architecture, one can see that it is possible for the CPU to have a direct interface to the memory. This is also true for other supercomputers, for example, the NEC SX-4,5,6 series, Fujitsu AP3000, and others. The advantage to this direct interface is that memory access is closer in performance to the CPU. In effect, all the memory is cache. The downside is that memory becomes expensive and because of cooling requirements, is necessarily further away. Early Cray machines had twisted pair cable interconnects, all of the same physical length. Light speed propagation delay is almost exactly 1 ns in 30 cm, so a 1 ft waveguide forces a delay of order one clock cycle, assuming a 1.0 GHz clock. Obviously, the further away the data are from the CPU, the longer it takes to get. Caches, then, tend to be very close to the CPU—on-chip, if possible. Table 1.1 indicates some cache sizes and access times for three machines we will be discussing in the SIMD Chapter 3.

1.2.1 *Cache designs*

So what is a cache, how does it work, and what should we know to intelligently program? According to a French or English dictionary, it is a safe place to hide things. This is perhaps not an adequate description of cache with regard to a computer memory. More accurately, it is a safe place for storage that is close by. Since bulk storage for data is usually relatively far from the CPU, the principle of data locality encourages having a fast data access for data being used, hence likely to be used next, that is, close by and quickly accessible. Caches, then, are high speed CMOS or BiCMOS memory but of much smaller size than the main memory, which is usually of DRAM type.

The idea is to bring data from memory into the cache where the CPU can work on them, then modify and write some of them back to memory. According to Hennessey and Patterson [71], about 25 percent of memory data traffic is writes, and perhaps 9–10 percent of all memory traffic. Instructions are only read, of course. The most common case, reading data, is the easiest. Namely, data read but not used pose no problem about what to do with them—they are ignored. A datum from memory to be read is included in a **cacheline** (block) and fetched as part of that line. Caches can be described as direct mapped or set associative:

- **Direct mapped** means a data block can go only one place in the cache.
- **Set associative** means a block can be anywhere within a set. If there are m sets, the number of blocks in a set is

$$n = (\text{cache size in blocks})/m,$$

and the cache is called an $n-$way set associative cache. In Figure 1.5 are three types namely, an 8-way or fully associative, a 2-way, and a direct mapped.

In effect, a direct mapped cache is set associative with each set consisting of only one block. Fully associative means the data block can go anywhere in the cache. A 4-way set associative cache is partitioned into sets each with 4 blocks; an 8-way cache has 8 cachelines (blocks) in each set and so on. The set where the cacheline is to be placed is computed by

$$(\text{block address}) \ \mathbf{mod} \ (m = \text{no. of sets in cache}).$$

The machines we examine in this book have both 4-way set associative and 8-way set associative caches. Typically, the higher the level of cache, the larger the number of sets. This follows because higher level caches are usually much larger than lower level ones and search mechanisms for finding blocks within a set tend to be complicated and expensive. Thus, there are practical limits on the size of a set. Hence, the larger the cache, the more sets are used. However, the block sizes may also change. The largest possible block size is called a **page** and is typically 4 kilobytes (kb). In our examination of SIMD programming on cache memory architectures (Chapter 3), we will be concerned with block sizes of 16 bytes, that is, 4 single precision floating point words. Data read from cache into vector registers (SSE or Altivec) must be aligned on cacheline boundaries. Otherwise, the data will be mis-aligned and mis-read: see Figure 3.19. Figure 1.5

shows an extreme simplification of the kinds of caches: a cache block (number 12) is mapped into a fully associative; a 4-way associative; or a direct mapped cache [71]. This simplified illustration has a cache with 8 blocks, whereas a real 8 kB, 4-way cache will have sets with 2 kB, each containing 128 16-byte blocks (cachelines).

Now we ask: where does the desired cache block actually go within the set? Two choices are common:

1. The block is placed in the set in a **random** location. Usually, the random location is selected by a hardware pseudo-random number generator. This location depends only on the initial state before placement is requested, hence the location is deterministic in the sense it will be reproducible. Reproducibility is necessary for debugging purposes.
2. The block is placed in the set according to a **least recently used** (LRU) algorithm. Namely, the block location in the set is picked which has not been used for the longest time. The algorithm for determining the least recently used location can be heuristic.

The machines we discuss in this book use an approximate LRU algorithm which is more consistent with the principle of data locality. A **cache miss rate** is the fraction of data requested in a given code which are not in cache and must be fetched from either higher levels of cache or from bulk memory. Typically it takes $c_M = O(100)$ cycles to get one datum from memory, but only $c_H = O(1)$ cycles to fetch it from low level cache, so the penalty for a cache miss is high and a few percent miss rate is not inconsequential.

To locate a datum in memory, an address format is partitioned into two parts (Figure 1.6):

- A block address which specifies which block of data in memory contains the desired datum, this is itself divided into two parts,
  - a **tag** field which is used to determine whether the request is a hit or a miss,
  - a **index** field selects the set possibly containing the datum.
- An offset which tells where the datum is relative to the beginning of the block.

Only the tag field is used to determine whether the desired datum is in cache or not. Many locations in memory can be mapped into the same cache block, so in order to determine whether a particular datum is in the block, the tag portion

Block address		Block offset
Tag	Index	

FIG. 1.6. *Data address in set associative cache memory.*

of the block is checked. There is little point in checking any other field since the index field was already determined before the check is made, and the offset will be unnecessary unless there is a hit, in which case the whole block containing the datum is available. If there is a hit, the datum may be obtained immediately from the beginning of the block using this offset.

1.2.1.1 *Writes*

Writing data into memory from cache is the principal problem, even though it occurs only roughly one-fourth as often as reading data. It will be a common theme throughout this book that **data dependencies** are of much concern in parallel computing. In writing modified data back into memory, these data cannot be written onto old data which should be subsequently used for processes issued earlier. Conversely, if the programming language ordering rules dictate that an updated variable is to be used for the next step, it is clear this variable must be safely stored before it is used. Since bulk memory is usually far away from the CPU, why write the data all the way back to their rightful memory locations if we want them for a subsequent step to be computed very soon? Two strategies are in use.

1. A **write through** strategy automatically writes back to memory any modified variables in cache. A copy of the data is kept in cache for subsequent use. This copy might be written over by other data mapped to the same location in cache without worry. A subsequent cache miss on the written through data will be assured to fetch valid data from memory because the data are freshly updated on each write.
2. A **write back** strategy skips the writing to memory until: (1) a subsequent read tries to replace a cache block which has been modified, or (2) these cache resident data are modified by the CPU. These two situations are more/less the same: cache resident data are not written back to memory until some process tries to modify them. Otherwise, the modification would write over computed information before it is saved.

It is well known [71] that certain processes, I/O and multi-threading, for example, want it both ways. In consequence, modern cache designs often permit both write-through and write-back modes [29]. Which mode is used may be controlled by the program.

1.2.2 *Pipelines, instruction scheduling, and loop unrolling*

For our purposes, the memory issues considered above revolve around the same basic problem—that of data dependencies. In Section 3.2, we will explore in more detail some coding issues when dealing with data dependencies, but the idea, in principle, is not complicated. Consider the following sequence of **C** instructions.

```
a[1] = f1(a[0]);
              .
              .
              .
a[2] = f2(a[1]);
              .
              .
              .
a[3] = f3(a[2]);
```

Array element a[1] is to be set when the first instruction is finished. The second, f2(a[1]), cannot issue until the result a[1] is ready, and likewise f3(a[2]) must wait until a[2] is finished. Computations f1(a[0]), f2(a[1]), and f3(a[2]) are not independent. There are data dependencies: the first, second, and last must run in a serial fashion and not concurrently. However, the computation of f1(a[0]) will take some time, so it may be possible to do other operations while the first is being processed, indicated by the dots. The same applies to computing the second f2(a[1]). **On modern machines, essentially all operations are pipelined**: several hardware stages are needed to do any computation. That multiple steps are needed to do arithmetic is ancient history, for example, from grammar school. What is more recent, however, is that it is possible to do multiple operands concurrently: as soon as a low order digit for one operand pair is computed by one stage, that stage can be used to process the same low order digit of the next operand pair. This notion of pipelining operations was also not invented yesterday: the University of Manchester *Atlas* project implemented

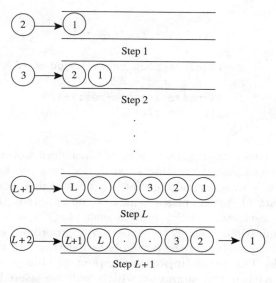

FIG. 1.7. *Pipelining: a pipe filled with marbles.*

such arithmetic pipelines as early as 1962 [91]. The terminology is an analogy to a short length of pipe into which one starts pushing marbles, Figure 1.7. Imagine that the pipe will hold L marbles, which will be symbolic for stages necessary to process each operand. To do one complete operation on one operand pair takes L steps. However, with multiple operands, we can keep pushing operands into the pipe until it is full, after which one result (marble) pops out the other end at a rate of one result/cycle. By this simple device, instead n operands taking L cycles each, that is, a total of $n \cdot L$ cycles, only $L + n$ cycles are required as long as the last operands can be flushed from the pipeline once they have started into it. The resulting speedup is $n \cdot L/(n + L)$, that is, L for large n. To program systems with pipelined operations to advantage, we will need to know how instructions are executed when they run concurrently. The schema is in principle straightforward and shown by loop unrolling transformations done either by the compiler or by the programmer. The simple loop

```
for(i=0;i<n;i++){
      b[i] = f(a[i]);
   }
```

is expanded into segments of (say) m is.

```
for(i=0;i<n;i+=m){
    b[i   ]  = f(a[i  ]);
    b[i+1]   = f(a[i+1]);
                .
                .
    b[i+m-1] = f(a[i+m-1]);
}
/* residual segment res = n mod m */
nms = n/m;  res = n%m;
for(i=nms*m;i<nms*m+res;i++){
    b[i]    = f(a[i]);
}
```

The first loop processes nms segments, each of which does m operations f(a[i]). Our last loop cleans up the remaining is when $n \neq nms \cdot m$, that is, a residual segment. Sometimes this residual segment is processed first, sometimes last (as shown) or for data alignment reasons, part of the res first, the rest last. We will refer to the instructions which process each f(a[i]) as a **template**. The problem of optimization, then, is to choose an appropriate depth of unrolling m which permits squeezing all the m templates together into the tightest time grouping possible. **The most important aspect of this procedure is prefetching data within the segment which will be used by subsequent segment elements in order to hide memory latencies**. That is, one wishes to hide the time it takes to get the data from memory into registers. Such data pre-fetching was called **bottom loading** in former times. Pre-fetching in its simplest form is for $m = 1$ and takes the form

```
t = a[0];              /* prefetch a[0] */
for(i=0;i<n-1; ){
    b[i] = f(t);
    t    = a[++i]; /* prefetch a[i+1] */
}
b[n-1] = f(t);
```

where one tries to hide the next load of a[i] under the loop overhead. We can go one or more levels deeper, as in Figure 1.8 or more. If the computation of f(ti) does not take long enough, not much memory access latency will be hidden under f(ti). In that case, the loop unrolling level m must be increased. In every case, we have the following highlighted purpose of loop unrolling:

The purpose of loop unrolling is to hide latencies, in particular, the delay in reading data from memory.

Unless the stored results will be needed in subsequent iterations of the loop (a data dependency), these stores may always be hidden: their meanderings into memory can go at least until all the loop iterations are finished. The next section illustrates this idea in more generality, but graphically.

1.2.2.1 *Instruction scheduling with loop unrolling*

Here we will explore only instruction issue and execution where these processes are concurrent. Before we begin, we will need some notation. Data are loaded into and stored from registers. We denote these registers by $\{R_i, \ i = 0\ldots\}$. Different machines have varying numbers and types of these: floating point registers, integer registers, address calculation registers, general purpose registers; and anywhere from say 8 to 32 of each type or sometimes blocks of such registers

```
t0 = a[0];              /* prefetch a[0] */
t1 = a[1];              /* prefetch a[1] */
for(i=0;i<n-2;i+=2){
    b[i  ] = f(t0);
    b[i+1] = f(t1);
    t0     = a[i+1]; /* prefetch a[i+1] */
    t1     = a[i+2]; /* prefetch a[i+2] */
}
b[n-2] = f(t0);
b[n-1] = f(t1);
```

FIG. 1.8. *Pre-fetching 2 data one loop iteration ahead (assumes $2|n$).*

which may be partitioned in different ways. We will use the following simplified notation for the operations on the contents of these registers:

$R_1 \leftarrow M$:   loads a datum from memory M into register R_1.
$M \leftarrow R_1$:   stores content of register R_1 into memory M.
$R_3 \leftarrow R_1 + R_2$:   add contents of R_1 and R_2 and store results into R_3.
$R_3 \leftarrow R_1 * R_2$:   multiply contents of R_1 by R_2, and put result into R_3.

More complicated operations are successive applications of basic ones. Consider the following operation to be performed on an array $\mathbf{A}$: $\mathbf{B} = f(\mathbf{A})$, where $f(\cdot)$ is in two steps:

$$B_i = f_2(f_1(A_i)).$$

Each step of the calculation takes some time and there will be **latencies** in between them where results are not yet available. If we try to perform multiple is together, however, say two, $B_i = f(A_i)$ and $B_{i+1} = f(A_{i+1})$, the various operations, memory fetch, f_1 and f_2, might run concurrently, and we could set up two **templates** and try to align them. Namely, by starting the $f(A_{i+1})$ operation steps one cycle after the $f(A_i)$, the two templates can be merged together. In Figure 1.9, each calculation $f(A_i)$ and $f(A_{i+1})$ takes some number (say m) of cycles ($m = 11$ as illustrated). If these two calculations ran sequentially, they would take twice what each one requires, that is, $2 \cdot m$. By merging the two together and aligning them to fill in the gaps, they can be computed in $m + 1$ cycles. This will work only if: (1) the separate operations can run independently and concurrently, (2) if it is possible to align the templates to fill in some of the gaps, and (3) there are enough registers. As illustrated, if there are only eight registers, alignment of two templates is all that seems possible at compile time. More than that and we run out of registers. As in Figure 1.8, going deeper shows us how to hide memory latencies under the calculation. By using look-ahead (prefetch) memory access when the calculation is long enough, memory latencies may be significantly hidden.

Our illustration is a dream, however. Usually it is not that easy. Several problems raise their ugly heads.

1. One might run out of registers. No matter how many there are, if the calculation is complicated enough, we will run out and no more unrolling is possible without going up in levels of the memory hierarchy.
2. One might run out of functional units. This just says that one of the $\{f_i, i = 1, \ldots\}$ operations might halt awaiting hardware that is busy. For example, if the multiply unit is busy, it may not be possible to use it until it is finished with multiplies already started.
3. A big bottleneck is memory traffic. If memory is busy, it may not be possible to access data to start another template.
4. Finally, finding an optimal algorithm to align these templates is no small matter. In Figures 1.9 and 1.10, everything fit together quite nicely. In general, this may not be so. In fact, it is known that finding an optimal

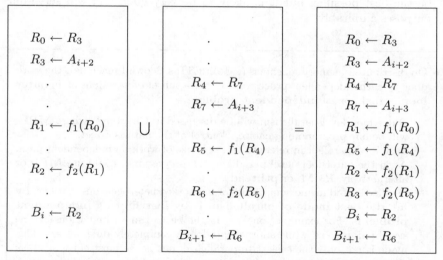

$$
\begin{array}{l}
R_0 \leftarrow A_i \\
\quad \cdot \\
\text{wait} \\
R_1 \leftarrow f_1(R_0) \\
\quad \cdot \\
R_2 \leftarrow f_2(R_1) \\
\quad \cdot \\
B_i \leftarrow R_2 \\
\quad \cdot
\end{array}
\quad \bigcup \quad
\begin{array}{l}
\quad \cdot \\
R_4 \leftarrow A_{i+1} \\
\quad \cdot \\
\text{wait} \\
R_5 \leftarrow f_1(R_4) \\
\quad \cdot \\
R_6 \leftarrow f_2(R_5) \\
\quad \cdot \\
B_{i+1} \leftarrow R_6
\end{array}
\quad = \quad
\begin{array}{l}
R_0 \leftarrow A_i \\
R_4 \leftarrow A_{i+1} \\
\text{wait} \\
R_1 \leftarrow f_1(R_0) \\
R_5 \leftarrow f_1(R_4) \\
R_2 \leftarrow f_2(R_1) \\
R_3 \leftarrow f_2(R_5) \\
B_i \leftarrow R_2 \\
B_{i+1} \leftarrow R_6
\end{array}
$$

FIG. 1.9. *Aligning templates of instructions generated by unrolling loops. We assume* $2\,|\,n$, *while loop variable* i *is stepped by 2.*

$$
\begin{array}{l}
R_0 \leftarrow R_3 \\
R_3 \leftarrow A_{i+2} \\
\quad \cdot \\
\quad \cdot \\
R_1 \leftarrow f_1(R_0) \\
\quad \cdot \\
R_2 \leftarrow f_2(R_1) \\
\quad \cdot \\
B_i \leftarrow R_2 \\
\quad \cdot
\end{array}
\quad \bigcup \quad
\begin{array}{l}
\quad \cdot \\
\quad \cdot \\
R_4 \leftarrow R_7 \\
R_7 \leftarrow A_{i+3} \\
\quad \cdot \\
R_5 \leftarrow f_1(R_4) \\
\quad \cdot \\
R_6 \leftarrow f_2(R_5) \\
\quad \cdot \\
B_{i+1} \leftarrow R_6
\end{array}
\quad = \quad
\begin{array}{l}
R_0 \leftarrow R_3 \\
R_3 \leftarrow A_{i+2} \\
R_4 \leftarrow R_7 \\
R_7 \leftarrow A_{i+3} \\
R_1 \leftarrow f_1(R_0) \\
R_5 \leftarrow f_1(R_4) \\
R_2 \leftarrow f_2(R_1) \\
R_3 \leftarrow f_2(R_5) \\
B_i \leftarrow R_2 \\
B_{i+1} \leftarrow R_6
\end{array}
$$

FIG. 1.10. *Aligning templates and hiding memory latencies by pre-fetching data. Again, we assume* $2\,|\,n$ *and the loop variable* i *is stepped by 2: compare with Figure 1.9.*

algorithm is an NP-complete problem. This means there is no algorithm which can compute an optimal alignment strategy and be computed in a time t which can be represented by a polynomial in the number of steps.

So, our little example is fun, but is it useless in practice? Fortunately the situation is not at all grim. Several things make this idea extremely useful.

1. Modern machines usually have multiple copies of each functional unit: add, multiply, shift, etc. So running out of functional units is only a bother but not fatal to this strategy.
2. Modern machines have lots of registers, even if only temporary storage registers. Cache can be used for this purpose if the data are not written through back to memory.
3. Many machines allow renaming registers. For example, in Figure 1.9, as soon as R_0 is used to start the operation $f_1(R_0)$, its data are in the f_1 pipeline and so R_0 is not needed anymore. It is possible to rename R_5 which was assigned by the compiler and call it R_0, thus providing us more registers than we thought we had.
4. While it is true that there is no **optimal algorithm** for unrolling loops into such templates and dovetailing them perfectly together, there are heuristics for getting a **good** algorithm, if not an optimal one. Here is the art of optimization in the compiler writer's work. The result may not be the best possible, but it is likely to be very good and will serve our purposes admirably.

- On distributed memory machines (e.g. on ETH's Beowulf machine), the work done by each independent processor is either a subset of iterations of an **outer loop**, a **task**, or an **independent problem**.

  — Outer loop level parallelism will be discussed in Chapter 5, where **MPI** will be our programming choice. Control of the data is direct.
  — Task level parallelism refers to large chunks of work on independent data. As in the outer-loop level paradigm, the programmer could use **MPI**; or alternatively, **PVM**, or **pthreads**.
  — On distributed memory machines or networked heterogeneous systems, **by far the best mode of parallelism is by distributing independent problems**. For example, one job might be to run a simulation for one set of parameters, while another job does a completely different set. This mode is not only the easiest to parallelize, but is the most efficient. Task assignments and scheduling are done by the batch queueing system.

- On shared memory machines, for example, on ETH's Cray SV-1 cluster, or our Hewlett-Packard HP9000 Superdome machine, both **task level** and **outer loop level** parallelism are natural modes. The programmer's job is to specify the independent tasks by various **compiler directives** (e.g., see Appendix C), but data management is done by system software. This mode of using directives is relatively easy to program, but has the disadvantage that parallelism is less directly controlled.

1.3   Multiple processors and processes

In the SIMD Section 3.2, we will return to loop unrolling and multiple data processing. There the context is vector processing as a method by which machines can concurrently compute multiple independent data. The above discussion about loop unrolling applies in an analogous way for that mode. Namely, special vector registers are used to implement the loop unrolling and there is a lot of hardware support. To conclude this section, we outline the considerations for multiple independent processors, each of which uses the same lower level instruction level parallelism discussed in Section 1.2.2. Generally, our programming methodology reflects the following viewpoint.

1.4   Networks

Two common network configurations are shown in Figures 1.11–1.13. Variants of Ω-networks are very commonly used in tightly coupled clusters and relatively modest sized multiprocessing systems. For example, in Chapter 4 we discuss the NEC SX-6 (Section 4.4) and Cray X1 (Section 4.3) machines which use such $\log(NCPUs)$ stage networks for each board (node) to tightly couple multiple CPUs in a cache coherent memory image. In other flavors, instead of $2 \rightarrow 2$ switches as illustrated in Figure 1.12, these may be $4 \rightarrow 4$ (see Figure 4.2) or higher order. For example, the former Thinking Machines C-5 used a quadtree network and likewise the HP9000 we discuss in Section 4.2. For a large number of

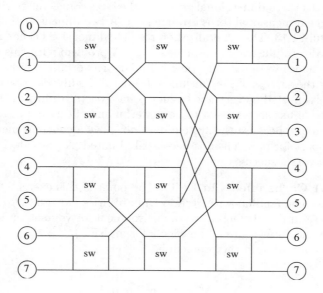

FIG. 1.11. Ω-network.

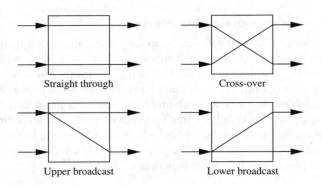

FIG. 1.12. *Ω-network switches from Figure 1.11.*

processors, cross-bar arrangements of this type can become unwieldy simply due to the large number of switches necessary and the complexity of wiring arrangements. As we will see in Sections 4.4 and 4.3, however, very tightly coupled **nodes** with say 16 or fewer processors can provide extremely high performance. In our view, such clusters will likely be the most popular architectures for supercomputers in the next few years. Between **nodes**, message passing on a sophisticated bus system is used. Between nodes, no memory coherency is available and data dependencies must be controlled by software.

Another approach, which places processors on tightly coupled grid, is more amenable to a larger number of CPUs. The very popular Cray T3-D, T3-E machines used a three-dimensional grid with the faces connected to their opposite faces in a three-dimensional torus arrangement. A two-dimensional illustration is shown in Figure 1.13. The generalization to three dimensions is not hard to imagine, but harder to illustrate in a plane image. A problem with this architecture was that the nodes were not very powerful. The network, however, is extremely powerful and the success of the machine reflects this highly effective design. Message passing is effected by very low latency primitives (**shmemput**, **shmemget**, etc.). This mode has shown itself to be powerful and effective, but lacks portability. Furthermore, because the system does not have a coherent memory, image compiler support for parallelism is necessarily limited. A great deal was learned from this network's success.

Exercise 1.1 Cache effects in FFT   The point of this exercise is to get you started: to become familiar with certain Unix utilities `tar`, `make`, `ar`, `cc`; to pick an editor; to set up a satisfactory work environment for yourself on the machines you will use; and to measure cache effects for an FFT.

The transformation in the problem is

$$y_l = \sum_{k=0}^{n-1} \omega^{\pm kl} x_k, \quad \text{for } l = 0, \ldots, n-1 \tag{1.1}$$

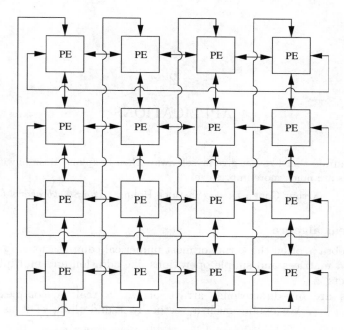

FIG. 1.13. *Two-dimensional nearest neighbor connected torus. A three-dimensional torus has six nearest neighbors instead of four.*

with $\omega = e^{2\pi i/n}$ equal to the nth root of unity. The sign in Equation (1.1) is given by the `sign` argument in `cfft2` and is a `float`. A sufficient background for this computation is given in Section 2.4.

What is to be done? From our anonymous ftp server

$$\text{http://www.inf.ethz.ch/~arbenz/book,}$$

in directory `Chapter1/uebung1`, using `get` download the `tar` file `uebung1.tar`

1. Un-tar this file into five source files, a `makefile`, and an NQS batch script (may need slight editing for different machines).
2. Execute `make` to generate:
    (a) `cfftlib.a` = library of modules for the FFT (*make lib*).
    (b) `cfftst` = test program (*make cfftst*).
3. Run this job on ALL MACHINES using (via `qsub`) the batch sumission script.
4. From the output on each, plot Mflops (million floating pt. operations/second) vs. problem size n. Use your favorite plotter—`gnuplot`, for example, or plot by hand on graph paper.
5. Interpret the results in light of Table 1.1.

APPLICATIONS

I am afraid that I rather give myself away when I explain. Results without causes are much more impressive.

Arthur Conan Doyle (Sherlock Holmes, *The Stockbroker's Clerk*)

2.1 Linear algebra

Linear algebra is often the kernel of most numerical computations. It deals with vectors and matrices and simple operations like addition and multiplication on these objects.

Vectors are one-dimensional arrays of say n real or complex numbers $x_0, x_1, \ldots, x_{n-1}$. We denote such a vector by x and think of it as a column vector,

$$\mathbf{x} = \begin{bmatrix} x_0 \\ x_1 \\ \vdots \\ x_{n-1} \end{bmatrix}. \tag{2.1}$$

On a sequential computer, these numbers occupy n consecutive memory locations. This is also true, at least conceptually, on a shared memory multiprocessor computer. On distributed memory multicomputers, the primary issue is how to distribute vectors on the memory of the processors involved in the computation.

Matrices are two-dimensional arrays of the form

$$A = \begin{bmatrix} a_{00} & a_{01} & \cdots & a_{0,m-1} \\ a_{10} & a_{11} & \cdots & a_{1,m-1} \\ \vdots & \vdots & & \vdots \\ a_{n-1,0} & a_{n-1,1} & \cdots & a_{n-1,m-1} \end{bmatrix}. \tag{2.2}$$

The $n \cdot m$ real (complex) matrix elements a_{ij} are stored in $n \cdot m$ (respectively $2 \cdot n \cdot m$ if `complex` datatype is available) consecutive memory locations. This is achieved by either stacking the columns on top of each other or by appending row after row. The former is called *column-major*, the latter *row-major* order. The actual procedure depends on the programming language. In Fortran, matrices are stored in column-major order, in C in row-major order. There is no principal difference, but for writing efficient programs one has to respect how matrices

Table 2.1 *Basic linear algebra subprogram prefix/suffix conventions.*

	Prefixes
S	Real
D	Double precision
C	Complex
Z	Double complex
	Suffixes
U	Transpose
C	Hermitian conjugate

are laid out. To be consistent with the libraries that we will use that are mostly written in Fortran, we will explicitly program in column-major order. Thus, the matrix element a_{ij} of the $m \times n$ matrix A is located $i + j \cdot m$ memory locations after a_{00}. Therefore, in our C codes we will write a[i+j*m]. Notice that there is no such simple procedure for determining the memory location of an element of a *sparse* matrix. In Section 2.3, we outline data descriptors to handle sparse matrices.

In this and later chapters we deal with one of the simplest operations one wants to do with vectors and matrices: the so-called saxpy operation (2.3). In Tables 2.1 and 2.2 are listed some of the acronyms and conventions for the basic linear algebra subprograms discussed in this book. The operation is one of the more basic, albeit most important of these:

$$\mathbf{y} = \alpha\mathbf{x} + \mathbf{y}. \tag{2.3}$$

Other common operations we will deal with in this book are the scalar (inner, or dot) product (Section 3.5.6) sdot,

$$s = \mathbf{x} \cdot \mathbf{y} = (\mathbf{x}, \mathbf{y}) = \sum_{i=0}^{n-1} x_i y_i, \tag{2.4}$$

matrix–vector multiplication (Section 5.6),

$$\mathbf{y} = A\mathbf{x}, \tag{2.5}$$

and matrix–matrix multiplication (Section 3.4.1),

$$C = AB. \tag{2.6}$$

In Equations (2.3)–(2.6), equality denotes assignment, that is, the variable on the left side of the equality sign is assigned the result of the expression on the right side.

Table 2.2 *Summary of the basic linear algebra subroutines.*

Level 1 BLAS	
_ROTG, _ROT	Generate/apply plane rotation
_ROTMG, _ROTM	Generate/apply modified plane rotation
_SWAP	Swap two vectors: $\mathbf{x} \leftrightarrow \mathbf{y}$
_SCAL	Scale a vector: $\mathbf{x} \leftarrow \alpha\mathbf{x}$
_COPY	Copy a vector: $\mathbf{x} \leftarrow \mathbf{y}$
_AXPY	_axpy operation: $\mathbf{y} \leftarrow \mathbf{y} + \alpha\mathbf{x}$
DOT	Dot product: $s \leftarrow \mathbf{x} \cdot \mathbf{y} = \mathbf{x}^*\mathbf{y}$
_NRM2	2-norm: $s \leftarrow \|\mathbf{x}\|_2$
_ASUM	1-norm: $s \leftarrow \|\mathbf{x}\|_1$
I_AMAX	Index of largest vector element: first i such that $\|x_i\| \geq \|x_k\|$ for all k
Level 2 BLAS	
_GEMV, _GBMV	General (banded) matrix–vector multiply: $\mathbf{y} \leftarrow \alpha A\mathbf{x} + \beta\mathbf{y}$
_HEMV, _HBMV, _HPMV	Hermitian (banded, packed) matrix–vector multiply: $\mathbf{y} \leftarrow \alpha A\mathbf{x} + \beta\mathbf{y}$
_SEMV, _SBMV, _SPMV	Symmetric (banded, packed) matrix–vector multiply: $\mathbf{y} \leftarrow \alpha A\mathbf{x} + \beta\mathbf{y}$
_TRMV, _TBMV, _TPMV	Triangular (banded, packed) matrix–vector multiply: $\mathbf{x} \leftarrow A\mathbf{x}$
_TRSV, _TBSV, _TPSV	Triangular (banded, packed) system solves (forward/backward substitution): $\mathbf{x} \leftarrow A^{-1}\mathbf{x}$
_GER, _GERU, _GERC	Rank-1 updates: $A \leftarrow \alpha\mathbf{x}\mathbf{y}^* + A$
_HER, _HPR, _SYR, _SPR	Hermitian/symmetric (packed) rank-1 updates: $A \leftarrow \alpha\mathbf{x}\mathbf{x}^* + A$
_HER2, _HPR2, _SYR2, _SPR2	Hermitian/symmetric (packed) rank-2 updates: $A \leftarrow \alpha\mathbf{x}\mathbf{y}^* + \alpha^*\mathbf{y}\mathbf{x}^* + A$
Level 3 BLAS	
_GEMM, _SYMM, _HEMM	General/symmetric/Hermitian matrix–matrix multiply: $C \leftarrow \alpha AB + \beta C$
_SYRK, _HERK	Symmetric/Hermitian rank-k update: $C \leftarrow \alpha AA^* + \beta C$
_SYR2K, _HER2K	Symmetric/Hermitian rank-k update: $C \leftarrow \alpha AB^* + \alpha^* BA^* + \beta C$
_TRMM	Multiple triangular matrix–vector multiplies: $B \leftarrow \alpha AB$
_TRSM	Multiple triangular system solves: $B \leftarrow \alpha A^{-1}B$

An important topic of this and subsequent chapters is the solution of the system of linear equations

$$A\mathbf{x} = \mathbf{b} \tag{2.7}$$

by Gaussian elimination with partial pivoting. Further issues are the solution of least squares problems, Gram–Schmidt orthogonalization, and QR factorization.

2.2 LAPACK and the BLAS

By 1976 it was clear that some standardization of basic computer operations on vectors was needed [92]. By then it was already known that coding procedures that worked well on one machine might work very poorly on others [124]. In consequence of these observations, Lawson, Hanson, Kincaid, and Krogh proposed a limited set of Basic Linear Algebra Subprograms (BLAS) to be optimized by hardware vendors, implemented in assembly language if necessary, that would form the basis of comprehensive linear algebra packages [93]. These so-called Level 1 BLAS consisted of vector operations and some attendant co-routines. The first major package which used these BLAS kernels was LINPACK [38]. Soon afterward, other major software libraries such as the IMSL library [145] and NAG [112] rewrote portions of their existing codes and structured new routines to use these BLAS. Early in their development, vector computers (e.g. [124]) saw significant optimizations using the BLAS. Soon, however, such machines were clustered together in tight networks (see Section 1.3) and somewhat larger kernels for numerical linear algebra were developed [40, 41] to include matrix–vector operations. Additionally, Fortran compilers were by then optimizing vector operations as efficiently as hand coded Level 1 BLAS. Subsequently, in the late 1980s, distributed memory machines were in production and shared memory machines began to have significant numbers of processors. A further set of matrix–matrix operations was proposed [42] and soon standardized [39] to form a Level 2. The first major package for linear algebra which used the Level 3 BLAS was LAPACK [4] and subsequently a scalable (to large numbers of processors) version was released as ScaLAPACK [12]. Vendors focused on Level 1, Level 2, and Level 3 BLAS which provided an easy route to optimizing LINPACK, then LAPACK. LAPACK not only integrated pre-existing solvers and eigenvalue routines found in EISPACK [133] (which did not use the BLAS) and LINPACK (which used Level 1 BLAS), but incorporated the latest dense and banded linear algebra algorithms available. It also used the Level 3 BLAS which were optimized by much vendor effort. In subsequent chapters, we will illustrate several BLAS routines and considerations for their implementation on some machines. Conventions for different BLAS are indicated by

- A **root** operation. For example, _axpy (2.3).
- A prefix (or combination prefix) to indicate the datatype of the operands, for example, saxpy for single precision _axpy operation, or isamax for the index of the maximum absolute element in an array of type **single**.

- A suffix if there is some qualifier, for example, `cdotc` or `cdotu` for conjugated or unconjugated complex dot product, respectively:

$$\texttt{cdotc(n,x,1,y,1)} = \sum_{i=0}^{n-1} x_i \bar{y}_i,$$

$$\texttt{cdotu(n,x,1,y,1)} = \sum_{i=0}^{n-1} x_i y_i,$$

where both **x** and **y** are vectors of complex elements.

Tables 2.1 and 2.2 give the prefix/suffix and root combinations for the BLAS, respectively.

2.2.1 *Typical performance numbers for the BLAS*

Let us look at typical representations of all three levels of the BLAS, `daxpy`, `ddot`, `dgemv`, and `dgemm`, that perform the basic operations (2.3)–(2.6). Additionally, we look at the rank-1 update routine `dger`. An overview on the number of memory accesses and floating point operations is given in Table 2.3. The Level 1 BLAS comprise basic vector operations. A call of one of the Level 1 BLAS thus gives rise to $\mathcal{O}(n)$ floating point operations and $\mathcal{O}(n)$ memory accesses. Here, n is the vector length. The Level 2 BLAS comprise operations that involve matrices *and* vectors. If the involved matrix is $n \times n$, then both the memory accesses and the floating point operations are of $\mathcal{O}(n^2)$. In contrast, the Level 3 BLAS have a higher order floating point operations than memory accesses. The most prominent operation of the Level 3 BLAS, matrix–matrix multiplication costs $\mathcal{O}(n^3)$ floating point operations while there are only $\mathcal{O}(n^2)$ reads and writes. The last column in Table 2.3 shows the crucial difference between the Level 3 BLAS and the rest.

Table 2.4 gives some performance numbers for the five BLAS of Table 2.3. Notice that the timer has a resolution of only 1 μs! Therefore, the numbers in Table 2.4 have been obtained by timing a loop inside of which the respective function is called many times. The Mflop/s rates of the Level 1 BLAS `ddot`

Table 2.3 *Number of memory references and floating point operations for vectors of length n.*

	Read	Write	Flops	Flops/mem access
ddot	$2n$	1	$2n$	1
daxpy	$2n$	n	$2n$	2/3
dgemv	$n^2 + n$	n	$2n^2$	2
dger	$n^2 + 2n$	n^2	$2n^2$	1
dgemm	$2n^2$	n^2	$2n^3$	2n/3

Table 2.4 *Some performance numbers for typical BLAS in Mflop/s for a 2.4 GHz Pentium 4.*

	$n = 100$	500	2000	10,000,000
ddot	1480	1820	1900	440
daxpy	1160	1300	1140	240
dgemv	1370	740	670	—
dger	670	330	320	—
dgemm	2680	3470	3720	—

and daxpy quite precisely reflect the ratios of the memory accesses of the two routines, $2n$ vs. $3n$. The high rates are for vectors that can be held in the on-chip cache of 512 MB. The low 240 and 440 Mflop/s with the very long vectors are related to the memory bandwidth of about 1900 MB/s (cf. Table 1.1).

The Level 2 BLAS dgemv has about the same performance as daxpy if the matrix can be held in cache ($n = 100$). Otherwise, it is considerably reduced. dger has a high volume of read and write operations, while the number of floating point operations is limited. This leads to a very low performance rate. The Level 3 BLAS dgemm performs at a good fraction of the peak performance of the processor (4.8 Gflop/s). The performance increases with the problem size. We see from Table 2.3 that the ratio of computation to memory accesses increases with the problem size. This ratio is analogous to a volume-to-surface area effect.

2.2.2 *Solving systems of equations with LAPACK*

2.2.2.1 *Classical Gaussian elimination*

Gaussian elimination is probably the most important algorithm in numerical linear algebra. In Chapter 3, in particular Section 3.4.2, we will review the classical form for Gaussian elimination because there we will be deeper into hardware considerations wherein the classical representation will seem more appropriate. Here and in subsequent sections, we hope it will be clear why Level 2 and Level 3 BLAS are usually more efficient than the vector operations found in the Level 1 BLAS. Given a rectangular $m \times n$ matrix A, it computes a lower triangular matrix L and an upper triangular matrix U, such that

$$PA = LU, \tag{2.8}$$

where P is an $m \times m$ permutation matrix, L is an $m \times m$ lower triangular matrix with ones on the diagonal and U is an $m \times n$ upper triangular matrix, that is, a matrix with nonzero elements only on and above its diagonal.

The algorithm is obviously well known [60] and we review it more than once due to its importance. The main code portion of an implementation of Gaussian elimination is found in Figure 2.1. The algorithm factors an $m \times n$ matrix in

```
info = 0;
for (j=0; j < min(M,N); j++){
    /* Find pivot and test for singularity */
    tmp = M-j;
    jp = j - 1 + idamax_(&tmp,&A[j+j*M],&ONE );
    ipiv[j] = jp;
    if (A[jp+j*M] != 0.0){
        /* Interchange actual with pivot row */
        if (jp != j) dswap_(&N,&A[j],&M,&A[jp],&M);
        /* Compute j-th column of L-factor */
        s = 1.0/A[j+j*M]; tmp = M-j-1;
        if (j < M) dscal_(&tmp,&s,&A[j+1+j*M],&ONE);
    }
    else if (info == 0) info = j;
    /* Rank-one update trailing submatrix */
    if (j < min(M,N)) {
        tmp = M-j-1; tmp2 = N-j-1;
        dger_(&tmp,&tmp2,&MDONE,&A[j+1+j*M],&ONE,
              &A[j+(j+1)*M],&M,&A[j+1+(j+1)*M],&M);
    }
}
```

FIG. 2.1. *Gaussian elimination of an $M \times N$ matrix based on Level 2 BLAS as implemented in the LAPACK routine* dgetrf.

$\min(m, n) - 1$ steps. In the algorithm of Figure 2.1, the step number is j. For illustrating a typical step of the algorithm, we chose $m = n + 1 = 6$. After completing the first two steps of Gaussian elimination, the first two columns of the lower triangular factor L and the two rows of the upper triangular factor U are computed.

$$
\begin{bmatrix}
1 \\
l_{10} & 1 \\
l_{20} & l_{21} & 1 \\
l_{30} & l_{31} & & 1 \\
l_{40} & l_{41} & & & 1 \\
l_{50} & l_{51} & & & & 1
\end{bmatrix}
\begin{bmatrix}
u_{00} & u_{01} & u_{02} & u_{03} & u_{04} \\
& u_{11} & u_{12} & u_{13} & u_{14} \\
& & \hat{a}_{22} & \hat{a}_{23} & \hat{a}_{24} \\
& & \hat{a}_{32} & \hat{a}_{33} & \hat{a}_{34} \\
& & \hat{a}_{42} & \hat{a}_{43} & \hat{a}_{44} \\
& & \hat{a}_{52} & \hat{a}_{53} & \hat{a}_{54}
\end{bmatrix}
\equiv L_1 U_1 = P_1 A. \quad (2.9)
$$

In the third step of Gaussian elimination, zeros are introduced below the first element in the *reduced matrix* $\hat{a}_{ij}$. Column three of L is filled below its diagonal element. Previously computed elements l_{ij} and u_{ij} are not affected: Their elements in L may be permuted, however!

The jth step of Gaussian elimination has three substeps.

1. Find the first index j_p of the largest element in modulus in the pivot column j. That is, $|\hat{a}_{j_p,j}| \geq |\hat{a}_{ij}|$ for all $i \geq j$. (This is done by function idamax in Figure 2.1.) Let $\widehat{P}_j$ be the $m \times m$ permutation matrix that swaps entries j and j_p in a vector of length m. Notice, that $\widehat{P}_j$ is the identity matrix if $j_p = j$.

   In the example in (2.9) we have $j = 2$. Applying P_2 yields

$$\widehat{P}_2 L_1 \widehat{P}_2^T \widehat{P}_2 U_1 = \widehat{P}_2 P_1 A = P_2 A, \qquad P_2 = \widehat{P}_2 P_1. \tag{2.10}$$

   Notice that $\widehat{P}_2$ swaps row $j = 2$ with row $j_p \geq 2$. Therefore, $\widehat{P}_2 L_1 \widehat{P}_2^T$ differs from L_1 only in swapped elements on columns 0 and 1 below row 1. $\widehat{P}_2$ applied to U_1 swaps two of the rows with elements $\hat{a}_{ik}$. After the permutation, $\hat{a}_{jj}$ is (one of) the largest element(s) of the first column of the reduced matrix. Therefore, if $\hat{a}_{jj} = 0$, then the whole column is zero.

   In the code fragment in Figure 2.1 the lower triangle of L without the unit diagonal and the upper triangle of U are stored in-place onto matrix A. Evidently, from (2.9), the elements of L_k below the diagonal can be stored where U_k has zero elements. Therefore, applying $\widehat{P}_j$ corresponds to a swap of two complete rows of A.

2. Compute the jth column of L,

$$l_{ij} = \hat{a}_{ij}/\hat{a}_{jj}, \quad i > j.$$

   This is executed in the Level 1 BLAS dscal.

3. Update the remainder of the matrix,

$$\hat{a}_{ik} = \hat{a}_{ik} - l_{ij}\hat{a}_{jk}, \quad i, k > j.$$

   This operation is a rank-one update that can be done with the Level 2 BLAS dger.

As we see in Table 2.4, the BLAS dger has quite a low performance. Also, please look at Figure 3.15. To use the high performance Level 3 BLAS routine dgemm, the algorithm has to be blocked!

2.2.2.2 *Block Gaussian elimination*

The essential idea to get a blocked algorithm is in *collecting* a number of steps of Gaussian elimination. The latter number is called *block size*, say b. Assume that we have arrived in the Gaussian elimination at a certain stage $j > 0$ as indicated in Figure 2.2(a). That is, we have computed (up to row permutations) the first j columns of the lower triangular factor L, indicated by L_0, and the first j rows of the upper triangular factor U, indicated by U_0. We wish to eliminate the next *panel* of b columns of the reduced matrix $\hat{A}$. To that end, split $\hat{A}$ in four

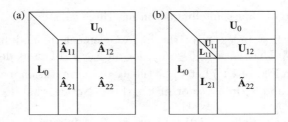

FIG. 2.2. *Block Gaussian elimination. (a) Before and (b) after an intermediate block elimination step.*

portions, wherein $\hat{A}_{11}$ comprises the $b \times b$ block in the upper left corner of $\hat{A}$. The sizes of the further three blocks become clear from Figure 2.2(a). The block Gaussian elimination step now proceeds similarly to the classical algorithm (see Figure 3.15 and p. 108) in three substeps

1. Factor the first panel of $\hat{A}$ by classical Gaussian elimination with column pivoting,

$$P \begin{bmatrix} \hat{A}_{11} \\ \hat{A}_{21} \end{bmatrix} = \begin{bmatrix} L_{11} \\ L_{21} \end{bmatrix} U_{11}.$$

   Apply the row interchanges P on the "rectangular portion" of L_0 and $\begin{bmatrix} \hat{A}_{12} \\ \hat{A}_{22} \end{bmatrix}$. (The rectangular portion of L_0 is the portion of L_0 on the left of $\hat{A}$.)

2. Compute U_{12} by forward substitution, $U_{12} = L_{11}^{-1} \hat{A}_{12}$. This can be done efficiently by a Level 3 BLAS as there are multiple right hand sides.

3. Update the rest of the matrix by a rank-b update.

$$\widetilde{A}_{22} = \hat{A}_{22} - L_{21} U_{12},$$

   by using matrix–matrix multiplication Level 3 BLAS routine `dgemm`.

Block Gaussian elimination as implemented in the LAPACK routine, `dgetrf`, is available from the NETLIB [111] software repository. Figure 2.3 shows the main loop in the Fortran subroutine `dgetrf` for factoring an $M \times N$ matrix. The block size is `NB`, and is determined by LAPACK and is determined by hardware characteristics rather than problem size.

The motivation for the blocking Gaussian elimination was that blocking makes possible using the higher performance Level 3 BLAS. Advantages of Level 3 BLAS over the Level 1 and Level 2 BLAS are the higher ratios of computations to memory accesses, see Tables 2.3 and 2.4. Let us examine the situation for Gaussian elimination. For simplicity let us assume that the cache can hold three $b \times b$ blocks, that is, $3b^2$ floating point numbers. Furthermore, we assume that n is divisible by b, $n = bm$. Then we investigate the jth block step, $1 \leq j \leq m$. We use the notation of Figure 2.2.

```
      DO 20 J=1, MIN(M,N), NB
         JB = MIN(MIN(M,N)-J+1,NB)

*        Factor diagonal and subdiagonal blocks and test for
*        exact singularity.
         CALL DGETF2(M-J+1, JB, A(J,J), LDA, IPIV(J), IINFO)

*        Adjust INFO and the pivot indices.
         IF(INFO.EQ.0 .AND. IINFO.GT.0)
     $      INFO = IINFO + J - 1
         DO 10 I = J, MIN(M,J+JB-1)
            IPIV(I) = J - 1 + IPIV(I)
   10    CONTINUE

*        Apply interchanges to columns 1:J-1.
         CALL DLASWP(J-1, A, LDA, J, J+JB-1, IPIV, 1)

         IF(J+JB.LE.N) THEN

*           Apply interchanges to columns J+JB:N.
            CALL DLASWP(N-J-JB+1, A(1,J+JB), LDA, J, J+JB-1,
     $                   IPIV, 1)

*           Compute block row of U.
            CALL DTRSM('Left', 'Lower', 'No transpose', 'Unit',
     $                JB, N-J-JB+1, ONE, A(J,J), LDA,
     $                A(J,J+JB), LDA)
            IF(J+JB.LE.M) THEN

*              Update trailing submatrix.
               CALL DGEMM('No transpose', 'No transpose',
     $                   M-J-JB+1, N-J-JB+1, JB, -ONE,
     $                   A(J+JB,J), LDA, A(J,J+JB), LDA,
     $                   ONE, A(J+JB,J+JB), LDA)
            END IF
         END IF
   20 CONTINUE
```

FIG. 2.3. *The main loop in the LAPACK routine* dgetrf, *which is functionally equivalent to* dgefa *from LINPACK.*

1. The in-place factorization $\hat{A}_{11} = L_{11}U_{11}$ costs b^2 reads and writes.
2. Keeping L_{11}/U_{11} in cache, the backward substitution $L_{21} \leftarrow \hat{A}_{21}U_{11}^{-1}$ needs the reading and storing of $b \cdot (m-j)b$ floating point numbers.
3. The same holds for the forward substitution $U_{12} \leftarrow L_{11}^{-1}\hat{A}_{12}$.
4. The rank-b update can be made panel by panel. Keeping the required block of U_{12} in cache, L_{21} and the panel are read; after the update, the

panel is stored in memory. Neglecting the access of U_{12}, this consumes $2b \cdot (m-j)b$ read and $2b \cdot (m-j)$ write operations *for each* of the $m-j$ panels.

Summing all the contributions of items (1)–(4) and taking $n = bm$ into account gives

$$\sum_{j=1}^{m} 2b^2(m-j) + 3b^2(m-j)^2 = \frac{n^3}{b} + \mathcal{O}(n^2).$$

Thus, the blocked algorithm executes $\frac{3}{2}b$ flops per memory access. This raw formula seems to show that b should be chosen as big as possible. However, we have derived it under the assumption that $3b^2$ floating point numbers can be stored in cache. This assumption gives an upper bound for b.

In Table 2.5 we have collected some timings of the LAPACK routine `dgesv` that comprises a full system solve of order n including factorization, forward and backward substitution. Our numbers show that it is indeed wise to block Gaussian elimination. A factor of three or more improvement in performance over the classical Gaussian elimination (see p. 108) can be expected if the block size is chosen properly. However, we get nowhere close to the performance of `dgemm`. The performance depends on the block size. The default block size on the Pentium 4 is 64. In Chapter 4, we will see that on shared memory machines, the block algorithm even more clearly shows its superiority.

2.3   Linear algebra: sparse matrices, iterative methods

In many situations, either an explicit representation of matrix A or its factorization is extremely large and thus awkward to handle, or such explicit representations do not exist at all. For example, A may be a general linear

Table 2.5 *Times (s) and speed in Mflop/s of* `dgesv` *on a P 4 (2.4 GHz, 1 GB). There is little improvement when $b \geq 16$.*

$n = 500$			$n = 1000$			$n = 2000$		
b	Time (s)	Speed	b	Time (s)	Speed	b	Time (s)	Speed
1	0.27	308	1	2.17	307	1	16.57	322
2	0.18	463	2	1.44	463	2	11.06	482
4	0.13	641	4	1.08	617	4	8.16	654
8	0.11	757	8	0.89	749	8	6.73	792
16	0.10	833	16	0.80	833	16	6.42	831
32	0.09	926	32	0.78	855	32	7.74	689
64	0.10	833	64	0.96	694	64	10.16	525

operator whose only definition is its effect on an explicit representation of a vector $\mathbf{x}$. In these situations, iterative methods for the solution of

$$Ax = b \tag{2.11}$$

are used. Direct methods such as Gaussian elimination may be suitable to solve problems of size $n \leq 10^5$. If A is very large and sparse, that is, most of A's elements are zero, then the factorization $A = LU$ in a direct solution may generate nonzero numbers in the triangular factors L and U in places that are zero in the original matrix A. This so-called **fill-in** can be so severe that storing the factors L and U needs so much more memory than A, so a direct method becomes very expensive or may even be impossible for lack of memory. In such cases, iterative methods are required to solve (2.11). Likewise, when no explicit representation of A exists, iterative methods are the only option. In iterative methods, a sequence $\mathbf{x}^{(0)}, \mathbf{x}^{(1)}, \mathbf{x}^{(2)}, \ldots$ is constructed that converges to the solution of (2.11) for some *initial vector* $\mathbf{x}^{(0)}$.

A second reason for choosing an iterative solution method is if it is not necessary to have a highly accurate solution. As the sequence $\mathbf{x}^{(0)}, \mathbf{x}^{(1)}, \mathbf{x}^{(2)}, \ldots$ converges to the solution, it is possible to discontinue the iterations if one considers one of the $\mathbf{x}^{(k)}$ accurate enough. For example, if A is a discretization of, say, a differential operator, then it makes no sense to solve the system of equations more accurately than the error that is introduced by the discretization. Or, often the determination of the elements of A is not highly accurate, so a highly accurate solution of (2.11) would be foolish. In the next section, we examine the so-called stationary iterative and conjugate-gradient methods.

2.3.1 *Stationary iterations*

Assume $\mathbf{x}^{(k)}$ is an approximation to the solution $\mathbf{x}$ of (2.11), $A\mathbf{x} = \mathbf{b}$. Then

$$\mathbf{x} = \mathbf{x}^{(k)} + \mathbf{e}^{(k)}, \tag{2.12}$$

where $\mathbf{e}^{(k)}$ is called the *error*. Multiplying (2.12) by A gives

$$A\mathbf{e}^{(k)} = A\mathbf{x} - A\mathbf{x}^{(k)} = \mathbf{b} - A\mathbf{x}^{(k)} =: \mathbf{r}^{(k)}. \tag{2.13}$$

Vector $\mathbf{r}^{(k)}$ is called the *residual* at $\mathbf{x}^{(k)}$. Determining the error $\mathbf{e}^{(k)}$ would require knowing $\mathbf{x}$, whereas the residual $\mathbf{r}^{(k)}$ is easily computed using known information once the approximation $\mathbf{x}^{(k)}$ is available. From (2.12) and (2.13) we see that

$$\mathbf{x} = \mathbf{x}^{(k)} + A^{-1}\mathbf{r}^{(k)}. \tag{2.14}$$

Of course, determining $\mathbf{e}^{(k)} = A^{-1}\mathbf{r}^{(k)}$ is as difficult as solving the original (2.11), so (2.14) is only of theoretical interest. Nevertheless, if A in (2.14) is replaced by a matrix, say M, where (1) M is a good approximation of A and (2) the system $M\mathbf{z} = \mathbf{r}$ can be solved cheaply, then one may expect that

$$\mathbf{x}^{(k+1)} = \mathbf{x}^{(k)} + M^{-1}\mathbf{r}^{(k)}, \quad \mathbf{r}^{(k)} = \mathbf{b} - A\mathbf{x}^{(k)} \tag{2.15}$$

gives a convergent sequence $\{\mathbf{x}^{(k)}\}$. Another way to write (2.15) is

$$M\mathbf{x}^{(k+1)} = N\mathbf{x}^{(k)} + \mathbf{b}, \quad N = M - A. \tag{2.16}$$

Iterations (2.15) and (2.16) are called stationary iterations because the rules to compute $\mathbf{x}^{(k+1)}$ from $\mathbf{x}^{(k)}$ do not depend on k. Matrix M is called a *preconditioner*. The error changes in each iteration according to

$$\mathbf{e}^{(k+1)} = \mathbf{x} - \mathbf{x}^{(k+1)} = \mathbf{x} - \mathbf{x}^{(k)} - M^{-1}\mathbf{r}^{(k)},$$
$$= \mathbf{e}^{(k)} - M^{-1}(\mathbf{b} - A\mathbf{x}^{(k)} - \mathbf{b} + A\mathbf{x}),$$
$$= \mathbf{e}^{(k)} - M^{-1}A\mathbf{e}^{(k)} = (I - M^{-1}A)\mathbf{e}^{(k)}.$$

The matrix $G = I - M^{-1}A$ is called the *iteration matrix*. The residuals satisfy

$$\mathbf{r}^{(k+1)} = (I - AM^{-1})\mathbf{r}^{(k)}. \tag{2.17}$$

The matrix $I - AM^{-1}$ is similar to $G = I - M^{-1}A$ which implies that it has the same eigenvalues as G. In fact, the eigenvalues of the iteration matrix are decisive for the convergence of the stationary iteration (2.15). Let $\rho(G)$ denote the *spectral radius* of G, that is, the largest eigenvalue of G in absolute value. Then the following statement holds [60].

The stationary iteration (2.15) converges for any $\mathbf{x}^{(0)}$ if and only if $\rho(G) < 1$.

Let us now look at the most widely employed stationary iterations.

2.3.2 Jacobi iteration

By splitting A into pieces, $A = L + D + U$, where D is diagonal, L is strictly lower triangular, and U is strictly upper triangular, the Jacobi iteration is obtained if one sets $M = D$ in (2.15).

$$\mathbf{x}^{(k+1)} = \mathbf{x}^{(k)} + D^{-1}\mathbf{r}^{(k)} = -D^{-1}(L + U)\mathbf{x}^{(k)} + D^{-1}\mathbf{b}. \tag{2.18}$$

Component-wise we have

$$x_i^{(k+1)} = \frac{1}{a_{ii}}\left(b_i - \sum_{j=1, j\neq i}^{n} a_{ij}x_j^{(k)}\right) = x_i^{(k)} + \frac{1}{a_{ii}}\left(b_i - \sum_{j=1}^{n} a_{ij}x_j^{(k)}\right).$$

Not surprisingly, the Jacobi iteration converges if A is *strictly diagonally dominant*, that is, if

$$a_{ii} > \sum_{j \neq i} |a_{ij}|, \quad \text{for all } i.$$

For a proof of this and similar statements, see [136]. A block Jacobi iteration is obtained if the diagonal matrix D in (2.18) is replaced by a block diagonal matrix.

2.3.3   *Gauss–Seidel (GS) iteration*

The GS iteration is obtained if we set $M = D + L$ in (2.15) with D and L as in the previous section. Thus, the iteration is

$$(D + L)\mathbf{x}^{(k+1)} = -U\mathbf{x}^{(k)} + \mathbf{b}. \tag{2.19}$$

Component-wise we have

$$x_i^{(k+1)} = \frac{1}{a_{ii}} \left(b_i - \sum_{j<i} a_{ij} x_j^{(k+1)} - \sum_{j>i} a_{ij} x_j^{(k)} \right).$$

The GS iteration converges if A is symmetric and positive definite [60]. A block GS iteration is obtained if the diagonal matrix D in (2.19) is replaced by a block diagonal matrix.

2.3.4   *Successive and symmetric successive overrelaxation*

Successive overrelaxation (SOR) is a modification of the GS iteration and has an adjustable parameter ω. Component-wise it is defined by

$$x_i^{(k+1)} = \frac{\omega}{a_{ii}} \left(b_i - \sum_{j<i} a_{ij} x_j^{(k+1)} - \sum_{j>i} a_{ij} x_j^{(k)} \right) + (1 - \omega) x_i^{(k)}, \quad 0 < \omega < 2.$$

In matrix notation, this is

$$M_\omega \mathbf{x}^{(k+1)} = N_\omega \mathbf{x}^{(k)} + \mathbf{b}, \qquad M_\omega = \frac{1}{\omega} D + L, \quad N_\omega = \frac{1 - \omega}{\omega} D - U, \tag{2.20}$$

where again D is the diagonal, L is the strictly lower triangular, and U is the strictly upper triangular portion of A. Usually $\omega \geq 1$, whence the term *over*relaxation. SOR becomes GS iteration if $\omega = 1$. If A is symmetric, that is, if $L = U^{\mathrm{T}}$, SOR can be symmetrized to become Symmetric Successive

Overrelaxation (SSOR). To that end, Equation (2.20) is defined as the first half-step

$$M_\omega \mathbf{x}^{(k+\frac{1}{2})} = N_\omega \mathbf{x}^{(k)} + \mathbf{b}, \tag{2.21}$$

of an iteration rule that is complemented by a backward SOR step

$$M_\omega^{\mathrm{T}} \mathbf{x}^{(k+1)} = N_\omega^{\mathrm{T}} \mathbf{x}^{(k+\frac{1}{2})} + \mathbf{b}. \tag{2.22}$$

Combining (2.21) and (2.22) yields

$$\frac{\omega}{2-\omega} M_\omega D^{-1} M_\omega^{\mathrm{T}} \mathbf{x}^{(k+1)} = \frac{\omega}{2-\omega} N_\omega^{\mathrm{T}} D^{-1} N_\omega \mathbf{x}^{(k)} + \mathbf{b}. \tag{2.23}$$

The symmetric GS iteration is obtained if $\omega = 1$ is set in the SSOR iteration (2.23),

$$(D+L)D^{-1}(D+L^{\mathrm{T}}) \mathbf{x}^{(k+1)} = LD^{-1}L^{\mathrm{T}} \mathbf{x}^{(k)} + \mathbf{b}. \tag{2.24}$$

(S)SOR converges if A is symmetric positive definite (spd) and $0 < \omega < 2$, see [136] or [113, p. 253ff.].

Remark 2.3.1 With the definitions in (2.20) we can rewrite (2.22),

$$M_\omega^{\mathrm{T}} \mathbf{x}^{(k+1)} = \frac{2-\omega}{\omega} D \mathbf{x}^{(k+\frac{1}{2})} - M_\omega \mathbf{x}^{(k+\frac{1}{2})} + \mathbf{b}.$$

As $M_\omega \mathbf{x}^{(k+\frac{1}{2})}$ is known from (2.21) we can omit the multiplication by L in (2.22). A similar simplification can be made to (2.21). These savings are called the **Conrad–Wallach trick**. Ortega [113] gives a different but enlightening presentation.

Example 2.3.2 Let A be the Poisson matrix for an $n \times n$ grid. A is symmetric positive definite and has the order n^2. A has a block-tridiagonal structure where the blocks have order n. The off-diagonal blocks are minus the identity. The diagonal blocks are themselves tridiagonal with diagonal elements 4 and off-diagonal elements -1. Table 2.6 gives the number of iteration steps needed to reduce the residual by the factor 10^6 by different stationary iteration methods and two problem sizes. The algorithm used for Example 2.3.2 takes the form given in Figure 2.4.

Test numbers for this example show typical behavior. GS iterations reduce the number of iterations to achieve convergence roughly by a factor of 2 compared

Table 2.6 *Iteration steps for solving the Poisson equation on a 31×31 and on a 63×63 grid with a relative residual accuracy of 10^{-6}.*

Solver	$n = 31^2$	$n = 63^2$
Jacobi	2157	7787
Block Jacobi	1093	3943
Gauss–Seidel	1085	3905
Block Gauss–Seidel	547	1959
SSOR ($\omega = 1.8$)	85	238
Block SSOR ($\omega = 1.8$)	61	132

Choose initial vector $\mathbf{x}_0$ and convergence tolerance τ.
Set $\mathbf{r}_0 = \mathbf{b} - A\mathbf{x}_0, \quad \rho_0 = \|\mathbf{r}_0\|, \quad k = 0$.
while $\rho_k > \tau \, \rho_0$ **do**
    Solve $M\mathbf{z}_k = \mathbf{r}_k$.
    $\mathbf{x}_{k+1} = \mathbf{x}_k + \mathbf{z}_k$.
    $\mathbf{r}_{k+1} = \mathbf{b} - A\mathbf{x}_{k+1}, \quad \rho_k = \|\mathbf{r}_k\|$.
    $k = k + 1$.
endwhile

FIG. 2.4. *Stationary iteration for solving $A\mathbf{x} = \mathbf{b}$ with preconditioner M.*

with the Jacobi method. So does blocking of Jacobi and GS iterations. SSOR further reduces the number of iterations. However, for difficult problems, it is often difficult or impossible to determine the optimal value of the relaxation parameter ω.

Notice that we have listed only iteration counts in Table 2.6 and not execution times. Each iteration of a stationary iteration consists of at least one multiplication with a portion of the system matrix A and the same number of solutions with the preconditioner M. Except for the Jacobi iteration, the solutions consist of solving one (or several as with SSOR) triangular systems of equations. Usually, these linear system solutions are the most time-consuming part of the algorithm.

Another typical behavior of stationary iterations is the growth of iteration counts as the problem size increases. When the problem size grows by a factor 4, the iteration count using the Jacobi or GS iterations grows by the same factor. The growth in iteration counts is not so large when using SSOR methods. Nevertheless, we conclude that stationary iterations are not usually viable solution methods for really large problems.

2.3.5 *Krylov subspace methods*

It can be easily deduced from (2.15) and (2.17) that

$$\mathbf{x}^{(k)} = \mathbf{x}^{(0)} + M^{-1}\mathbf{r}^{(k-1)} + M^{-1}\mathbf{r}^{(k-2)} + \cdots + M^{-1}\mathbf{r}^0,$$

$$= \mathbf{x}^{(0)} + M^{-1}\sum_{j=0}^{k-1}(I - AM^{-1})^j\mathbf{r}^{(0)},$$

$$= \mathbf{x}^{(0)} + \sum_{j=0}^{k-1}G^j\mathbf{z}^{(0)}, \qquad \mathbf{z}^{(j)} = M^{-1}\mathbf{r}^{(j)}. \qquad (2.25)$$

Here, $G = I - M^{-1}A$ is the iteration matrix defined on p. 30. Vectors $\mathbf{z}^{(j)}$ are called preconditioned residuals. Thus, the kth iterate $\mathbf{x}^{(k)}$ shifted by $\mathbf{x}^{(0)}$ is a particular element of the *Krylov subspace* $\mathcal{K}_k(G, \mathbf{z}^{(0)})$ which is defined as the linear space spanned by these powers of G applied to $\mathbf{z}^{(0)}$:

$$\mathcal{K}_k(G, \mathbf{z}^{(0)}) := \operatorname{span}\{\mathbf{z}^{(0)}, G\mathbf{z}^{(0)}, \dots, G^{k-1}\mathbf{z}^{(0)}\}.$$

In Krylov subspace methods, the approximations $\mathbf{x}^{(k)}$ are found by some criterion applied to *all* vectors in $\mathcal{K}_k(G, \mathbf{z}^{(0)})$. In this book, we consider only the two most important Krylov subspace methods: the Generalized Minimal RESidual method (GMRES) for solving arbitrary (nonsingular) systems and the Preconditioned Conjugate Gradient (PCG) method for solving symmetric positive definite systems of equations. In GMRES, $\mathbf{x}^{(k)}$ is chosen to minimize $\|\mathbf{z}^{(k)}\|_2$. The preconditioned conjugate gradient method determines $\mathbf{x}^{(k)}$ such that the residual $\mathbf{r}^{(k)}$ is orthogonal to $\mathcal{K}_k(G, \mathbf{z}^{(0)})$.

If the vectors $G^j\mathbf{z}^{(0)}$ become closely aligned with an eigenvector corresponding to the absolute largest eigenvalue of G, the set $\{\mathbf{z}^{(0)}, G\mathbf{z}^{(0)}, \dots, G^{k-1}\mathbf{z}^{(0)}\}$ become a poorly conditioned basis for the Krylov subspace $\mathcal{K}_k(G, \mathbf{z}^{(0)})$. Therefore, a considerable amount of work in Krylov subspace methods is devoted to the construction of a good basis of $\mathcal{K}_k(G, \mathbf{z}^{(0)})$. In GMRES and PCG this is done by a modified Gram–Schmidt orthogonalization procedure [63]. In the context of Krylov subspaces, the Gram–Schmidt orthogonalization procedure is called Lanczos' algorithm if G is symmetric and positive definite, and Arnoldi's algorithm otherwise.

For a more comprehensive discussion of Krylov subspace methods, the reader is referred to [36]. Table 2.7 lists the most important of such methods, together with the properties of the system matrix required for their applicability.

2.3.6 *The generalized minimal residual method (GMRES)*

The GMRES is often the algorithm of choice for solving the equation $A\mathbf{x} = \mathbf{b}$. Here, we consider a variant, the *preconditioned* equation

$$M^{-1}A\mathbf{x} = M^{-1}\mathbf{b}, \qquad (2.26)$$

Table 2.7 *Some Krylov subspace methods for* $A\mathbf{x} = \mathbf{b}$ *with nonsingular* A. *On the left is its name and on the right the matrix properties it is designed for [11, 63, 127].*

Algorithm	Matrix type
GMRES	Arbitrary
Bi-CG, Bi-CGSTAB, QMR	Arbitrary
CG	Symmetric positive definite
MINRES, SYMMLQ	Symmetric
QMRS	J-symmetric

where the preconditioner M is in some sense a good approximation of A and systems of the form $M\mathbf{z} = \mathbf{r}$ can be solved much more easily than $A\mathbf{x} = \mathbf{b}$.

In GMRES, for $k = 1, 2, \ldots$, an orthogonal basis $\{\mathbf{q}_1, \mathbf{q}_2, \ldots, \mathbf{q}_k\}$ is constructed from the Krylov subspace $\mathcal{K}_k(\mathbf{z}_0, M^{-1}A)$. Notice that $\mathcal{K}_k(\mathbf{z}_0, M^{-1}A) = \mathcal{K}_k(\mathbf{z}_0, G)$. Here, $\mathbf{z}_0 = M^{-1}\mathbf{r}_0$, where $\mathbf{r}_0 = \mathbf{b} - A\mathbf{x}_0$ for some initial vector $\mathbf{x}_0$. The algorithm proceeds recursively in that computation of the orthogonal basis of $\mathcal{K}_{k+1}(\mathbf{z}_0, M^{-1}A)$ makes use of the already computed orthogonal basis of $\mathcal{K}_k(\mathbf{z}_0, M^{-1}A)$.

To see how this works, assume $\mathbf{q}_1, \mathbf{q}_2, \ldots, \mathbf{q}_k$ have already been computed. Normalized vector $\mathbf{q}_1$ is chosen by $\mathbf{q}_1 = \mathbf{z}_0/\|\mathbf{z}_0\|_2$. We get $\mathbf{q}_{k+1}$ in the following way:

- Compute the auxiliary vector $\mathbf{y}_k = M^{-1}A\mathbf{q}_k$. It can be shown that $\mathbf{y}_k$ is linear combination of $(M^{-1}A)^k\mathbf{q}_k$ and of $\mathbf{q}_1, \ldots, \mathbf{q}_k$.
- Construct a new vector $\mathbf{y}_k'$ from $\mathbf{y}_k$, orthogonal to $\mathbf{q}_1, \mathbf{q}_2, \ldots, \mathbf{q}_k$, by

$$\mathbf{y}_k' = \mathbf{y}_k - \sum_{j=1}^{k} \mathbf{q}_j h_{jk}, \quad h_{jk} = \mathbf{q}_j^{\mathrm{T}} \mathbf{y}_k. \tag{2.27}$$

- Normalize $\mathbf{y}_k'$ to make $\mathbf{q}_{k+1}$,

$$h_{k+1,k} = \|\mathbf{y}_k'\|_2, \qquad \mathbf{q}_{k+1} = \mathbf{y}_k'/h_{k+1,k} \tag{2.28}$$

Let $Q_k = [\mathbf{q}_1, \mathbf{q}_2, \ldots, \mathbf{q}_k]$. Then, (2.27) and (2.28) for $j = 1, \ldots, k$ can be collected in the form

$$M^{-1}AQ_k = Q_{k+1}H_{k+1,k} = Q_k H_{k,k} + h_{k+1,k}\mathbf{q}_{k+1}\mathbf{e}_k^{\mathrm{T}} \tag{2.29}$$

with

$$H_{k+1,k} = \begin{bmatrix} h_{11} & h_{12} & \cdots & h_{1,k} \\ h_{21} & h_{22} & \cdots & h_{2,k} \\ & h_{3,2} & \cdots & h_{3,k} \\ & & \ddots & \vdots \\ & & & h_{k+1,k} \end{bmatrix}.$$

$H_{k,k}$ is obtained by deleting the last row from $H_{k+1,k}$. Unit vector $\mathbf{e}_k$ is the last row of the $k \times k$ identity matrix. $H_{k+1,k}$ and $H_{k,k}$ are called *Hessenberg* matrices [151]. They are upper triangular matrices with an additional nonzero first lower off-diagonal.

If $h_{k+1,k} = \|\mathbf{y}'_k\|_2$ is very small we may declare the iterations to have converged. Then $M^{-1}AQ_k = Q_kH_{k,k}$ and $\mathbf{x}_k$ is in fact the solution $\mathbf{x}$ of (2.26).

In general, the approximate solution $\mathbf{x}_k = Q_k\mathbf{y}_k$ is determined such that $\|M^{-1}\mathbf{b} - M^{-1}A\mathbf{x}_k\|_2$ becomes minimal. We have

$$
\begin{aligned}
\|M^{-1}(\mathbf{b} - A\mathbf{x}_k)\|_2 &= \|\|\mathbf{b}\|_2\mathbf{q}_1 - M^{-1}AQ_k\mathbf{y}_k\|_2, \\
&= \|\|\mathbf{b}\|_2Q_{k+1}\mathbf{e}_1 - Q_{k+1}H_{k+1,k}\mathbf{y}_k\|_2, \\
&= \|\|\mathbf{b}\|_2\mathbf{e}_1 - H_{k+1,k}\mathbf{y}_k\|_2, \quad\quad\quad (2.30)
\end{aligned}
$$

where the last equality holds since Q_{k+1} has orthonormal columns. Thus, $\mathbf{y}_k$ is obtained by solving the small $k + 1 \times k$ least squares problem

$$
H_{k+1,k}\mathbf{y}_k = \|\mathbf{b}\|_2\mathbf{e}_1. \quad\quad\quad (2.31)
$$

Since $H_{k+1,k}$ is a Hessenberg matrix, the computation of its QR factorization only costs k Givens rotations. Furthermore, the QR factorization of $H_{k+1,k}$ can be computed in $\mathcal{O}(k)$ floating point operations from the QR factorization of $H_{k,k-1}$.

The GMRES method is very memory consumptive. In addition to the matrices A and M, $m + \mathcal{O}(1)$ vectors of length n have to be stored because all the vectors $\mathbf{q}_j$ are needed to compute $\mathbf{x}_k$ from $\mathbf{y}_k$. A popular way to limit the memory consumption of GMRES is to *restart* the algorithm after a certain number, say, m, of iteration steps. In the GMRES(m) algorithm, the approximate solution $\mathbf{x}_m$ is used as the initial approximation $\mathbf{x}_0$ of a completely new GMRES run. Independence of the GMRES runs gives additional freedom. For example, it is possible to change the preconditioner every iteration, see [36].

We give a possible implementation of GMRES in Figure 2.5. Notice that the application of Givens rotations set to zero the nonzeros below the diagonal of $H_{k,k}$. Vector $\mathbf{s}_{1,\dots,m}$ denotes the first m elements of $\mathbf{s}$. The absolute value $|s_m|$ of the last component of $\mathbf{s}$ equals the norm of the *preconditioned* residual. If one checks this norm as a convergence criterion, it is easy to test for convergence at each iteration step [11].

2.3.7   *The conjugate gradient (CG) method*

If the system matrix A and the preconditioner M are both symmetric and positive definite, then $M^{-1}A$ appearing in the preconditioned system (2.26) is symmetric positive and definite with respect to the M-inner product $\langle\mathbf{x},\mathbf{y}\rangle \equiv \mathbf{x}^{\mathrm{T}}M\mathbf{y}$.

Choose an initial guess $\mathbf{x}_0$, $\mathbf{r}_0 = \mathbf{b} - A\mathbf{x}_0$, $\rho_0 = \|\mathbf{r}_0\|$.
while 1 **do**
    Compute preconditioned residual $\mathbf{z}_0$ from $M\mathbf{z}_0 = \mathbf{r}_0$.
    $\mathbf{q}_1 = \mathbf{z}_0/\|\mathbf{z}_0\|$, $\mathbf{s} = \|\mathbf{z}_0\|_2\mathbf{e}_1$.
    for $k = 1, 2, \ldots, m$ **do**
        Solve $M\mathbf{y}_k = A\mathbf{q}_k$.
        for $j = 1, \ldots, k$ **do**
            $h_{jk} = \mathbf{q}_j^T\mathbf{y}_k$, $\mathbf{y}_k = \mathbf{y}_k - \mathbf{q}_j h_{jk}$
        end
        $h_{k+1,k} = \|\mathbf{y}_k\|_2$, $\mathbf{q}_{k+1} = \mathbf{y}_k/h_{k+1,k}$.
        Apply $J_1, \ldots, J_{k-1}$ on the last column of $H_{k+1,k}$.
        Generate and apply a Givens rotation J_k acting on the last
            two rows of $H_{k+1,k}$ to annihilate $h_{k+1,k}$.
        $\mathbf{s} = J_k\mathbf{s}$
    end
    Solve the upper triangular system $H_{m,m}\mathbf{t} = \mathbf{s}_{1..m}$.
    $\mathbf{x}_m = \mathbf{x}_0 + [\mathbf{q}_1, \mathbf{q}_2, \ldots, \mathbf{q}_m]\,\mathbf{t}$, $\mathbf{r}_m = \mathbf{b} - A\mathbf{x}_m$
    if $\|\mathbf{r}_m\|_2 < \epsilon \cdot \rho_0$ **then**
        Return with $\mathbf{x} = \mathbf{x}_m$ as the approximate solution
    end
    $\mathbf{x}_0 = \mathbf{x}_m$, $\mathbf{r}_0 = \mathbf{r}_m$
end

FIG. 2.5. *The preconditioned GMRES(m) algorithm.*

In fact, for all $\mathbf{x}, \mathbf{y}$, we have

$$\langle \mathbf{x}, M^{-1}A\mathbf{y} \rangle_M = \mathbf{x}^T M(M^{-1}A\mathbf{y}) = \mathbf{x}^T A\mathbf{y},$$
$$= \mathbf{x}^T A M^{-1}M\mathbf{y} = (M^{-1}A\mathbf{x})^T M\mathbf{y} = \langle M^{-1}A\mathbf{x}, \mathbf{y} \rangle_M.$$

If we execute the GMRES algorithm using this M-inner product, then the Hessenberg matrix $H_{k,k}$ becomes symmetric, that is, tridiagonal. This implies that $\mathbf{y}_k$ in (2.27) has to be explicitly made orthogonal only to $\mathbf{q}_k$ and $\mathbf{q}_{k-1}$ to become orthogonal to *all* previous basis vectors $\mathbf{q}_1, \mathbf{q}_2, \ldots, \mathbf{q}_k$. So, for the expansion of the sequence of Krylov subspaces only three basis vectors have to be stored in memory at a time. This is the Lanczos algorithm.

Like GMRES, the **Lanczos algorithm** constructs an (M-)orthonormal basis of a Krylov subspace where the generating matrix is symmetric. In contrast, the CG method, first suggested by Hestenes and Stiefel [72], targets directly improving approximations $\mathbf{x}_k$ of the solution $\mathbf{x}$ of (2.26). $\mathbf{x}_k$ is improved along a search direction, $\mathbf{p}_{k+1}$, such that the functional $\varphi = \frac{1}{2}\mathbf{x}^T A\mathbf{x} - \mathbf{x}^T\mathbf{b}$ becomes minimal at the new approximation $\mathbf{x}_{k+1} = \mathbf{x}_k + \alpha_k\mathbf{p}_{k+1}$. φ has its global minimum

> Choose $\mathbf{x}_0$ and a convergence tolerance ε.
> Set $\mathbf{r}_0 = \mathbf{b} - A\mathbf{x}_0$ and solve $M\mathbf{z}_0 = \mathbf{r}_0$.
> Set $\rho_0 = \mathbf{z}_0^T \mathbf{r}_0$, $\mathbf{p}_1 = \mathbf{z}_0$.
> **for** $k = 1, 2, \ldots$ **do**
> $\qquad \mathbf{q}_k = A\mathbf{p}_k$.
> $\qquad \alpha_k = \rho_{k-1}/\mathbf{p}_k^T \mathbf{q}_k$.
> $\qquad \mathbf{x}_k = \mathbf{x}_{k-1} + \alpha_k \mathbf{p}_k$.
> $\qquad \mathbf{r}_k = \mathbf{r}_{k-1} - \alpha_k \mathbf{q}_k$.
> $\qquad$ Solve $M\mathbf{z}_k = \mathbf{r}_k$.
> $\qquad$ **if** $\|\mathbf{r}_k\| < \varepsilon \|\mathbf{r}_0\|$ **then** exit.
> $\qquad \rho_k = \mathbf{z}_k^T \mathbf{r}_k$.
> $\qquad \beta_k = \rho_k/\rho_{k-1}$.
> $\qquad \mathbf{p}_{k+1} = \mathbf{z}_k + \beta_k \mathbf{p}_k$.
> **end**

FIG. 2.6. *The preconditioned conjugate gradient algorithm.*

at $\mathbf{x}$. The **preconditioned conjugate gradient** (PCG) algorithm is shown in Figure 2.6. In the course of the algorithm, residual and preconditioned residual vectors $\mathbf{r}_k = \mathbf{b} - A\mathbf{x}_k$ and $\mathbf{z}_k = M^{-1}\mathbf{r}_k$, respectively, are computed. The iteration is usually stopped if the norm of the actual residual $\mathbf{r}_k$ has dropped below a small fraction ε of the initial residual $\mathbf{r}_0$. Lanczos and CG algorithms are closely related. An elaboration of this relationship is given in Golub and Van Loan [60].

Both GMRES and CG have a finite termination property. That is, at step n, the algorithms will terminate. However, this is of little practical value since to be useful the number of iterations needed for convergence must be much lower than n, the order of the system of equations. The *convergence rate* of the CG algorithm is given by

$$\|\mathbf{x} - \mathbf{x}_k\|_A \leq \|\mathbf{x} - \mathbf{x}_0\|_A \left(\frac{\sqrt{\kappa} - 1}{\sqrt{\kappa} + 1} \right)^k,$$

where $\kappa = \|M^{-1}A\| \|A^{-1}M\|$ is the *condition number* of $M^{-1}A$. In general, κ is close to unity only if M is a good preconditioner for A.

Example 2.3.3 We consider the same problem as in Example 2.3.2 but now use the conjugate gradient method as our solver preconditioned by one step of a stationary iteration. Table 2.8 lists the number of iteration steps needed to reduce the residual by the factor $\varepsilon = 10^{-6}$. The numbers of iteration steps have been reduced by at least a factor of 10. Because the work per iteration step is not much larger with PCG than with stationary iterations, the execution times are similarly reduced by large factors.

Table 2.8 *Iteration steps for solving the Poisson equation on a 31×31 and on a 63×63 grid with an relative residual accuracy of 10^{-6}. PCG with preconditioner as indicated.*

Preconditioner	$n = 31^2$	$n = 63^2$
Jacobi	76	149
Block Jacobi	57	110
Symmetric Gauss–Seidel	33	58
Symmetric block Gauss–Seidel	22	39
SSOR ($\omega = 1.8$)	18	26
Block SSOR ($\omega = 1.8$)	15	21

2.3.8 *Parallelization*

The most time consuming portions of PCG and GMRES are the matrix–vector multiplications by system matrix A and solving linear systems with the preconditioner M. Computations of inner products and vector norms can become expensive, however, when vectors are distributed over memories with weak connections. Thus, in this section we consider parallelizing these three crucial operations. We assume that the sparse matrices are distributed block row-wise over the processors. Accordingly, vectors are distributed in blocks.

While we fix the way we store our data, we do not fix in advance the numbering of rows and columns in matrices. We will see that this numbering can strongly affect the parallelizability of the crucial operations in PCG and GMRES.

2.3.9 *The sparse matrix vector product*

There are a number of ways sparse matrices can be stored in memory. For an exhaustive overview on sparse storage formats see [73, p. 430ff.]. Here, we only consider the popular *compressed sparse row* (CSR, or Yale storage) format. It is the basic storage mechanism used in SPARSKIT [128] or PETSc [9] where it is called generalized sparse AIJ format. Another convenient format, particularly when A is *structurally* symmetric (i.e. if $a_{ij} \neq 0 \rightarrow a_{ji} \neq 0$) is the BLSMP storage from Kent Smith [95].

In the CSR format, the *nonzero* elements of an $n \times m$ matrix are stored row-wise in a list `val` of length nnz equal to the number of nonzero elements of the matrix. Together with the list `val` there is an index list `col_ind`, also of length nnz, and another index list `col_ptr` of length $n + 1$. List element `col_ind[i]` holds the column index of the matrix element stored in `val[i]`. List item `col_ptr[j]` points to the location in `val` where the first nonzero matrix element of row j is stored, while `col_ptr[n]` points to the memory location right

```
for (i=0; i < n; i++){
    y[i] = 0.0;
    for (j=col_ptr[i]; j < col_ptr[i+1]; j++)
        y[i] = y[i] + val[j]*x[col_ind[j]];
}
```

FIG. 2.7. *Sparse matrix–vector multiplication* $\mathbf{y} = A\mathbf{x}$ *with the matrix A stored in the CSR format.*

behind the last element in `val`. For illustration, let

$$A = \begin{bmatrix} 1 & 0 & 0 & 0 & 0 \\ 0 & 2 & 5 & 0 & 0 \\ 0 & 3 & 6 & 0 & 9 \\ 0 & 4 & 0 & 8 & 0 \\ 0 & 0 & 7 & 0 & 10 \end{bmatrix}.$$

Then,

$$\mathtt{val} = [1, 2, 5, 3, 6, 9, 4, 8, 7, 10],$$
$$\mathtt{col\_ind} = [1, 2, 3, 2, 3, 5, 2, 4, 3, 5],$$
$$\mathtt{col\_ptr} = [1, 2, 4, 7, 9].$$

If A is symmetric, then it is only necessary to store either the upper or the lower triangle.

A matrix–vector multiplication $\mathbf{y} = A\mathbf{x}$ can be coded in the way shown in Figure 2.7. Here, the elements of the vector $\mathbf{x}$ are addressed *indirectly* via the index array `col_ptr`. We will revisit such indirect addressing in Chapter 3, Section 3.2.2 where the `x[col_ptr[j]]` fetches are called **gather** operations. Indirect addressing can be very slow due to the irregular memory access pattern. Block CSR storage, however, can improve performance significantly [58]. Parallelizing the matrix–vector product is straightforward. Using OpenMP on a shared memory computer, the outer loop is parallelized with a compiler directive just as in the dense matrix–vector product, for example, Section 4.8.1. On a distributed memory machine, each processor gets a block of rows. Often each processor gets $\lceil n/p \rceil$ rows such that the last processor possible has less work to do. Sometimes, for example, in PETSc [9], the rows are distributed so that each processor holds (almost) the same number of rows or nonzero elements. The vectors $\mathbf{x}$ and $\mathbf{y}$ are distributed accordingly. Each processor executes a code segment as given in Figure 2.7 to compute its segment of $\mathbf{y}$. However, there will be elements of vector $\mathbf{x}$ stored on other processors that may have to be gathered. Unlike the dense case, where each processor needs to get data from every other processor and thus calls `MPI_Allgather`, in the sparse case there are generally

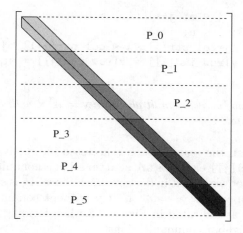

FIG. 2.8. *Sparse matrix with band-like nonzero structure row-wise block distributed on six processors.*

just a few nonzero elements required from the other processor memories. Furthermore, not all processors need the same, or same amount of, data. Therefore, a call to MPI_Alltoallv may be appropriate.

Very often communication can be reduced by reordering the matrix. For example, if the nonzero elements of the matrix all lie inside a band as depicted in Figure 2.8, then a processor needs only data from nearest neighbors to be able to form its portion of $A\mathbf{x}$.

It is in principle possible to hide some communication latencies by a careful coding of the necessary send and receive commands. To see this, we split the portion A_i of the matrix A that is local to processor i in three submatrices. A_{ii} is the diagonal block that is to be multiplied with the local portion $\mathbf{x}_i$ of $\mathbf{x}$. $A_{i,i-1}$ and $A_{i,i+1}$ are the submatrices of A_i that are to be multiplied with $\mathbf{x}_{i-1}$ and $\mathbf{x}_{i+1}$, the portions of $\mathbf{x}$ that reside on processors $i-1$ and $i+1$, respectively. Then, by proceeding in the following three steps

- **Step 1:** Form $\mathbf{y}_i = A_{ii}\mathbf{x}_i$ (these are all local data) and concurrently receive $\mathbf{x}_{i-1}$.
- **Step 2:** Update $\mathbf{y}_i \leftarrow \mathbf{y}_i + A_{i,i-1}\mathbf{x}_{i-1}$ and concurrently receive $\mathbf{x}_{i+1}$.
- **Step 3:** Update $\mathbf{y}_i \leftarrow \mathbf{y}_i + A_{i,i+1}\mathbf{x}_{i+1}$.

some fraction of the communication can be hidden under the computation. This technique is called *latency hiding* and exploits non-blocking communication as implemented in MPI_Isend and MPI_Irecv (see Appendix D). An analogous latency hiding in the SIMD mode of parallelism is given in Figure 3.6, where it is usually more effective.

In Figure 2.7 we have given a code snippet for forming $\mathbf{y} = A\mathbf{x}$. We have seen, that the vector $\mathbf{x}$ was accessed indirectly. If one multiplies with A^{T}, that is, if one

```
for (j=0; j < m; j++) y[i] = 0.0;
for (i=0; i < n; i++){
    for (j=col_ptr[i]; j < col_ptr[i+1]; j++)
        y[row_ind[j]] = y[row_ind[j]] + val[j]*x[i];
}
```

FIG. 2.9. *Sparse matrix–vector multiplication* $\mathbf{y} = A^{\mathrm{T}}\mathbf{x}$ *with the matrix A stored in the CSR format.*

forms $\mathbf{y} = A^{\mathrm{T}}\mathbf{x}$, then the *result* vector is accessed indirectly, see Figure 2.9. In this case, y[row_ind[j]] elements are **scattered** in a nonuniform way back into memory, an operation we revisit in Section 3.2.2. Since A^{T} is stored column-wise, we first form local portions $\mathbf{y}_i = A_i^{\mathrm{T}}\mathbf{x}_i$ of $\mathbf{y}$ without communication. If A has a banded structure as indicated in Figure 2.8, then forming $\mathbf{y} = \sum \mathbf{y}_i$ involves only the nearest neighbor communications.

If only the upper or lower triangle of a symmetric matrix is stored, then both matrix–vector multiplies have to be used, one for multiplying with the original matrix, one for multiplying with its transpose.

Remark 2.3.4 The above matrix–vector multiplications should, of course, be constructed on a set of sparse BLAS. Work on a set of sparse BLAS is in progress [43].

2.3.10 *Preconditioning and parallel preconditioning*

2.3.10.1 *Preconditioning with stationary iterations*

As you can see in Figures 2.5 and 2.6, both GMRES and PCG require the solution of a system of equations $M\mathbf{z} = \mathbf{r}$, where M is the preconditioner. Since M approximates A it is straightforward to execute a fixed number of steps of stationary iterations to approximately solve $A\mathbf{z} = \mathbf{r}$.

Let $A = M_1 - N_1$ be a splitting of A, where M_1 is an spd matrix. As we derived in Section 2.3.1, the corresponding stationary iteration for solving $A\mathbf{z} = \mathbf{r}$ is given by

$$M_1\mathbf{z}^{(k)} = N_1\mathbf{z}^{(k-1)} + \mathbf{r} \quad \text{or} \quad \mathbf{z}^{(k)} = G\mathbf{z}^{(k-1)} + \mathbf{c}, \tag{2.32}$$

where $G = M_1^{-1}N_1 = I - M_1^{-1}A$ is the iteration matrix and $\mathbf{c} = M_1^{-1}\mathbf{r}$. If the iteration is started with $\mathbf{z}^{(0)} = \mathbf{0}$, then we have seen in (2.25) that

$$\mathbf{z}^{(k)} = \sum_{j=0}^{k-1} G^j\mathbf{c} = \sum_{j=0}^{k-1} G^j M_1^{-1}\mathbf{r}, \quad k > 0. \tag{2.33}$$

Sum $\sum_{j=0}^{k-1} G^j$ is a truncated approximation to $A^{-1}M_1 = (I - G)^{-1} = \sum_{j=0}^{\infty} G^j$. Thus, if the preconditioner M is defined by applying m steps of a stationary iteration, then

$$\mathbf{z} = M^{-1}\mathbf{r} = (I + G + \cdots + G^{m-1})M_1^{-1}\mathbf{r}. \tag{2.34}$$

This preconditioner is symmetric if A and M_1 are also symmetric.

We note that the preconditioner is *not* applied in the form (2.34), but as the iteration given in (2.32). Frequently, the preconditioner consists of only one step of the iteration (2.32). In that case, $M = M_1$.

2.3.10.2   *Jacobi preconditioning*

In Jacobi preconditioning, we set $M_1 = D = \text{diag}(A)$. If $m = 1$ in (2.32)–(2.34), then

$$\mathbf{z} = \mathbf{z}^{(1)} = D^{-1}\mathbf{r},$$

which is easy to parallelize. $D^{-1}\mathbf{r}^{(k)}$ corresponds to an elementwise vector–vector or Hadamard product. To improve its usually mediocre quality without degrading the parallelization property, Jacobi preconditioning can be replaced by block Jacobi preconditioning. The diagonal M_1 is replaced by a block diagonal M_1 such that each block resides entirely on one processor.

2.3.10.3   *Parallel Gauss–Seidel preconditioning*

Gauss–Seidel preconditioning is defined by

$$z_i^{(k+1)} = \frac{1}{a_{ii}}\left(c_i - \sum_{j<i} a_{ij} z_j^{(k+1)} - \sum_{j>i} a_{ij} z_i^{(k)} \right), \qquad (2.35)$$

from Section 2.3.3. Each step of the GS iteration requires the solution of a triangular system of equations. From the point of view of computational complexity and parallelization, SOR and GS are very similar.

If the lower triangle of L is dense, then GS is tightly recursive. In the case where L is sparse, the degree of parallelism depends on the sparsity pattern. Just like solving tridiagonal systems, the degree of parallelism can be improved by permuting A. Note that the original matrix A is permuted and not L. L inherits the sparsity pattern of the lower triangle of A.

The best known permutation is probably the *checkerboard* or *red-black* ordering for problems defined on rectangular grids. Again (Example 2.3.2), let A be the matrix that is obtained by discretizing the Poisson equation $-\Delta u = f$ (Δ is the Laplace operator) on a square domain by 5-point finite differences in a 9×9 grid. The grid and the sparsity pattern of the corresponding matrix A is given in Figure 2.10 for the case where the grid points are numbered in lexicographic order, that is, row by row. Since there are elements in the first lower off-diagonal of A, and thus of L, the update of $z_i^{(k+1)}$ in (2.35) has to wait until $z_{i-1}^{(k+1)}$ is known. If the unknowns are *colored* as indicated in Figure 2.11(left) and first the white (red) unknowns are numbered and subsequently the black unknowns, the

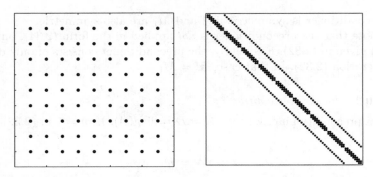

FIG. 2.10. *9 × 9 grid (left) and sparsity pattern of the corresponding Poisson matrix (right) if grid points are numbered in lexicographic order.*

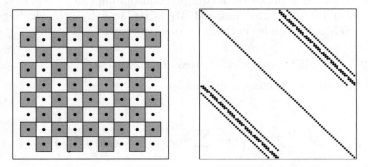

FIG. 2.11. *9 × 9 grid (left) and sparsity pattern of the corresponding Poisson matrix (right) if grid points are numbered in checkerboard (often called red-black) ordering. Note that the color red is indicated as white in the figure.*

sparsity pattern is changed completely, cf. Figure 2.11(right). Now the matrix has a 2×2 block structure,

$$A = \begin{bmatrix} D_{\mathrm{w}} & A_{\mathrm{wb}} \\ A_{\mathrm{bw}} & D_{\mathrm{b}} \end{bmatrix},$$

where the diagonal blocks are diagonal. Here, the indices "w" and "b" refer to white (red) and black unknowns. With this notation, one step of SOR becomes

$$
\begin{aligned}
\mathbf{z}_{\mathrm{w}}^{(k+1)} &= D_{\mathrm{w}}^{-1}(\mathbf{b}_{\mathrm{w}} - A_{\mathrm{wb}}\mathbf{z}_{\mathrm{b}}^{(k)}), \\
\mathbf{z}_{\mathrm{b}}^{(k+1)} &= D_{\mathrm{b}}^{-1}(\mathbf{b}_{\mathrm{b}} - A_{\mathrm{bw}}\mathbf{z}_{\mathrm{w}}^{(k+1)}).
\end{aligned}
\tag{2.36}
$$

This structure admits parallelization if both the black and the white (red) unknowns are distributed evenly among the processors. Each of the two steps in (2.36) then comprises a sparse matrix–vector multiplication and a multiplication with the inverse of a diagonal matrix. The first has been discussed in the previous section; the latter is easy to parallelize, again as a Hadamard product.

2.3.10.4   Domain decomposition

Instead of coloring single grid points, one may prefer to color groups of grid points or grid points in subdomains as indicated in Figure 2.12—again for the Poisson equation on the square grid. To formalize this approach, let us denote the whole computational domain Ω and the subdomains Ω_i, $i = 1, \ldots, d$. We require that Ω is covered by the Ω_i, $\Omega = \cup_i \Omega_i$. This means that each point $\mathbf{x} \in \Omega$: in particular, each grid point is an element of at least one of the subdomains. This approach is called *domain decomposition* [132]. In the example in Figure 2.12, all subdomains are mutually disjoint: $\Omega_i \cap \Omega_j = \emptyset$, if $i \neq j$. In Figure 2.13, the subdomains overlap.

Let R_j be the matrix consisting of those columns of the identity matrix that correspond to the numbers of the grid points in Ω_j. (R_j^{T} extracts from a vector those components that belong to subdomain Ω_j.) Then $\Omega = \cup_j \Omega_j$ implies that each column of the identity matrix appears in at least one of the R_j. Furthermore, if the subdomains do not overlap, then each column of the identity matrix appears in exactly one of the R_j. By means of the R_js, the blocks on the diagonal of A and the residuals corresponding to the jth subdomain are

$$A|_{\Omega_j} = A_j = R_j^{\mathrm{T}} A R_j,$$
$$(\mathbf{b} - A\mathbf{z}^{(k)})|_{\Omega_j} = R_j^{\mathrm{T}}(\mathbf{b} - A\mathbf{z}^{(k)}). \tag{2.37}$$

When we step through the subdomains, we update those components of the approximation $\mathbf{z}^{(k)}$ corresponding to the respective domain. This can be

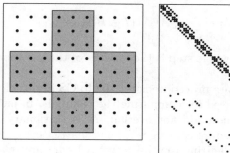

FIG. 2.12. *9 × 9 grid (left) and sparsity pattern of the corresponding Poisson matrix (right) if grid points are arranged in checkerboard (red-black) ordering.*

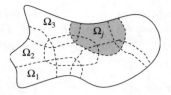

FIG. 2.13. *Overlapping domain decomposition.*

written as

$$\mathbf{z}^{(k+i/d)} = \mathbf{z}^{(k+(i-1)/d)} + R_j A_j^{-1} R_j^{\mathrm{T}} (\mathbf{b} - A\mathbf{z}^{(k+(i-1)/d)}),$$

$$\equiv \mathbf{z}^{(k+(i-1)/d)} + B_j \mathbf{r}^{(k+(i-1)/d)}, \quad i = 1, \ldots, d. \tag{2.38}$$

We observe that $P_j := B_j A$ is an A-orthogonal projector, that is

$$P_j = P_j^2, \qquad AP_j = P_j^{\mathrm{T}} A.$$

Iteration (2.38) is called a *multiplicative Schwarz* procedure [130]. The adjective "multiplicative" comes from the behavior of the iteration matrices. From (2.38) we see that

$$\mathbf{e}^{(k+j/d)} = (I - R_j (R_j^{\mathrm{T}} A R_j)^{-1} R_j^{\mathrm{T}} A)\mathbf{e}^{(k+(j-1)/d)} = (I - B_j A)\mathbf{e}^{(k+(j-1)/d)}.$$

Thus,

$$\mathbf{e}^{(k+1)} = (I - B_d A) \cdots (I - B_1 A)\mathbf{e}^{(k)}.$$

The iteration matrix of the whole step is the *product* of the iteration matrices of the single steps.

The multiplicative Schwarz procedure is related to GS iteration wherein only the most recent values are used for computing the residuals. In fact, it *is* block GS iteration if the subdomains do not overlap. As a stationary method, the multiplicative Schwarz procedure converges for spd matrices.

The problems with parallelizing multiplicative Schwarz are related to those parallelizing GS and the solution is the same, *coloring*. Let us color the subdomains such that domains that have a common edge (or even overlap) do not have the same color. From Figure 2.12 we see that two colors are enough in the case of the Poisson matrix on a rectangular grid. More generally, if we have q

colors, then

$$\mathbf{x}^{(k+1/q)} = \mathbf{x}^{(k)} + \sum_{j\in\text{color}_1} B_j\mathbf{r}^{(k)},$$

$$\mathbf{x}^{(k+2/q)} = \mathbf{x}^{(k+1/q)} + \sum_{j\in\text{color}_2} B_j\mathbf{r}^{(k+1/q)},$$

$$\vdots$$

$$\mathbf{x}^{(k+1)} = \mathbf{x}^{(k+1-1/q)} \sum_{j\in\text{color}_q} B_j\mathbf{r}^{(k+1-1/q)}.$$

As subdomains with the same color do not overlap, the updates corresponding to domains that have the same color can be computed simultaneously.

An *additive Schwarz* procedure is given by

$$\mathbf{z}^{(k+1)} = \mathbf{z}^{(k)} + \sum_{j=1}^{d} B_j\mathbf{r}^{(k)}, \quad \mathbf{r}^{(k)} = \mathbf{b} - A\mathbf{z}^{(k)}. \tag{2.39}$$

If the domains do not overlap, then the additive Schwarz preconditioner coincides with the block Jacobi preconditioner $\text{diag}(A_1, \ldots, A_d)$. If the Ω_j do overlap as in Figure 2.13, the additive Schwarz iteration may diverge as a stationary iteration but can be useful as a preconditioner in a Krylov subspace method. Additive Schwarz preconditioners are, as the related Jacobi iterations, easily parallelized. Nevertheless, in (2.39) care has to be taken when updating grid points corresponding to overlap regions.

2.3.10.5   *Incomplete Cholesky factorization/ICCG(0)*

Very popular preconditioners are obtained by *incomplete factorizations* [129].

A direct solution of $A\mathbf{z} = \mathbf{r}$, when A is spd, involves finding a version of the square root of A, $A = LL^\mathrm{T}$, which in most situations will generate a lot of fill-in. This may render the direct solution infeasible with regard to operations count and memory consumption.

An incomplete LU or Cholesky factorization can help in this situation. Incomplete factorizations are obtained by ignoring some of the fill-in. Thus,

$$A = LL^\mathrm{T} + R, \quad R \neq O.$$

R is nonzero at places where A is zero. One of the most used incomplete Cholesky factorizations is called IC(0), see Figure 2.14. Here, the sparsity structure of the lower triangular portion of the incomplete Cholesky factor is a priori specified to be the structure of the original matrix A. The incomplete LU factorization ILU(0) for nonsymmetric matrices is defined in a similar way.

The incomplete Cholesky LU factorization can be parallelized quite like the original LU or Cholesky factorization. It is simplified because the zero structure of the triangular factor is known in advance.

```
for k = 1, ..., n do
    l_{kk} = √(a_{kk});
    for i = k + 1, ..., n do
        l_{ik} = l_{ik}/l_{kk};
        for j = k + 1, ..., n do
            if a_{ij} = 0 then l_{ij} = 0 else
                a_{ij} = a_{ij} − l_{ik}l_{kj};
            endif
        endfor
    endfor
endfor
```

FIG. 2.14. *The incomplete Cholesky factorization with zero fill-in.*

2.3.10.6 *Sparse approximate inverses (SPAI)*

SPAI preconditioners are obtained by finding the solution of

$$\min_K \|I - AK\|^2_{\mathbf{F}} = \sum_{i=1}^n \|\mathbf{e}_i - A\mathbf{k}_i\|,$$

where K has a given sparsity structure. Here, $\mathbf{k}_i = K\mathbf{e}_i$ is the ith column of K. SPAI preconditioners are quite expensive to compute. However, their set-up parallelizes nicely since the columns of K can be computed independent of each other. Likewise, SPAI preconditioners also parallelize well in their application.

As the name says, SPAI is an approximate inverse of A. Therefore, in the iterative solver, we *multiply* with K. With our previous notation, $K = M^{-1}$.

$$M\mathbf{z} = \mathbf{r} \iff \mathbf{z} = M^{-1}\mathbf{r} = K\mathbf{r}.$$

There are variants of SPAI in which the number of the zeros per column are increased until $\|\mathbf{e}_i - A\mathbf{k}_i\| < \tau$ for some τ [65]. There are also symmetric SPAI preconditioners [88] that compute a sparse approximate inverse of a Cholesky factor.

2.3.10.7 *Polynomial preconditioning*

A preconditioner of the form

$$M = p(A) = \sum_{j=0}^{m-1} \gamma_j A^j$$

is called a *polynomial preconditioner*. The polynomial $p(A)$ is determined to approximate A^{-1}, that is, $p(\lambda) \approx \lambda^{-1}$ for $\lambda \in \sigma(A)$. Here, $\sigma(A)$ denotes the set of eigenvalues of A. See Saad [129] for an overview.

Polynomial preconditioners are easy to implement, in particular, on parallel or vector processors as they just require matrix–vector multiplication and no inner products. However, iterative Krylov subspace methods such as CG or GMRES construct approximate solutions in a Krylov subspace with the same number of matrix–vector products that satisfy some optimality properties. Therefore, a (inner) Krylov subspace method is generally more effective than a polynomial preconditioner.

2.4 Fast Fourier Transform (FFT)

According to Gilbert Strang, the idea of FFT originated with Karl Friedrich Gauss around 1805. However, the algorithm suitable for digital computers was invented by Cooley and Tukey in 1965 [21]. It is this latter formulation which became one of the most famous algorithms in computation developed in the twentieth century. There is a vast literature on FFT and readers serious about this topic should consult Van Loan's book [96] not only for its comprehensive treatment but also for the extensive bibliography. Additionally, E. Oran Brigham's two books [15] and [16], have clear-headed concise discussions of symmetries, and perhaps more important, how to use the FFT.

Our intent here is far more modest. Even the topic of parallel algorithms for FFT has an enormous literature—and again, Van Loan's book [96] does well in the bibliographic enumeration of this narrower topic. In fact, it was known to Gauss that the splitting we show below was suitable for parallel computers. Computers in his case were women, whom he acknowledged were not only fast but accurate (*schnell und präzis*).

Written in its most basic form, the discrete Fourier Transform is simply a linear transformation

$$\mathbf{y} = W_n \mathbf{x},$$

where $\mathbf{x}, \mathbf{y} \in \mathbf{C}^n$ are complex n-vectors, and $n^{-1/2} W_n$ is a unitary matrix. The matrix elements of W_n are

$$w_{p,q} = \mathrm{e}^{(2\pi i/n)pq} \equiv \omega^{pq},$$

where $\omega = \exp(2\pi i/n)$ is the nth root of unity. For convenience, we number the elements according to the C numbering convention: $0 \leq p, q \leq n - 1$. As written, the amount of computation is that of matrix times vector multiply, $O(n^2)$. What makes the FFT possible is that W_n has many symmetries. In our superficial survey here, we treat only the classic case where n, the dimension of the problem, is a power of 2: $n = 2^m$ for some integer $m \geq 0$. If n is a product of small prime factors, $n = 2^r 3^s 5^t \ldots$, the generalized prime factor algorithm can be used [141]. If n contains large primes, the usual procedure is to pad the vector to a convenient larger size, and use a convolution procedure. For example see Van Loan's [96, section 4.2.6].

Here are some obvious symmetries:

$$w_{p,n-q} = \bar{w}_{p,q}, \qquad w_{n-p,q} = \bar{w}_{p,q}, \qquad\qquad (2.40)$$

$$w_{p,q+n/2} = (-1)^p w_{p,q}, \qquad w_{p+n/2,q} = (-1)^q w_{p,q}, \qquad (2.40a)$$

$$w_{p,q+n/4} = i^p w_{p,q}, \qquad w_{p+n/4,q} = i^q w_{p,q}. \qquad\qquad (2.40b)$$

Because of the first pair of symmetries, only $n/2$ elements of W are independent, the others being linear combinations (frequently very simple) of these $n/2$. As above, $\omega = \exp(2\pi i/n)$ is the nth root of unity. The first row of the matrix W_n is all ones. Now call the set $\mathbf{w} = \{1, \omega, \omega^2, \omega^3, \ldots, \omega^{n/2-1}\}$; then the second row of W_n is $w_{1,q=0\ldots n-1} = \{\mathbf{w}, -\mathbf{w}\}$. The first half of the third row is every other element of the second row, while the next half of the third row is just the negative of the first half, and so forth. The point is that only $\mathbf{w}$, the first $n/2$ powers of ω, are needed. Historically, the pre-computed roots of unity, $\mathbf{w} = (1, \omega, \omega^2, \ldots, \omega^{n/2-1})$, with $\omega = \exp(2\pi i/n)$, were called "twiddle factors."

Let us see how the FFT works: the output is

$$y_p = \sum_{q=0}^{n-1} \omega^{pq} x_q, \quad p = 0, \ldots, n-1.$$

Gauss's idea is to split this sum into even/odd parts:

$$y_p = \sum_{q \text{ even}} \omega^{p \cdot q} x_q + (\text{odd}),$$

$$= \sum_{r=0}^{n/2-1} \omega_n^{p \cdot (2r)} x_{2r} + \sum_{r=0}^{n/2-1} \omega_n^{p \cdot (2r+1)} x_{2r+1},$$

$$= \sum_{r=0}^{n/2-1} \omega_{n/2}^{p \cdot r} x_{2r} + \omega_n^p \sum_{r=0}^{n/2-1} \omega_{n/2}^{p \cdot r} x_{2r+1},$$

$$\mathbf{y} = W_{n/2} \mathbf{x}_{\text{even}} + \text{diag}(\mathbf{w}_n) W_{n/2} \mathbf{x}_{\text{odd}},$$

$$\mathbf{y}_{n/2} = W_{n/2} \mathbf{x}_{\text{even}} - \text{diag}(\mathbf{w}_n) W_{n/2} \mathbf{x}_{\text{odd}},$$

where $\text{diag}(\mathbf{w}_n) = \text{diag}(1, \omega, \omega^2, \ldots, \omega^{n/2-1})$. The $\mathbf{y}_{n/2}$ is the second half of $\mathbf{y}$ and the minus sign is a result of (2.40a). Already you should be able to see what happens: the operation count: $\mathbf{y} = W_n \mathbf{x}$ has $8n^2$ real operations (*, +). Splitting gives

$$\underbrace{8\left(\frac{n}{2}\right)^2}_{\text{even}} + \underbrace{6n}_{\text{diag} *} + \underbrace{8\left(\frac{n}{2}\right)^2}_{\text{odd}} = 4n^2 + 6n,$$

a reduction in floating point operations of nearly $1/2$. A variant of this idea (called splitting in the time domain) is to split the output and is called decimation in the frequency domain. We get

$$y_{2\cdot r} = \sum_{q=0}^{n-1} \omega_n^{2\cdot r \cdot q} x_q,$$

$$= \sum_{q=0}^{n/2-1} \cdot \omega_{n/2}^{r\cdot q}(x_q + x_{n/2+q}),$$

$$\mathbf{y}_{\text{even}} = W_{n/2}(\mathbf{x} + \mathbf{x}_{n/2}), \tag{2.41}$$

$$y_{2\cdot r+1} = \sum_{q=0}^{n-1} \omega_n^{(2r+1)\cdot q} x_q,$$

$$= \sum_{q=0}^{n/2-1} \omega_{n/2}^{r\cdot q}\omega_n^q(x_q - x_{(n/2)+q}),$$

$$\mathbf{y}_{\text{odd}} = W_{n/2}\left[\text{diag}(\mathbf{w}_n)(\mathbf{x} - \mathbf{x}_{n/2})\right]. \tag{2.42}$$

In both forms, time domain or frequency domain, the idea of separating the calculation into even/odd parts can then be repeated. In the first stage, we end up with two $n/2 \times n/2$ transforms and a diagonal scaling. Each of the two transforms is of $O((n/2)^2)$, hence the savings of $1/2$ for the calculation. Now we split each $W_{n/2}$ transformation portion into two $W_{n/4}$ operations (four altogether), then into eight $W_{n/8}$, and so forth until the transforms become W_2 and we are done.

Let us expand on this variant, *decimation in frequency*, in order to see how it works in more general cases. For example, if $n = 2^{m_1}3^{m_2}5^{m_3}\cdots$ can be factored into products of small primes, the resulting algorithm is called the general prime factor algorithm (GPFA) [141]. To do this, we write the above splitting in matrix form: as above,

$$\mathbf{y}_{\text{even}} = \{y_{2\cdot r}|r = 0,\ldots,n/2-1\},$$

$$\mathbf{y}_{\text{odd}} = \{y_{2\cdot r+1}|r = 0,\ldots,n/2-1\},$$

$$\mathbf{x}^+ = \{x_r + x_{r+n/2}|r = 0,\ldots,n/2-1\},$$

$$\mathbf{x}^- = \{x_r - x_{r+n/2}|r = 0,\ldots,n/2-1\},$$

and

$$D = \text{diag}(\mathbf{w}_n) = \text{diag}(1,\omega,\omega^2,\ldots,\omega^{n/2-1}),$$

to get

$$\left(\begin{array}{c} \mathbf{y}_{\text{even}} \\ \mathbf{y}_{\text{odd}} \end{array} \right) = \left(\begin{array}{cc} W_{n/2} & \\ & W_{n/2} \end{array} \right) \left(\begin{array}{cc} I_{n/2} & \\ & D_{n/2} \end{array} \right) \left(\begin{array}{c} \mathbf{x}^{+} \\ \mathbf{x}^{-} \end{array} \right). \tag{2.43}$$

Now some notation is required. An operation $\otimes$ between two matrices is called a Kronecker (or "outer") product, which for matrix A $(p \times p)$ and matrix B $(q \times q)$, is written as

$$\underbrace{A}_{p \times p} \otimes \underbrace{B}_{q \times q} = \left[\begin{array}{cccc} a_{0,0}B & a_{0,1}B & \cdots & a_{0,p-1}B \\ a_{1,0}B & a_{1,1}B & \cdots & a_{1,p-1}B \\ & & \cdots & \\ a_{p-1,0}B & a_{p-1,1}B & \cdots & a_{p-1,p-1}B \end{array} \right]$$

and of course $A \otimes B \neq B \otimes A$. A little counting shows that where $l = l_0 + l_1 p$ and $m = m_0 + m_1 p$ with $0 \leq m_0, l_0 < p$ and $0 \leq m_1, l_1 < q$, that $(A_p \otimes B_q)_{lm} = A_{l_0 m_0} B_{l_1 m_1}$. Using this notation, we may write (2.43) in a slightly more compact form:

$$\left(\begin{array}{c} \mathbf{y}_{\text{even}} \\ \mathbf{y}_{\text{odd}} \end{array} \right) = \left(I_2 \otimes W_{n/2} \right) \text{diag}(I_{n/2}, D) \left(\begin{array}{c} \mathbf{x}^{+} \\ \mathbf{x}^{-} \end{array} \right), \tag{2.44}$$

where I_2 is the 2×2 unit matrix. Furthermore, noting that

$$W_2 = \left(\begin{array}{cc} 1 & 1 \\ 1 & -1 \end{array} \right),$$

we get an even more concise form

$$\left(\begin{array}{c} \mathbf{y}_{\text{even}} \\ \mathbf{y}_{\text{odd}} \end{array} \right) = \left(I_2 \otimes W_{n/2} \right) \text{diag}(I_{n/2}, D) \left(W_2 \otimes I_{n/2} \right) \mathbf{x}. \tag{2.45}$$

All that remains is to get everything into the right order by permuting $(\mathbf{y}_{\text{even}}, \mathbf{y}_{\text{odd}}) \to \mathbf{y}$. Such permutations are called index digit permutations and the idea is as follows. If the dimension of the transform can be written in the form $n = p \cdot q$ (only two factors for now), then a permutation P_q^p takes an index $l = l_0 + l_1 p \to l_1 + l_0 q$, where $0 \leq l_0 < p$ and $0 \leq l_1 < q$. We have

$$\left(P_q^p \right)_{kl} = \delta_{k_0 l_1} \delta_{k_1 l_0}, \tag{2.46}$$

where $k = k_0 + k_1 q$, $l = l_0 + l_1 p$, with the ranges of the digits $0 \leq k_0, l_1 < p$ and $0 \leq k_1, l_0 < q$. Notice that the decimation for k, l is switched, although they both have the same $0 \leq k, l < n$ range. With this definition of P_q^p, we get a very compact form for (2.43)

$$\mathbf{y} = P_2^{n/2} \left(I_2 \otimes W_{n/2} \right) \text{diag}(I_{n/2}, D) \left(W_2 \otimes I_{n/2} \right) \mathbf{x}. \tag{2.47}$$

To finish up our matrix formulation, we state without proof the following identity which may be shown from (2.46) [141]. Using the above dimensions of A and B ($p \times p$ and $q \times q$, respectively),

$$(A \otimes B)\, P_q^p = P_q^p \,(B \otimes A)\,. \tag{2.48}$$

So, finally we get a commuted form

$$\mathbf{y} = \left(W_{n/2} \otimes I_2\right) P_2^{n/2} \,\mathrm{diag}(I_{n/2}, D) \left(W_2 \otimes I_{n/2}\right) \mathbf{x}\,. \tag{2.49}$$

As in (2.41) and (2.42), the $O(n^2)$ computation has been reduced by this procedure to two $O((n/2)^2)$ computations, plus another $O(n)$ due to the diagonal factor. This is easy to see from (2.47) because the $I_2 \otimes W_{n/2}$ is a direct sum of two $W_{n/2}$ multiplies, each of which is $O((n/2)^2)$, the diagonal $\mathrm{diag}(1, D)$ factor is $O(n)$. The remaining two $W_{n/2}$ operations may be similarly factored, the next four $W_{n/4}$ similarly until $n/2$ independent W_2 operations are reached and the factorization is complete. Although this factorized form looks more complicated than (2.41) and (2.42), it generalizes to the case $n = n_1 \cdot n_2 \cdots n_k$, where any n_j may be repeated (e.g. $n_j = 2$ for the binary radix case $n = 2^m$).

Here is a general result, which we do not prove [141]. Having outlined the method of factorization, interested readers should hopefully be able to follow the arguments in [96] or [141] without much trouble. A general formulation can be written in the above notation plus two further notations, where $n = \prod_{i=1}^{k} n_i$:

$$m_j = \prod_{i=1}^{j-1} n_i \quad \text{and} \quad l_j = \prod_{i=j+1}^{k} n_i,$$

which are the products of all the previous factors up to j and of all the remaining factors after j, respectively. One variant is [141]:

$$W_n = \prod_{j=k}^{1} \left(P_{l_j}^{n_j} \otimes I_{m_j}\right) \left(D_{l_j}^{n_j} \otimes I_{m_j}\right) \left(W_{n_j} \otimes I_{n/n_j}\right). \tag{2.50}$$

In this expression, the diagonal matrix $D_{l_j}^{n_j}$ generalizes $\mathrm{diag}(1, D)$ in (2.49) appropriate for the next recursive steps:

$$D_q^p = \bigoplus_{l=0}^{p-1} (\mathbf{w}_q)^l = \begin{pmatrix} (\mathbf{w}_q)^0 & & & \\ & (\mathbf{w}_q)^1 & & \\ & & \ddots & \\ & & & (\mathbf{w}_q)^{p-1} \end{pmatrix},$$

where $\mathbf{w}_q = \mathrm{diag}(1, \omega, \omega^2, \ldots, \omega^{q-1})$. Not surprisingly, there is a plethora of similar representations, frequently altering the order of reads/writes for various desired properties—in-place, unit-stride, in order, and so forth [96].

In any case, the point of all this is that by using such factorizations one can reduce the floating point operation count from $O(n^2)$ to $O(n \cdot \log(n))$, a significant savings. Perhaps more to the point for the purposes in this book is that they also reduce the memory traffic by the same amount—from $O(n^2)$ to $O(n \cdot \log(n))$. This is evident from (2.50) in that there are k steps, each of which requires $O(n)$ operations: each W_{n_j} is independent of n and may be optimally hand-coded.

Now we wish to answer the following questions:

1. Is this recursive factorization procedure stable?
2. What about the efficiency of more general n-values than $n = 2^m$?

The answers are clear and well tested by experience:

1'. The FFT is very stable: first because W_n is unitary up to a scaling, but also because the number of floating point operations is sharply reduced from $O(n^2)$ to $O(n \cdot \log n)$, thus reducing rounding errors.
2'. It turns out that small prime factors, $n_j > 2$, in $n = n_1 \cdot n_2 \cdots n_k$, are often more efficient than for $n_j = 2$. Figure 3.21 shows that the computation ("volume") for $n_j = 2$ is very simple, whereas the input/output data ("surface area") is high relative to the computation. The (memory traffic)/(floating point computation) ratio is higher for $n_j = 2$ than for $n_j > 2$. Unfortunately, if some n_j is too large, coding for this large prime factor becomes onerous. Additionally, large prime factor codings also require a lot of registers—so some additional memory traffic (even if only to cache) results. Frequently, only radices 2–5 are available and larger prime factor codings use variants of Rader's ([96], theorem 4.2.9) or Bluestein's ([96], section 4.2.3) methods. These involve computing a slightly larger composite value than n_j which contains smaller prime factors. Optimal choices of algorithms depend on the hardware available and problem size [55].

What we have not done in enough detail is to show where the partial results at each step are stored. This is important. In Cooley and Tukey's formulation, without permutations, the partial results are stored into the same locations as the operands. Although convenient operationally, this may be inconvenient to use. What happens in the classical Cooley–Tukey algorithm is that the results come out numbered in **bit-reversed** order. To be specific: when $n = 8$, the input vector elements are numbered $0, 1, 2, 3, 4, 5, 6, 7$ or by their bit patterns $000, 001, 010, 011, 100, 101, 110, 111$; and the results come out numbered $0, 4, 2, 6, 1, 5, 3, 7$. The output bit patterns of the indices of these re-ordered elements are **bit-reversed**: $001 \rightarrow 100, 011 \rightarrow 110, \ldots$, etc. This is not always inconvenient, for if one's larger calculation is a convolution, both operand vectors come out in the same bit-reversed order so multiplying them element by element does not require any re-ordering. Furthermore, the inverse operation can start from this weird order and get back to the original order by reversing the procedure. However, when using FFT for filtering, solving PDEs, and most other situations, it is well to have an ordered-in, ordered-out algorithm. Hence, that is what we will do in Sections 3.5.4 and 3.6. Clever choices of P_q^p (2.50) for each recursive factorization will result in an ordered-in/ordered-out algorithm. In addition, these algorithms illustrate some important points about data dependencies and strides in memory which we hope our dear readers will find edifying. It turns out that a single post-processing step to re-order the bit-reversed output ([140]) is nearly as expensive as the FFT itself—a reflection on the important point we made in the introduction (Section 1.1): memory traffic is the most important consideration on today's computing machinery.

2.4.1 *Symmetries*

As we have just shown, by splitting either the input or output into even and odd parts, considerable savings in computational effort ensue. In fact, we can go further: if the input sequence has certain symmetries, Equations (2.40) may be used to reduce the computational effort even more. Consider first the case when the n-dimensional input contains only real elements. It follows that the output $\mathbf{y} = W_n \mathbf{x}$ satisfies a complex conjugate condition: we have

$$\bar{y}_k = \sum_{j=0}^{n-1} \bar{\omega}^{jk} \bar{x}_j = \sum_{j=0}^{n-1} \bar{\omega}^{jk} x_j,$$

$$= \sum_{j=0}^{n-1} \omega^{-jk} x_j = \sum_{j=0}^{n-1} \omega^{(n-j)k} x_j,$$

$$= y_{n-k}, \tag{2.51}$$

because $\mathbf{x}$ is real. Thus, the second half of the output sequence $\mathbf{y}$ is the complex conjugate of the first half read in backward order. This is entirely sensible because there are only n independent real input elements, so there will be only n independent real output elements in the complex array $\mathbf{y}$. A procedure first outlined by Cooley *et al.* (see [138]) reduces an n-dimensional FFT to an $n/2$-dimensional complex FFT plus post-processing step of $O(n)$ operations. When n is even, then

$$\mathbf{z} = W_{n/2} \mathbf{x}, \text{ we pretend } \mathbf{x} \in \mathbf{C}^{n/2}$$

$$y_k = \frac{1}{4}(z_k + \bar{z}_{(n/2)-k}) + \frac{1}{4i}\omega^k(z_k - \bar{z}_{(n/2)-k}). \tag{2.52}$$

for $k = 0, \ldots, n/2$. Another helpful feature of this algorithm is that the complex portion $\mathbf{z} = \bar{W}_{n/2} \mathbf{x}$ simply *pretends* that the real input vector $\mathbf{x}$ is complex (i.e. that storage follows the Fortran convention $\mathbf{x} = (\Re x_0, \Im x_0, \Re x_1, \Im x_1, \ldots)$) and processing proceeds on that pretense, that is, no re-ordering is needed. The inverse operation is similar but has a pre-processing step followed by an

$n/2$-dimensional complex FFT. The un-normalized inverse is $\mathbf{x} = \bar{W}_{n/2}\mathbf{y}$: for $j = 0, \ldots, n/2 - 1$,

$$z_j = y_j + \bar{y}_{(n/2)-j} + i\bar{\omega}^j (y_j - \bar{y}_{(n/2)-j}) \tag{2.53}$$

$$\mathbf{x} = \bar{W}_{n/2}\mathbf{z}, \text{ again pretend } \mathbf{z} \in \mathbf{C}^{n/2}.$$

Cost savings reduce the $O(n \cdot \log(n))$ operation count to

$$O\left(\frac{n}{2}\log\left(\frac{n}{2}\right)\right) + O(n).$$

Both parts, the $n/2$-dimensional FFT and $O(n)$ operation post(pre)-processing steps are both parallelizable and may be done in place if the $W_{n/2}$ FFT algorithm is in place. Even more savings are possible if the input sequence $\mathbf{x}$ is not only real, but either symmetric or skew-symmetric.

If the input sequence is real $\mathbf{x} \in \mathbf{R}^n$ and satisfies

$$x_{n-j} = x_j, \text{ satisfies for } j = 0, \ldots, n/2 - 1,$$

then Dollimore's method [138] splits the n-dimensional FFT into three parts, an $O(n)$ pre-processing, an $O(n/4)$ dimensional complex FFT, and finally another $O(n)$ dimensional post-processing step. We get, for $j = 0, \ldots, n/2 - 1$,

$$e_j = (x_j + x_{(n/2)-j}) - 2\sin\left(\frac{2\pi j}{n}\right)(x_j - x_{(n/2)-j}),$$

$$\mathbf{y} = \text{RCFFT}_{n/2}(\mathbf{e}),$$

$$y_j = y_{j-2} - 2y_j, \text{ for } j = 3, 5, 7, \ldots, n/2 - 1.$$

Here $\text{RCFFT}_{n/2}$ is an $n/2$-dimensional FFT done by the CTLW procedure (2.52). This is equivalent to a cosine transform [96] (Section 4.4). If the input sequence is real and skew-symmetric

$$x_j = -x_{n-j}$$

the appropriate algorithm is again from Dollimore [138]. The computation is first for $j = 0, \ldots, n/2 - 1$, a pre-processing step, then an $n/4$-dimensional complex FFT, and another $O(n)$ post-processing step:

$$o_j = (x_j - x_{(n/2)-j}) - \sin\left(\frac{2\pi j}{n}\right)(x_j + x_{(n/2)-j}),$$

$$\mathbf{y} = \text{CRFFT}_{n/2}(\mathbf{o}),$$

$$\Re(\mathbf{y}) \leftrightarrow \Im(\mathbf{y}), \text{ swap real and imaginary parts },$$

$$y_j = 2y_j + y_{j-2}, \quad j = 3, 5, 7, \ldots, n/2 - 1.$$

The routine $\text{CRFFT}_{n/2}$ is an $n/2$-dimensional **half-complex** inverse to the **real$\rightarrow$half-complex** routine RCFFT (2.53). The expression **half-complex** means that the sequence satisfies the complex-conjugate symmetry (2.51) and thus only $n/4$ elements of the complete $n/2$ total are needed. The skew-symmetric transform is equivalent to representation as a Fourier *sine* series.

A complete test suite for each of these four symmetric FFT cases can be downloaded from our web-server [6] in either Fortran (`master.f`) or C (`master.c`). An important point about each of these symmetric cases is that each step is parallelizable: either vectorizable, or by sectioning (see Sections 3.2 and 3.2.1) both parallelizable and vectorizable.

2.5 Monte Carlo (MC) methods

In the early 1980s, it was widely thought that MC methods were ill-suited for both vectorization (SIMD) and parallel computing generally. This perspective considered existing codes whose logical construction had an outermost loop which counted the sample. All internal branches to simulated physical components were like `goto` statements, very unparallel in viewpoint. To clarify: a sample path (a particle, say) started at its source was simulated to its end through various branches and decisions. Because of the many branches, these codes were hard to vectorize. Worse, because they ran one particle to completion as an outer loop, distributing a sample datum of one particle/CPU on distributed memory machines resulted in a poorly load balanced simulation. After a little more thought, however, it has become clear that MC methods are nearly ideal simulations for parallel environments (e.g. see [120]). Not only can such simulations often vectorize in inner loops, but by splitting up the sample N into pieces, the pieces (subsamples) may be easily distributed to independently running processors. Each subsample is likely to have relatively the same distribution of short and long running sample data, hence improving the load balance. Furthermore, in many cases, integration problems particularly, domains may be split into subdomains of approximately equal volume. After this "attitude readjustment," it is now generally agreed that MC simulations are nearly an ideal paradigm for parallel computing. A short list of advantages shows why:

1. The intersection between the concept of statistical independence of data streams and the concept of data independence required for parallel execution is nearly inclusive. Independently seeded data should be statistically independent and may be run as independent data streams.

2. Because of the independence of each sample path (datum), inter processor communication is usually very small. Only final statistics require communication.

3. Distributed memory parallelism (MIMD) is complemented by instruction level parallelism (SIMD): there is no conflict between these modes. Vectorizing tasks running on each independent processor only makes the whole job run faster.

4. If subsamples (say $N/ncpus$) are reasonably large, load balancing is also good. Just because one particular path may take a longer (or shorter)

time to run to termination, each subsample will on average take nearly the same time as other independent subsamples running on other independent processors.

5. If a processor fails to complete its task, the total sample size is reduced but the simulation can be run to completion anyway. For example, if one CPU fails to complete its $N/ncpus$ subsample, the final statistic will consist of a sample of size $N \cdot (1 - 1/ncpus)$ not N, but this is likely to be large enough to get a good result. Hence such MC simulations can be **fault tolerant**. It is not fault tolerant to divide an integration domain into independent volumes, however.

2.5.1 *Random numbers and independent streams*

One of the most useful purposes for MC is numerical integration. In one dimension, there are far more accurate procedures [33] than MC. However, MC in one dimension provides some useful illustrations. Let us look at the bounded interval case,

$$F = \int_a^b f(x)\, dx,$$

which we approximate by the estimate

$$F = (b - a)\langle f \rangle \equiv (b - a)\boldsymbol{E}f,$$

$$\approx |A| \frac{1}{N} \sum_{i=1}^N f(x_i). \tag{2.54}$$

Here we call $|A| = (b - a)$ the "volume" of the integration domain, and all the x_is are uniformly distributed random numbers in the range $a < x_i < b$. Expectation values $\boldsymbol{E}f = \langle f \rangle$ mean the average value of f in the range $a < x < b$. Writing

$$x = (b - a)z,$$
$$g(z) = f((a - b)z)$$

gives us (2.54) again with $F = |A|\boldsymbol{E}g$, where $g(z)$ is averaged over the unit interval (i.e. on $z \in U(0,1)$). By other trickery, it is easy to do infinite ranges as well. For example,

$$H = \int_0^\infty h(x)\, dx$$

may also be transformed into the bounded interval by

$$x = \frac{z}{1 - z}, \quad 0 < z < 1,$$

to get

$$H = \int_0^1 \frac{1}{(1 - z)^2} h\left(\frac{z}{1 - z}\right) dz. \tag{2.55}$$

The doubly infinite case is almost as easy, where $x = (u-1)/u + u/(u-1)$,

$$K = \int_{-\infty}^{\infty} k(x)\,\mathrm{d}x = \int_0^1 \frac{2u^2 - 2u + 1}{u^2(1-u)^2} k\left(\frac{2u-1}{u(1-u)}\right)\,\mathrm{d}u. \qquad (2.56)$$

To be useful in (2.55), we need $h(x)/(1-z)^2$ to be bounded as $z \to 1$. Likewise, in (2.56) we require that $k(x)/u^2$ and $k(x)/(1-u)^2$ must be bounded as $z \to 0$ and $z \to 1$, respectively. With care, one-dimensional integrals (finite or infinite ranges) may be scaled $0 < z < 1$. Not surprisingly, range rescaling is appropriate for multiple dimension problems as well—provided the ranges of integration are fixed. If the ranges of some coordinates depend on the value of others, the integrand may have to be replaced by $f(x) \to f(x)\chi_A(x)$, where $\chi_A(x)$ is the indicator function: $\chi_A(x) = 1$ if $x \in A$, and zero otherwise ($x \notin A$).

Quite generally, a multiple dimension integral of $f(x)$ over a measurable Euclidean subset $A \subset R^n$ is computed by

$$I = \int_A f(x)\,\mathrm{d}^n x,$$
$$= |A|\mathbf{E}f,$$
$$\approx |A|\frac{1}{N}\sum_{i=1}^{N} f(x_i), \qquad (2.57)$$

where $|A|$ is again the volume of the integration region, when this is appropriate (i.e. A is bounded). Also, $\mathbf{E}f$ is the expected value of f in A, estimated by MC as an average over uniformly distributed sample points $\{x_i | i = 1, \ldots, N\}$. For an infinite volume, the problem is usually written as

$$\mathbf{E}f = \int f(x)p(x)\,\mathrm{d}^n x,$$
$$= \langle f \rangle_p,$$
$$\approx \frac{1}{N}\sum_{i=1}^{N} f(x_i). \qquad (2.58)$$

In this case, the sample points are not drawn uniformly but rather from the distribution density p which is a weighting function of $x = (x_1, x_2, \ldots, x_n)$. The volume element is $\mathrm{d}^n x = \mathrm{d}x_1\mathrm{d}x_2\cdots\mathrm{d}x_n$. Density p is subject to the normalization condition

$$\int p(x)\,\mathrm{d}^n x = 1.$$

If $p(x) = \chi_A(x)/|A|$, we get the previous bounded range situation and uniformly distributed points inside domain A. In a common case, p takes the form

$$p(x) = \frac{e^{-S(x)}}{\int e^{-S(x)} d^n x},\qquad (2.59)$$

which we discuss in more detail in Section 2.5.3.2.

Sometimes x may be high dimensional and sampling it by acceptance/ rejection (see Section 2.5.3.1) from the probability density $p(x)$ becomes difficult. A good example is taken from statistical mechanics: $S = E/kT$, where E is the system energy for a configuration x, k is Boltzmann's constant, and T is the temperature. The denominator in this Boltzmann case (2.59), $Z = \int \exp(-S) \, d^n x$, is called the **partition function**. We will consider simulations of such cases later in Section 2.5.3.2.

2.5.2 *Uniform distributions*

From above we see that the first task is to generate random numbers in the range $0.0 < x < 1.0$. Most computer mathematics libraries have generators for precisely this uniformly distributed case. However, several facts about random number generators should be pointed out immediately.

1. Few general purpose computer mathematical library packages provide quality parallel or vectorized random number generators.
2. In general purpose libraries, routines are often function calls which return one random number $0.0 < x < 1.0$ at a time. In nearly all parallel applications, this is very inefficient: typical function call overheads are a few microseconds whereas the actual computation requires only a few clock cycles. That is, computation takes only a few nanoseconds. As we will discuss later, the computations are usually simple, so procedure call overhead will take most of the CPU time if used in this way.
3. Many random number generators are poor. Do not trust any of them completely. More than one should be tried, with different initializations, and the results compared. Your statistics should be clearly reproducible.
5. Parallel random number generators are available and if used with care will give good results [102, 120, 134]. In particular, the **SPRNG** generator suite provides many options in several data formats [134].

Two basic methods are in general use, with many variants of them in practice. An excellent introduction to the theory of these methods is Knuth [87, vol. 2]. Here, our concern will be parallel generation using these two basics. They are

1. Linear congruential (LC) generators which use integer sequences

$$x_n = a \cdot x_{n-1} + b \bmod \text{ wordsize (or a prime)}$$

to return a value $((\text{float})x_n)/((\text{float})\text{wordsize})$. For example, wordsize $= 2^{24}$ (single precision IEEE arithmetic) or wordsize $= 2^{53}$ (double precision IEEE). Additionally, if a is chosen to be odd, b may be set to zero. The choice of the **multiplier** a is not at all trivial, and unfortunately there are not many really good choices [87].

2. Lagged Fibonacci (LF) sequences

$$x_n = x_{n-p} \otimes x_{p-q} \bmod 1.0, \tag{2.60}$$

where the **lags** p, q must be chosen carefully, and the operator $\otimes$ can be one of several variants. Some simple choices are $p = 607$, $q = 273$, and $\otimes$ is floating point add ($+$). There are better choices for both the lags and the operator $\otimes$, but they use more memory or more computation. Other operators have been chosen to be subtract, multiply, bit-wise exclusive or ($\oplus$), and structures like $x_{n-p} \otimes x_{n-q} \equiv x_{n-p} \oplus M x_{n-q}$, where M is a bit-matrix [103]. In these latter cases, the operations are integer, with the routine returning a floating point result normalized to the wordsize, that is, the returned value is $0.0 < x < 1.0$.

The LC methods require only one initial value (x_0). Because the generator is a one-step recurrence, if any x_i in the sequence repeats, the whole series repeats in exactly the same order. Notice that the LC method is a one-step recursion and will not parallelize easily as written above. It is easy to parallelize by creating streams of such recurrences, however. The so-called **period** of the LC method is less than **wordsize**. This means that a sequence generated by this procedure repeats itself after this number (period). To put this in perspective, using IEEE single precision floating point arithmetic, the maximal period of an LC generator is 2^{24}. On a machine with a 1 GHz clock and assuming that the basic LC operation takes 10 cycles, the random number stream repeats itself every 10 s! This says that the LC method cannot be used with single precision IEEE wordsize for any serious MC simulation. Repeating the same random sample statistics over and over again is a terrible idea. Clearly, in IEEE double precision (53 bits of mantissa, not 24), the situation is much better since 2^{53} is a very large number. Other more sophisticated implementations can give good results. For example, the 59-bit NAG [68] `C05AGF` library routine generates good statistics, but returns only one result/call.

The LF method, and its generalizations (see p. 63), requires memory space for a buffer. Using a circular buffer, $\max(p, q)$ is the storage required for this procedure. The LF method, can be vectorized along the direction of the recurrence to a maximum segment length (VL in Chapter 3) of $\min(p, q)$ at a time. Here is a code fragment to show how the buffer is filled. We assume $LAGP = p > q = LAGQ$ for convenience [14, 104].

```
kP = 0;
kQ = LAGP - LAGQ;
for(i=0;i<LAGQ;i++){
    t        = buff[i] + buff[kQ+i];
```

```
    buff[i] = t - (double)((int) t);
}
kP = LAGQ;
kQ = 0;
for(i=0;i<LAGP-LAGQ;i++){
    t           = buff[i+kP] + buff[i+kQ];
    buff[i + kP] = t - (double)((int) t);
}
```

Uniformly distributed numbers x are taken from `buff` which is refilled as needed. The maximal periods of LF sequences are extremely large $(\frac{1}{2}\texttt{wordsize} \cdot (2^{p\vee q} - 1))$ because the whole buffer of length $\max(p,q)$ must repeat for the whole sequence to repeat. These sequences are not without their problems, however. Hypercubes in dimension $p \vee q$ can exhibit correlations, so long lags are recommended—or a more sophisticated operator $\otimes$. In our tests [62, 123], the Mersenne Twister [103] shows good test results and the latest implementations are sufficiently fast. M. Lüscher's `RANLUX` [98] in F. James' implementation [79] also tests well at high "luxury" levels (this randomly throws away some results to reduce correlations). Furthermore, this routine sensibly returns many random numbers per call.

In our parallel thinking mode, we see obvious modifications of the above procedures for parallel (or vector) implementations of $i = 1, 2, \ldots, VL$ independent streams

$$x_n^{[i]} = a \cdot x_{n-1}^{[i]} \ \mathbf{mod} \ \text{wordsize}, \tag{2.61}$$

or the Percus–Kalos [118] approach, where $p^{[i]}$ are independent primes for each stream $[i]$:

$$x_n^{[i]} = a \cdot x_{n-1}^{[i]} + p^{[i]} \ \mathbf{mod} \ \text{wordsize} \tag{2.62}$$

and

$$x_n^{[i]} = x_{n-p}^{[i]} \otimes x_{n-q}^{[i]} \ \text{mod} \ 1.0. \tag{2.63}$$

The difficulty is in verifying whether the streams are statistically independent. It is clear that each i counts a distinct sample datum from an independent initial seed (LC), or seeds (LF). A simple construction shows why one should expect that parallel implementations of (2.61) and (2.63) should give independent streams, however. Crucial to this argument is that the generator should have a very long period, much longer than the wordsize. Here is how it goes: if the period of the random number generator (RNG) is extremely long (e.g. $2^{23} \cdot (2^{p\wedge q} - 1)$ for a p,q lagged Fibonacci generator in single precision IEEE arithmetic), then any possible overlap between initial buffers (of length $p \vee q$) is very unlikely. Furthermore, since the parallel simulations are also unlikely to

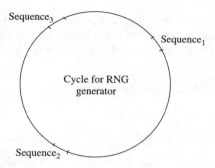

FIG. 2.15. *Graphical argument why parallel RNGs should generate parallel streams: if the cycle is astronomically large, none of the user sequences will overlap.*

use even an infinitesimal fraction of the period, the likelihood of overlap of the independent sequences is also very small. Figure 2.15 shows the reasoning. If the parallel sequences (labeled 1, 2, 3 in Figure 2.15) are sufficiently small relative to the period (cycle), the probability of overlap is tiny, hence the sequences can be expected to be independent. One cannot be convinced entirely by this argument and much testing is therefore required [62, 134]. Very long period generators of the LF type [123, 134] and variants [61, 79], when used in parallel with initial buffers filled by other generators (e.g. **ggl**) seem to give very satisfactorily independent streams.

An inherently vector procedure is a matrix method [66, 67] for an array of results **x**:

$$\mathbf{x}_n = M\mathbf{x}_{n-1} \bmod p,$$

where p is prime, M is a matrix of "multipliers" whose elements must be selected by a spectral test [87]. For vectors of large size, finding a suitable matrix M is a formidable business, however.

Finally, more general procedures than (2.60) can be constructed which use more terms. The idea is again to construct a primitive polynomial in the field of integers modulo wordsize. Some polynomials were given by Gonnet [61] who tested them for primality by the method of Lenstra *et al.* [94] using Maple [47]: one example is

$$x_n = (c_5 x_{n-5} + c_{43} x_{n-43} + c_{97} x_{n-97} + c_{128} x_{n-128}) \bmod 2^{53}.$$

In this expression, the coefficients are: $c_5 = 8, c_{43} = 128, c_{97} = \frac{1}{64}$, and $c_{128} = 1$. This generator has now been well tested with the Helsinki suite (see [62, 83]).

For our purposes, a particularly useful package **SPRNG** written by Mascagni and co-workers contains parallel versions of six pseudorandom number generators [134]. This suite contains parallel generators of the following types (p is a user selected prime):

- Combined multiple recursive generator:

$$x_n = a \cdot x_{n-1} + p \bmod 2^{64}$$

$$y_n = 107374182 \cdot y_{n-1} + 104480 \cdot y_{n-5} \bmod 2147483647$$

$$z_n = (x_n + 2^{32} \cdot y_n) \bmod 2^{64} \quad (n\text{th result})$$

- Linear congruential 48–bit (2.61): $x_n = a \cdot x_{n-1} + b \bmod 2^{48}$
- LC 64–bit (2.61): $x_n = a \cdot x_{n-1} + b \bmod 2^{64}$
- LC with prime modulus (2.61): $x_n = a \cdot x_{n-1} \bmod (2^{61} - 1)$
- Modified LF (2.60):
  $x_n = x_{n-p} + x_{n-q} \bmod 2^{32} \quad$ (1st sequence)
  $y_n = y_{n-p} + y_{n-q} \bmod 2^{32} \quad$ (2nd sequence)
  $z_n = x_n \oplus y_n \qquad\qquad\quad$ (nth result)
- LF with integer multiply (2.60): $x_n = x_{n-p} \times x_{n-q} \bmod 2^{64}$.

This suite has been extensively tested [35] and ported to a wide variety of machines including Cray T-3E, IBM SP2, HP Superdome, SFI Origin2000, and all Linux systems.

2.5.3 *Non-uniform distributions*

Although uniform generators from Section 2.5.2 form the base routine for most samplings, other non-uniformly distributed sequences must be constructed from uniform ones. The simplest method, when it is possible, is by direct inversion. Imagine that we wish to generate sequences distributed according to the density $p(x)$, where x is a real scalar. The cumulative probability distribution is

$$P[x < z] = P(z) = \int_{-\infty}^{z} p(t) \, dt. \tag{2.64}$$

Direct inversion may be used when the right-hand side of this expression (2.64) is known and can be inverted. To be more precise: since $0 \leq P(x) \leq 1$ is monotonically increasing ($p(x) \geq 0$), if $u = P(x)$, then $P^{-1}(u)$ exists. The issue is whether this inverse is easily found. If it is the case that P^{-1} is easily computed, then to generate a sequence of mutually independent, non-uniformly distributed random numbers, one computes

$$x_i = P^{-1}(u_i), \tag{2.65}$$

where $u_1, u_2, \ldots$ is a sequence of uniformly distributed, mutually independent, real numbers $0.0 < u_i < 1.0$: see [34, theorem 2.1].

Example 2.5.1 An easy case is the exponential density $p(x) = \lambda \exp(-\lambda x), x > 0$ because $P(x) = u = 1 - \exp(-\lambda x)$ is easily inverted for $x = P^{-1}(u)$. The sequence generated by $x_i = -\log(u_i/\lambda)$ will be exponentially distributed. This follows because if $\{u_i\}$ are uniformly distributed in $(0,1)$, so are $\{1 - u_i\}$.

Things are not usually so simple because computing P^{-1} may be painful.

A normally distributed sequence is a common case:

$$P[x < z] = \frac{1}{\sqrt{2\pi}} \int_{-\infty}^{z} e^{-t^2/2}\, dt = \frac{1}{2} + \frac{1}{2}\mathrm{erf}\left(\frac{z}{\sqrt{2}}\right).$$

Here the inversion of the error function `erf` is no small amount of trouble, particularly in parallel. Thus, a better method for generating normally distributed random variables is required. Fortunately a good procedure, the Box–Muller method, is known and even better suited for our purposes since it is easily parallelized. It generates two normals at a time

$$
\begin{aligned}
t_1 &= 2\pi u_1, &&// \;\; u_1 \in U(0,1), \\
t_2 &= \sqrt{-2\ln(u_2)}, &&// \;\; u_2 \in U(0,1), \\
z_1 &= \cos(t_1) \cdot t_2, \\
z_2 &= \sin(t_1) \cdot t_2.
\end{aligned}
\tag{2.66}
$$

An essential point here is that the library functions `sqrt`, `log`, `cos`, and `sin` must have parallel versions. Usually, this means SIMD (see Chapter 3) modes wherein multiple streams of operands may be computed concurrently. We have already briefly discussed parallel generation of the uniformly distributed variables u_1, u_2 (2.60), that is, p. 61, and (2.61), (2.63). Function `sqrt` may be computed in various ways, but the essence of the thing starts with a range reduction: where $x = 2^k x_0$, $1/2 < x_0 \leq 1$, then

$$\sqrt{x} = 2^{k/2}\sqrt{x_0} = 2^{(k-1)/2}\sqrt{2 \cdot x_0},$$

where its second form is used when k is odd [49]. Since the floating point representation of x is $x = [k : x_0]$ (in some biased exponent form), computing the new exponent, either $k/2$ or $(k-1)/2$, is effected by masking out the biased exponent, removing the bias (see Overton [114], Chapter 4) and shifting it right one bit. The new mantissa, either $\sqrt{x_0}$ or $\sqrt{2 \cdot x_0}$, involves computing only the square root of an argument between $1/2$ and 2. A Newton method is usually chosen to find the new mantissa: where we want $y = \sqrt{x_0}$, this takes the recursive form

$$y_{n+1} = \frac{1}{2}\left(y_n + \frac{x_0}{y_n}\right).$$

For purposes of parallelization, a fixed number of Newton steps is used (say $n = 0, \ldots, 3$, the number depending on the desired precision and the accuracy of the initial approximation y_0). Newton steps are then repeated on multiple data:

$$y_{n+1}^{[i]} = \frac{1}{2}\left(y_n^{[i]} + \frac{x_0^{[i]}}{y_n^{[i]}}\right),$$

where $i = 1, \ldots, VL$, the number of independent square roots to be calculated, see Section 3.2.

Computing $\log x$ is also easily parallelized. Again, writing $x = 2^k \cdot x_0$, one computes $\log x = \log_2(e)\log_2(x)$ from $\log_2(x)$ by

$$\log_2(x) = k + \log_2(x_0).$$

The range of x_0 is $1/2 < x_0 \leq 1$. The log function is slowly varying so either polynomial or rational approximations may be used. Assuming a rational approximation, parallel implementations for VL independent arguments ($i = 1, \ldots, VL$) would look like:

$$\log_2\left(x^{[i]}\right) = k^{[i]} + \log_2\left(x_0^{[i]}\right),$$

$$\log_2\left(x_0^{[i]}\right) = \frac{P\left(x_0^{[i]}\right)}{Q\left(x_0^{[i]}\right)},$$

where P and Q are relatively low order polynomials (about 5–6, see Hart et al. [49]). Also, see Section 3.5.

Finally, cos and sin: because standard Fortran libraries support complex arithmetic and exp(z) for a complex argument z requires both cos and sin, most intrinsic libraries have a function which returns both given a common argument. For example, the **Linux** routine in /lib/libm.so sincos returns both sin and cos of one argument, and the Cray intrinsic Fortran library contains a routine COSS which does the same thing. In the Intel **MKL** library [28], the relevant functions are vsSinCos and vdSinCos for single and double, respectively. It costs nearly the same to compute both cos and sin as it does to compute either. To do this, first the argument x is ranged to $0 \leq x_1 < 2\pi$: $x = x_1 + m \cdot 2\pi$, by division modulo 2π. In the general case, for large arguments this ranging is the biggest source of error. However, for our problem, x is always ranged $0 < x < 2\pi$. The remaining computation $\cos x_1$ (likewise $\sin x_1$) is then ranged $0 \leq x_1 < \frac{\pi}{2}$ using modular arithmetic and identities among the circular functions. Once this ranging has been done, a sixth to seventh order polynomial in x_1^2 is used: in parallel form (see Section 3.5),

$$\cos\left(x_1^{[i]}\right) = P\left(\left(x_1^{[i]}\right)^2\right), \text{ for } i = 1, \ldots, VL.$$

By appropriate ranging and circular function identities, computing cos is enough to get both cos and sin, see Hart et al. [49, section 6.4]. Also, see Luke [97, section 3.3, particularly table 3.6].

So, the Box–Muller method illustrates two features: (1) generating normal random variables is easily done by elementary functions, and (2) the procedure is relatively easy to parallelize if appropriate approximations for the elementary functions are used. These approximations are not novel to the parallel world, but are simply selections from well-known algorithms that are appropriate for parallel implementations. Finally, an interesting number: univariate normal generation computed on the NEC SX-4 in vector mode costs

$$(\text{clock cycles})/(\text{normal}) \approx 7.5,$$

which includes uniformly distributed variables, see Section 2.5.2 [123]. To us, this number is astonishingly small but apparently stems from the multiplicity of independent arithmetic units: 8 f.p. add and 8 f.p. multiply units. In any case, the Box–Muller method is faster than the *polar method* [87] which depends on acceptance rejection, hence if/else processing, see Section 3.2.8. On the machines we tested (Macintosh G-4, HP9000, Pentium III, Pentium 4, Cray SV-1, and NEC SX-4), Box–Muller was always faster and two machine results are illustrated in Figure 2.16. Label **pv BM** means that ggl was used to generate two arrays of uniformly distributed random variables which were subsequently used in a vectorized loop. Intel compiler icc vectorized the second part of the split loop

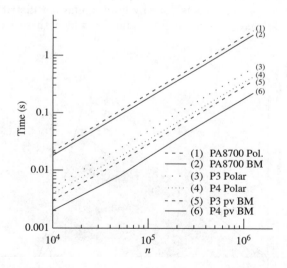

FIG. 2.16. *Timings for Box–Muller method vs. polar method for generating univariate normals. Machines are PA8700, Pentium III, and Pentium 4. The label* **Polar** *indicates the polar method, while* **pv BM** *means a "partially" vectorized Box–Muller method. Uniforms were generated by* ggl *which does not vectorize easily, see Section 2.5.2. The compilers were* icc *on the Pentiums and* gcc *on the PA8700.*

nicely but the library does not seem to include a vectorized RNG. On one CPU of *Stardust* (an HP9000), `gcc -O3` produced faster code than both the native `cc -O3` and `guidec -O4` [77]. On Cray SV-2 machines using the `ranf` RNG, the speedups are impressive—Box–Muller is easily a factor of 10 faster. See Section 3.5.7 for the relevant compiler switches used in Figure 2.16.

2.5.3.1 *Acceptance/rejection methods*

In this book we wish to focus on those aspects of MC relating parallel computing. In Equation (2.66), we showed the Box–Muller method for normals and remarked that this procedure is superior to the so-called polar method for parallel computing. While there remains some dispute about the tails of the distributions of Box–Muller and polar methods, experience shows that if the underlying uniform generator is of high quality, the results of these two related procedures are quite satisfactory, see Gentle [56, section 3.1.2]. Here, we show why the Box–Muller method is superior to acceptance/rejection polar method, while at the same time emphasize why branching (`if`/`else` processing) is the antithesis of parallelism [57]. First we need to know what the acceptance/rejection (AR) method is, and then we give some examples.

The idea is due to von Neumann and is illustrated in Figure 2.17. We wish to sample from a probability density function $p(x)$, whose cumulative distribution is difficult to invert (2.65). This is done by finding another distribution function, say $q(x)$, which is easy to sample from and for which there exists a constant

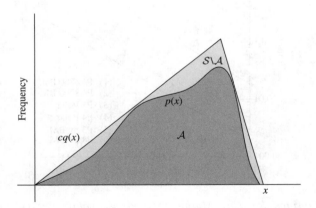

FIG. 2.17. *AR method: the lower curve represents the desired distribution density* $p(x)$, *while the covering is* $cq(x)$. *Distribution density* $q(x)$ *must be easy to sample from and* $c > 1$. *The set* $\mathcal{S} = \{(x,y) : 0 \le y \le cq(x)\}$ *covers the set* $\mathcal{A} = \{(x,y) : 0 \le y \le p(x)\}$ *and points* (x,y) *are uniformly distributed in both* $\mathcal{A}$ *and* $\mathcal{S}$.

$1 < c < \infty$ such that $0 \leq p(x) \leq cq(x)$ for all x in the domain of functions $p(x), q(x)$. Here is the general algorithm:

> **P1:** pick x from p.d.f. $q(x)$
>   pick $u \in U(0, 1)$
> $y = u \cdot c \cdot q(x)$
>   **if** $(y \leq p(x))$ **then**
>   accept x
>   **else**
>   goto **P1**
>   **fi**

Here is the proof that this works [99].

Theorem 2.5.2 *Acceptance/rejection samples according to the probability density $p(x)$.*

Proof   Given x is taken from the distribution q, y is thus uniformly distributed in the range $0 \leq y \leq cq(x)$. The joint probability density function is therefore

$$p_{[xy]}(x, y) = q(x)h(y|x),$$

where $h(y|x)$ is the conditional probability density for y given x. Since y is uniformly distributed, $h(y|x)$ does not depend on y, and is then $h(y|x) = 1/(cq(x))$, for $\int_0^{cq(x)} h \, dy = 1$. We get $p_{[xy]}(x, y) = 1/c$, a constant. For this reason, these (x, y) points are uniformly distributed in the set

$$\mathcal{S} = \{(x, y) \colon 0 \leq y \leq cq(x)\}.$$

Now, let $\mathcal{A} \subset \mathcal{S}$,

$$\mathcal{A} = \{(x, y) \colon 0 \leq y \leq p(x)\},$$

which contains the $(x, y) \in \mathcal{S}$ under the curve p as shown in Figure 2.17. Since $\mathcal{A} \subset \mathcal{S}$, the points $(x, y) \in \mathcal{A}$ are uniformly distributed, hence the probability density function for these (x, y) is a constant (the $X \to \infty$ limit of the next expression shows it must be 1). Therefore,

$$P[x \leq X] = \int_{-\infty}^X dx \int_0^{p(x)} dy = \int_{-\infty}^X p(x) \, dx.$$

Hence x is distributed according to the density $p(x)$, which is von Neumann' result. $\qquad\square$

The generalization of AR to higher dimensional spaces, $x \to \mathbf{x}$, involves only a change in notation and readers are encouraged to look at Madras' proof [99].

The so-called *acceptance ratio* is given by

$$\text{Acceptance ratio} = \frac{\text{Number of } x \text{ accepted}}{\text{Number of } x \text{ tried}} = \frac{1}{c} < 1.$$

The polar method, which again generates two univariate normals (z_1, z_2) is a good illustration. Here is the algorithm:

P1: pick $u_1, u_2 \in U(0, 1)$
$\quad\quad v_1 = 2u_1 - 1$
$\quad\quad v_2 = 2u_2 - 1$
$\quad\quad S = v_1^2 + v_2^2$
$\quad\quad$**if** $(S < 1)$**then**
$\quad\quad\quad\quad z_1 = v_1\sqrt{-2\log(S)/S}$
$\quad\quad\quad\quad z_2 = v_2\sqrt{-2\log(S)/S}$
$\quad\quad$**else**
$\quad\quad\quad\quad$goto **P1**
$\quad\quad$**fi**

and the inscription method is shown in Figure 2.18. This is a simple example of AR, and the acceptance ratio is $\pi/4$. That is, for any given randomly chosen point in the square, the chance that (v_1, v_2) will fall within the circle is the ratio of the areas of the circle to the square.

The basic antithesis is clear: if processing on one independent datum follows one instruction path while another datum takes an entirely different one, each may take different times to complete. Hence, they cannot be processed

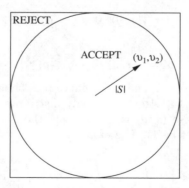

FIG. 2.18. *Polar method for normal random variates. A circle of radius one is inscribed in a square with sides equal to two. Possible (v_1, v_2) coordinates are randomly selected inside the square: if they fall within the circle, they are accepted; if the fall outside the circle, they are rejected.*

concurrently and have the results ready at the same time. Our essential point regarding parallel computing here is that independent possible (v_1, v_2) pairs may take different computational paths, thus they cannot be computed concurrently in a synchronous way. On independent processors, of course, the lack of synchrony is not a problem but requesting one z_1, z_2 pair from an independent CPU is asking for a very small calculation that requires resource management, for example, a job scheduling operating system intervention. On older architectures where cos, sin, and other elementary functions were expensive, the polar method was superior. We will be more expansive about branch processing (the if statement above) in Chapter 3.

In a general context, AR should be avoided for small tasks. For larger tasks, distributed over multiple independent processors, the large inherent latencies (see Section 3.2.1) of task assignment become insignificant compared to the (larger) computation. Conversely, the tiny computation of the z_1, z_2 pair by the polar method is too small compared to the overhead of task assignment. In some situations, AR cannot be avoided. An indirect address scheme (see Section 3.2.2 regarding scatter/gather operations) can be a way to index accepted points but not rejected ones. An integer routine fische which returns values distributed according to a Poisson distribution, $p(n, \mu) = e^{-mu}\mu^n/n!$, uses this idea. You can download this from the zufall package on NETLIB [111] or from our ftp server [6] .

If a branch is nearly always taken (i.e. $c \sim 1$), the results using AR for small tasks can be effective. For example, Figure 2.19 shows a stratified sampling method for Gaussian random variables by Marsaglia and Tsang [100]. Their idea is to construct a set of strips which cover one half of the symmetric distribution, each with the same area: see Figure 2.19(a). Unlike the diagram, the code actually has 256 strips, not 8. The lowest lying strip, handing the tail, uses Marsaglia's method [101]. The returned normal is given an random sign. Each strip area is the same, so the strips may be picked uniformly. The rejection rate is very small. The computation is in effect a table lookup to find the strip parameters which are pre-initialized. Their method is extremely fast as Figure 2.19 shows, but there are problems with the existing code [100]: the uniform random number generator is in-line thus hard to change.

There is an important point here, apparently not lost on Marsaglia and Tsang, for a procedure call costs at least 1–5 μs. Furthermore, as written, the code is only suitable for 32-bit floating point, again not easily modified. The speed performance is quite impressive, however, so this method holds considerable promise. To us, the lesson to be learned here is that a parallel method may be faster than a similar sequential one, but a better algorithm wins.

Not to put too fine a point on possible AR problems, but the following calculation shows that completely aside from parallel computing, AR can occasionally fail miserably when the dimension of the system is high enough that the acceptance ratio becomes small. Our example problem here is to sample uniformly inside, or on, the surface of, a unit n-sphere. Here is the AR version for interior sampling:

P1: pick $u_1, u_2, \ldots, u_n$ each $u_j \in U(0,1)$
$\qquad v_1 = 2u_1 - 1$
$\qquad v_2 = 2u_2 - 1$
$\qquad \ldots$
$\qquad v_n = 2u_n - 1$
$\qquad S = v_1^2 + v_2^2 + \cdots + v_n^2$
$\qquad$**if** $(S < 1)$**then**
$\qquad\qquad$accept points $\{v_1, v_2, \ldots, v_n\}$
$\qquad$**else**
$\qquad\qquad$goto **P1**
$\qquad$**fi**

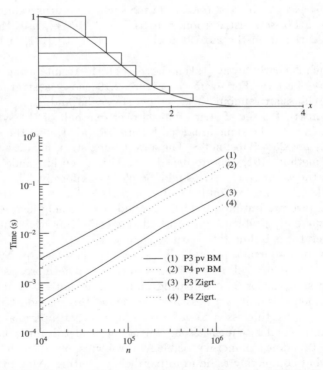

FIG. 2.19. *Box–Muller vs. Ziggurat method. (top) A simplified diagram of the stratified sampling used in the procedure [100]. In the actual code, there are 256 strips, not 8. (bottom) Comparative performance of Box–Muller vs. Ziggurat on a Pentium III and Pentium 4.*

Alas, here the ratio of volume of an inscribed unit radius n-sphere to the volume of a side $= 2$ covering n-cube (see Figure 2.18) gets small fast:

$$\frac{\text{Volume of unit } n\text{-sphere}}{\text{Volume of } n\text{-cube}} = \frac{\Omega_n \int_0^1 \mathrm{d}r\, r^{n-1}}{2^n},$$

$$\sim \frac{1}{\sqrt{2\pi}} \alpha^n \left(\frac{n}{2}\right)^{-(n+1)/2},$$

for large n. Constant $\alpha = \sqrt{e\pi}/2 \approx 1.46$ and Ω_n is the solid angle volume of an n-sphere [46, p. 234],

$$\Omega_n = \frac{2\pi^{n/2}}{\Gamma(n/2)}.$$

Hence, using Stirling's approximation, we see a rapidly decreasing acceptance ratio for large n. The following table shows how bad the acceptance ratio gets even for relatively modest n values.

n	2	3	4	10	20
Ratio	0.785	0.524	0.308	0.0025	0.25×10^{-7}

A vastly better approach is given in Devroye [34, section 4.2]. This is an **isotropic** algorithm for both surface or interior sampling. If interior points are desired, the density function for isotropically distributed points is $p(r) = k \cdot r^{n-1}$. Since $\int_0^1 p(r)\,\mathrm{d}r = 1$, then $k = n$ and $P[|x| < r] = r^n$. Sampling of $|x|$ takes the form $|x| = u^{1/n}$ from (2.65).

```
for i = 1, ..., n {
    z_i = box-muller
}
r = √∑_{i=1}^n z_i^2
// project onto surface
for i = 1, ..., n {
    x_i = z_i/r
}
if (interior points) {
// sample radius according to P = r^n
    u ∈ U(0, 1)
    r = u^{1/n}
    for i = 1, ..., n {
        x_i = rx_i
    }
}
```

A plot of the timings for both the AR and *isotropic* procedures is shown in Figure 2.20.

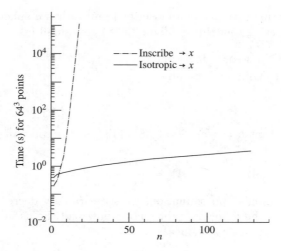

FIG. 2.20. *Timings on NEC SX-4 for uniform interior sampling of an n-sphere. Lower curve (isotropic method) uses n normals* **z**, *while the absurdly rising curve shows the inscription method.*

2.5.3.2 *Langevin methods*

Earlier in this chapter, we mentioned a common computation in quantum and statistical physics—that of finding the partition function and its associated Boltzmann distribution, Equation (2.59). The usual problem of interest is to find the expected (mean) value of a physical variable, say $f(\mathbf{x})$, where $\mathbf{x}$ may be very high dimensional. In an extreme case, $n = \dim[\mathbf{x}] \sim 6 \cdot N_A$, where N_A is the Avogadro's number ($N_A \approx 6.022 \times 10^{23}$) and the 6 refers to the 3 space + 3 momentum degrees of freedom of the N_A particles. For the foreseeable future, computing machinery will be unlikely to handle N_A particles, but already astrophysical simulations are doing $O(10^8)$—an extremely large number whose positions and velocities each must be integrated over many timesteps. Frequently, physicists are more interested in statistical properties than about detailed orbits of a large number of arbitrarily labeled particles. In that case, the problem is computing the expected value of f, written (see (2.59))

$$\boldsymbol{E}f = \frac{\int e^{-S(\mathbf{x})} f(x)\, d^n x}{Z}, \tag{2.67}$$

where the partition function $Z = \int e^{-S(\mathbf{x})}\, d^n x$ normalizes e^{-S}/Z in (2.59). For our simplified discussion, we assume the integration region is all of $\mathbf{E}^n$, the Euclidean space in n-dimensions. For an arbitrary **action** $S(\mathbf{x})$, generating configurations of $\mathbf{x}$ according to the density $p(\mathbf{x}) = e^{-S(\mathbf{x})}/Z$ can be painful unless S is say Gaussian, which basically means the particles have no interactions. A relatively general method exists, however, when $S(\mathbf{x}) > 0$ has the contraction property that when $|\mathbf{x}|$ is large enough,

$$\mathbf{x} \cdot \frac{\partial S}{\partial \mathbf{x}} > 1. \tag{2.68}$$

In this situation, it is possible to generate samples of $\mathbf{x}$ according to $p(\mathbf{x})$ by using Langevin's equation [10]. If S has the above contraction property and some smoothness requirements [86, 106], which usually turn out to be physically reasonable, a Langevin process $\mathbf{x}(t)$ given by the following equation will converge to a stationary state:

$$d\mathbf{x}(t) = -\frac{1}{2}\frac{\partial S}{\partial \mathbf{x}}\,dt + d\mathbf{w}(t), \tag{2.69}$$

where $\mathbf{w}$ is a Brownian motion, and the stationary distribution will be $p(\mathbf{x})$. Equation (2.69) follows from the Fokker–Planck equation (see [10], equation 11.3.15) and (2.79) below. What are we to make of $\mathbf{w}$? Its properties are as follows.

1. The probability density for $\mathbf{w}$ satisfies the heat equation:

$$\frac{\partial p(\mathbf{w}, t)}{\partial t} = \frac{1}{2}\triangle p(\mathbf{w}, t),$$

where $\triangle$ is the Laplace operator in n-dimensions. That is

$$\triangle p = \sum_{i=1}^{n} \frac{\partial^2 p}{\partial w_i^2}.$$

2. The $t = 0$ initial distribution for p is $p(\mathbf{x}, t = 0) = \delta(\mathbf{x})$
3. Its increments $d\mathbf{w}$ (when $t \to t + dt$) satisfy the equations:

$$\boldsymbol{E}dw_i(t) = 0,$$
$$\boldsymbol{E}dw_i(t)\,dw_j(s) = \delta_{ij}\delta(s - t)\,dt\,ds.$$

In small but finite form, these equations are

$$\boldsymbol{E}\Delta w_i(t_k) = 0, \tag{2.70}$$
$$\boldsymbol{E}\Delta w_i(t_k)\Delta w_j(t_l) = h\delta_{ij}\delta_{kl}, \tag{2.71}$$

where h is the time step $h = \Delta t$.

In these equations, $\delta_{ij} = 1$, if $i = j$ and zero otherwise: the δ_{ij} are the elements of the identity matrix in n-dimensions; and $\delta(\mathbf{x})$ is the Dirac delta function—zero everywhere except $\mathbf{x} = \mathbf{0}$, but $\int \delta(\mathbf{x})\,d^n x = 1$. Item (1) says $\mathbf{w}(t)$ is a diffusion process, which by item (2) means $\mathbf{w}(0)$ starts at the origin and diffuses out with a mean square $\boldsymbol{E}|\mathbf{w}|^2 = n \cdot t$. Item (3) says increments $d\mathbf{w}$ are only locally correlated.

There is an intimate connection between parabolic (and elliptic) partial differential equations and stochastic differential equations. Here is a one-dimensional version for the case of a continuous Markov process y,

$$p(y|x,t) = \text{transition probability of } x \to y, \text{ after time } t. \qquad (2.72)$$

The important properties of $p(y|x,t)$ are

$$\int p(y|x,t)\,\mathrm{d}y = 1, \qquad (2.73)$$

$$p(z|x,t_1+t_2) = \int p(z|y,t_2)p(y|x,t_1)\,\mathrm{d}y, \qquad (2.74)$$

where (2.73) says that x must go somewhere in time t, and (2.74) says that after t_1, x must have gone somewhere (i.e. y) and if we sum over all possible ys, we will get all probabilities. Equation (2.74) is known as the Chapman–Kolmogorov–Schmoluchowski equation [10] and its variants extend to quantum probabilities and gave rise to Feynman's formulation of quantum mechanics, see Feynman–Hibbs [50]. We would like to find an evolution equation for the transition probability $p(y|x,t)$ as a function of t. To do so, let $f(y)$ be an arbitrary smooth function of y, say $f \in C^\infty$. Then using (2.74)

$$\int f(y)\frac{\partial p(y|x,t)}{\partial t}\,\mathrm{d}y$$

$$= \lim_{\Delta t \to 0} \frac{1}{\Delta t} \int f(y)\left(p(y|x,t+\Delta t) - p(y|x,t)\right)\,\mathrm{d}y,$$

$$= \lim_{\Delta t \to 0} \frac{1}{\Delta t} \int f(y)\left(\int p(y|z,\Delta t)p(z|x,t)\,\mathrm{d}z - p(y|x,t)\right)\,\mathrm{d}y.$$

For small changes Δt, most of the contribution to $p(y|z,\Delta t)$ will be near $y \sim z$, so we expand $f(y) = f(z) + f_z(z)(z-y) + \frac{1}{2}f_{zz}(z)(y-z)^2 + \cdots$ to get

$$\int f(y)\frac{\partial p(y|x,t)}{\partial t}\,\mathrm{d}y$$

$$= \lim_{\Delta t \to 0} \frac{1}{\Delta t}\left\{ \int \left(\int (f(z)p(y|z,\Delta t)p(z|x,t)\,\mathrm{d}z\right)\,\mathrm{d}y \right.$$

$$+ \int \left(\frac{\partial f(z)}{\partial z}(y-z)p(y|z,\Delta t)p(z|x,t)\,\mathrm{d}z\right)\,\mathrm{d}y$$

$$+ \int \left(\frac{1}{2}\frac{\partial^2 f(z)}{\partial z^2}(y-z)^2 p(y|z,\Delta t)p(z|x,t)\,\mathrm{d}z\right)\,\mathrm{d}y$$

$$\left. + O((y-z)^3) - \int f(y)p(y|x,t)\,\mathrm{d}y \right\}. \qquad (2.75)$$

If most of the contributions to the $z \to y$ transition in small time increment Δt are around $y \sim z$, one makes the following assumptions [10]

$$\int p(y|z, \Delta t)(y - z)\, \mathrm{d}y = b(z)\Delta t + o(\Delta t), \qquad (2.76)$$

$$\int p(y|z, \Delta t)(y - z)^2\, \mathrm{d}y = a(z)\Delta t + o(\Delta t), \qquad (2.77)$$

$$\int p(y|z, \Delta t)(y - z)^m\, \mathrm{d}y = o(\Delta t), \text{ for } m > 2.$$

Substituting (2.76) and (2.77) into (2.75), we get using (2.73) and an integration variable substitution, in the $\Delta t \to 0$ limit

$$\int f(z)\frac{\partial p(z|x,t)}{\partial t}\, \mathrm{d}z = \int p(z|x,t)\left\{\frac{\partial f}{\partial z}b(z) + \frac{1}{2}\frac{\partial^2 f}{\partial z^2}a(z)\right\}\, \mathrm{d}z,$$

$$= \int f(z)\left\{-\frac{\partial}{\partial z}[b(z)p(z|x,t)] + \frac{1}{2}\frac{\partial^2}{\partial z^2}[a(z)p(z|x,t)]\right\}\, \mathrm{d}z. \tag{2.78}$$

In the second line of (2.78), we integrated by parts and assumed that the large $|y|$ boundary terms are zero. Since $f(y)$ is perfectly arbitrary, it must be true that

$$\frac{\partial p(y|x,t)}{\partial t} = -\frac{\partial}{\partial y}[b(y)p(y|x,t)] + \frac{1}{2}\frac{\partial^2}{\partial y^2}[a(y)p(y|x,t)]. \tag{2.79}$$

Equation (2.79) is the *Fokker–Planck equation* and is the starting point for many probabilistic representations of solutions for partial differential equations. Generalization of (2.79) to dimensions greater than one is not difficult. The coefficient $b(y)$ becomes a vector (drift coefficients) and $a(y)$ becomes a symmetric matrix (diffusion matrix).

In our example (2.69), the coefficients are

$$\mathbf{b}(\mathbf{x}) = -\frac{1}{2}\frac{\partial S}{\partial \mathbf{x}}$$

and

$$a(\mathbf{x}) = \mathbb{I}, \text{ the identity matrix.}$$

The Fokker–Planck equation for (2.69) is thus

$$\frac{\partial p}{\partial t} = \frac{1}{2}\frac{\partial}{\partial \mathbf{x}} \cdot \left\{\frac{\partial S}{\partial \mathbf{x}}p + \frac{\partial p}{\partial \mathbf{x}}\right\}.$$

And the stationary state is when $\partial p/\partial t \to 0$, so as $t \to \infty$

$$\frac{\partial S}{\partial \mathbf{x}}p + \frac{\partial p}{\partial \mathbf{x}} = \text{constant} = 0,$$

if p goes to zero at $|\mathbf{x}| \to \infty$. Integrating once more,

$$p(\mathbf{x}, t \to \infty) = \frac{e^{-S(\mathbf{x})}}{Z},$$

where $1/Z$ is the normalization constant, hence we get (2.68).

How, then, do we simulate Equation (2.69)? We only touch on the easiest way here, a simple forward Euler method:

$$\Delta\mathbf{w} = \sqrt{h}\xi,$$

$$\Delta\mathbf{x} = -\frac{h}{2}\left(\frac{\partial S}{\partial \mathbf{x}}\right)_k + \Delta\mathbf{w},$$

$$\mathbf{x}_{k+1} = \mathbf{x}_k + \Delta\mathbf{x}. \tag{2.80}$$

At each timestep of size h, a new vector of mutually independent, univariate, and normally distributed random numbers ξ is generated each by the Box–Muller method (see Equation (2.66)) and the increments are simulated by $\Delta\mathbf{w} = \sqrt{h}\xi$.

The most useful parallel form is to compute a sample N of such vectors, $i = 1, \ldots, N$ per time step:

$$\Delta\mathbf{w}^{[i]} = \sqrt{h}\xi^{[i]},$$

$$\Delta\mathbf{x}^{[i]} = -\frac{h}{2}\left(\frac{\partial S}{\partial \mathbf{x}}\right)_k^{[i]} + \Delta\mathbf{w}^{[i]},$$

$$\mathbf{x}_{k+1}^{[i]} = \mathbf{x}_k^{[i]} + \Delta\mathbf{x}^{[i]}. \tag{2.81}$$

If S is contracting, that is, (2.68) is positive when $|\mathbf{x}|$ is large, then $\mathbf{x}(t)$ will converge to a stationary process and $\boldsymbol{E}f$ in (2.67) may be computed by a long time average [117]

$$\boldsymbol{E}f \approx \frac{1}{T}\int_0^T f(\mathbf{x}(t))\,\mathrm{d}t,$$

$$\approx \frac{1}{mN}\sum_{k=1}^m\sum_{i=1}^N f\left(\mathbf{x}_k^{[i]}\right). \tag{2.82}$$

Two features of (2.82) should be noted: (1) the number of time steps chosen is m, that is, $T = m \cdot h$; and (2) we can accelerate the convergence by the sample average over N. The convergence rate, measured by the variance, is $O(1/mN)$: the statistical error is $O(1/\sqrt{mN})$. Process $\mathbf{x}(t)$ will become stationary when m is large enough that $T = h \cdot m$ will exceed the relaxation time of the dynamics: to lowest order this means that relative to the smallest eigenvalue $\lambda_{\text{small}} > 0$ of the Jacobian $[\partial^2 S/\partial x_i \partial x_j]$, $T\lambda_{\text{small}} \gg 1$.

There are several reasons to find (2.82) attractive. If n, the size of the vectors $\mathbf{x}$ and $\mathbf{w}$, is very large, $N = 1$ may be chosen to save memory. The remaining $i = 1$ equation is also very likely to be easy to parallelize by usual matrix methods for large n. Equation (2.80) is an explicit equation—only old data $\mathbf{x}_k$ appears on the right-hand side. The downside of such an explicit formulation is that Euler methods can be unstable for a large stepsize h. In that situation, higher order methods, implicit or semi-implicit methods, or small times steps can be used [86, 106, 123]. In each of these modifications, parallelism is preserved.

To end this digression on Langevin equations (stochastic differential equations), we show examples of two simple simulations. In Figure 2.21, we show 32 simulated paths of a two-dimensional Brownian motion. All paths begin at the origin, and the updates per time step take the following form. Where,

$$\mathbf{w} = \begin{pmatrix} w_1 \\ w_2 \end{pmatrix},$$

the updates at each time step are

$$\mathbf{w}_{k+1} = \mathbf{w}_k + \sqrt{h} \begin{pmatrix} \xi_1 \\ \xi_2 \end{pmatrix}.$$

The pair ξ are generated at each step by (2.66) and $h = 0.01$.

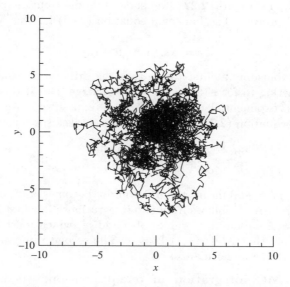

FIG. 2.21. *Simulated two-dimensional Brownian motion. There are 32 simulated paths, with timestep $h = 0.1$ and 100 steps: that is, the final time is $t = 100h$.*

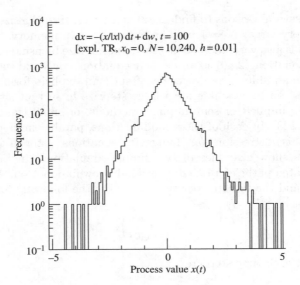

FIG. 2.22. *Convergence of the optimal control process. The parameters are* $N = 10,240$ *and time step* $h = 0.01$. *Integration was by an explicit trapezoidal rule [119].*

And finally, in Figure 2.22, we show the distribution of a converged optimal control process. The Langevin equation (2.80) for this one-dimensional example is

$$dx = -\text{sign}(x)\, dt + dw.$$

It may seem astonishing at first to see that the drift term, $-\text{sign}(x)\, dt$, is sufficiently contracting to force the process to converge. But it does converge and to a symmetric exponential distribution, $p \sim \exp(-2|x|)$. Again, this is the Fokker–Planck equation (2.79) which in this case takes the form:

$$\frac{\partial p}{\partial t} = \frac{\partial}{\partial x}[\text{sign}(x)p] + \frac{1}{2}\frac{\partial^2}{\partial x^2}p, \xrightarrow[t\to\infty]{} 0.$$

The evolution $\partial p/\partial t \to 0$ means the distribution becomes stationary (time independent), and $p = e^{-2|x|}$ follows from two integrations. The first is to a constant in terms of $x = \pm\infty$ boundary values of p and p', which must both be zero if p is normalizable, that is, $\int p(x,t)\, dx = 1$. The second integration constant is determined by the same normalization.

Exercise 2.1   MC integration in one-dimension. As we discussed in Section 2.5, MC methods are particularly useful to do integrations. However, we also pointed out that the statistical error is proportional to $N^{-1/2}$, where N is the sample size. This statistical error can be large since $N^{-1/2} = 1$ percent when $N = 10^4$. The keyword here is *proportional*. That is, although the statistical error is $k \cdot N^{-1/2}$ for some constant k, this constant can be reduced significantly. In this exercise, we want you to try some *variance reduction* schemes.

What is to be done?
The following integral

$$I_0(x) = \frac{1}{\pi} \int_0^\pi e^{-x \cos \zeta} \, d\zeta$$

is known to have a solution $I_0(x)$, the zeroth order modified Bessel function with argument x, see, for example, Abramowitz and Stegun [2], or any comparable table.

1. The method of *antithetic variables* applies in any given domain of integration where the integrand is monotonic [99]. Notice that for all positive x, the integrand $\exp(-x \cos \zeta)$ is monotonically decreasing on $0 \leq \zeta \leq \pi/2$ and is symmetric around $\zeta = \pi/2$. So, the antithetic variates method applies if we integrate only to $\zeta = \pi/2$ and double the result. For $x = 1$, the antithetic variates method is

   $$I_0(1) \approx I_+ + I_-$$

   $$= \frac{1}{N} \sum_{i=1}^{N} e^{-\cos \pi u_i/2} + \frac{1}{N} \sum_{i=1}^{N} e^{-\cos \pi(1-u_i)/2}.$$

   Try the $I_+ + I_-$ antithetic variates method for $I_0(1)$ and compute the variance (e.g. do several runs with different seeds) for both this method and a *raw* integration for the same size N—and compare the results.

2. The method of *control variates* also works well here. The idea is that an integral

   $$I = \int_0^1 g(u) \, du$$

   can be rewritten for a control variate ϕ as

   $$I = \int_0^1 (g(u) - \phi(u)) \, du + \int_0^1 \phi(u) \, du,$$

   $$\approx \frac{1}{N} \sum_{i=1}^{N} [g(u_i) - \phi(u_i)] + I_\phi,$$

   where I_ϕ is the same as I except that g is replaced by ϕ. The method consists in picking a useful ϕ whose integral I_ϕ is known. A good one for the modified Bessel function is

   $$\phi(u) = 1 - \cos(\pi u/2) + \tfrac{1}{2}(\cos(\pi u/2))^2,$$

the first three terms of the Taylor series expansion of the integrand. Again, we have chosen $x = 1$ to be specific. For this ϕ compute $I_0(1)$. Again compare with the results from a *raw* procedure without the control variate. By doing several runs with different seeds, you can get variances.

Exercise 2.2   **Solving partial differential equations by MC.** This assignment is to solve a three-dimensional partial differential equation inside an elliptical region by MC simulations of the Feynman–Kac formula. The following partial differential equation is defined in a three-dimensional ellipsoid E:

$$\tfrac{1}{2}\Delta u(x,y,z) - v(x,y,z)u(x,y,z) = 0, \qquad (2.83)$$

where the ellipsoidal domain is

$$D = \left\{ (x,y,z) \in \mathbb{R}^3;\, \frac{x^2}{a^2} + \frac{y^2}{b^2} + \frac{z^2}{c^2} < 1 \right\}.$$

The potential is $v(x,y,z) = 2\left(\dfrac{x^2}{a^4} + \dfrac{y^2}{b^4} + \dfrac{z^2}{c^4} \right) + \dfrac{1}{a^2} + \dfrac{1}{b^2} + \dfrac{1}{c^2}$. Our Dirichlet boundary condition is

$$u = g(\mathbf{x}) = 1 \quad \text{when} \quad \mathbf{x} \in \partial D.$$

The goal is to solve this boundary value problem at $\mathbf{x} = (x,y,z)$ by a MC simulation. At the heart of the simulation lies the Feynman–Kac formula, which in our case ($g = 1$) is

$$u(x,y,z) = \boldsymbol{E}g(\mathbf{X}(\tau)) \exp\left(-\int_0^\tau v(\mathbf{X}(s))\,\mathrm{d}s \right),$$

$$= \boldsymbol{E}\exp\left(-\int_0^\tau v(\mathbf{X}(s))\,\mathrm{d}s \right),$$

$$= \boldsymbol{E}Y(\tau),$$

which describes the solution u in terms of an expectation value of a stochastic process Y. Here $\mathbf{X}(s)$ is a Brownian motion starting from $\mathbf{X}(0) = \mathbf{x}$ and τ is its exit time from D (see Section 2.5.3.2) and for convenience, Y is defined as the exponential of the integral $-\int_0^t v(\mathbf{X}(s))\,\mathrm{d}s$.

The simulation proceeds as follows.

- Starting at some interior point $\mathbf{X}(0) = \mathbf{x} \in D$.
- Generate N realizations of $\mathbf{X}(t)$ and integrate the following system of stochastic differential equations ($\mathbf{W}$ is a Brownian motion)

$$\mathrm{d}\mathbf{X} = \mathrm{d}\mathbf{W},$$

$$\mathrm{d}Y = -v(\mathbf{X}(t))Y\,\mathrm{d}t.$$

- Integrate this set of equations until $\mathbf{X}(t)$ exits at time $t = \tau$.
- Compute $u(\mathbf{x}) = \boldsymbol{E}Y(\mathbf{X}(\tau))$ to get the solution.

The initial values for each realization are $\mathbf{X}(0) = (x, y, z)$ (for $\mathbf{X}$) and $Y(0) = 1$ (for Y), respectively. A simple integration procedure uses an explicit trapezoidal rule for each step $n \rightarrow n+1$ (i.e. $t \rightarrow t+h$):

$$\mathbf{X}_n = \mathbf{X}_{n-1} + \sqrt{h}\xi,$$

$$Y_{\mathrm{e}} = (1 - v(\mathbf{X}_{n-1})h)Y_{n-1}, \quad \text{(an Euler step)},$$

$$Y_n = Y_{n-1} - \frac{h}{2}\left[v(\mathbf{X}_n)Y_{\mathrm{e}} + v(\mathbf{X}_{n-1})Y_{n-1}\right] \quad \text{(trapezium)},$$

where h is the step size and ξ is a vector of three roughly normally distributed independent random variables each with mean 0 and variance 1. A inexpensive procedure is (three new ones for each coordinate $k = 1, \ldots, 3$: $\xi = (\xi_1, \xi_2, \xi_3)$ at each time step)

$$\xi_k = \pm\sqrt{3}, \text{ each with probability } 1/6,$$

$$= 0, \text{ with probability } 2/3.$$

At the end of each time step, check if $\mathbf{X}_n \in D$: if $(X_1/a)^2 + (X_2/b)^2 + (X_3/c)^2 \geq 1$, this realization of $\mathbf{X}$ exited the domain D. Label this realization i. For each $i = 1, \ldots, N$, save the values $Y^{(i)} = Y(\tau)$. When all N realizations i have exited, compute

$$u_{\mathrm{mc}}(\mathbf{x}) = \frac{1}{N}\sum_{i=1}^{N} Y^{(i)}.$$

This is the MC solution $u_{\mathrm{mc}}(\mathbf{x}) \approx u(\mathbf{x})$ to (2.83) for $\mathbf{x} = (x, y, z)$.

What is to be done?
The assignment consists of

(1) implement the MC simulation on a serial machine and test your code;
(2) for several initial values of $\mathbf{x} \in D$, compute the RMS error compared to the known analytic solution given below. For example, $m = 50\text{--}100$ values $\mathbf{x} = (x, 0, 0), -a < x < a$. See note (b).

Note: This problem will be revisited in Chapter 5.
Hints

(a) The exact solution of the partial differential equation is (easily seen by two differentiations)

$$u(x, y, z) = \exp\left(\frac{x^2}{a^2} + \frac{y^2}{b^2} + \frac{z^2}{c^2} - 1\right). \tag{2.84}$$

(b) Measure the accuracy of your solution by computing the root mean square error between the exact solution $u(\mathbf{x})$ (2.84) and the numerical approximation $u_{\mathrm{mc}}(\mathbf{x})$ given by the MC integration method for m (say $m = 50$ or 100) starting points $\mathbf{x}_i \in D$:

$$\mathrm{rms} = \sqrt{\frac{1}{m} \sum_{i=1}^{m} (u(\mathbf{x}_i) - u_{\mathrm{mc}}(\mathbf{x}_i))^2}.$$

(c) For this problem, a stepsize of $1/1000 \leq h \leq 1/100$ should give a reasonable result.

(d) A sensible value for N is $10,000$ ($\sim$ 1–2 percent statistical error).

(e) Choose some reasonable values for the ellipse (e.g. $a = 3, b = 2, c = 1$).

3

SIMD, SINGLE INSTRUCTION MULTIPLE DATA

Pluralitas non est ponenda sine neccesitate

William of Occam (1319)

3.1 Introduction

The **single instruction, multiple data** (SIMD) mode is the simplest method
of parallelism and now becoming the most common. In most cases this SIMD
mode means the same as **vectorization**. Ten years ago, vector computers were
expensive but reasonably simple to program. Today, encouraged by multimedia
applications, vector hardware is now commonly available in Intel Pentium III
and Pentium 4 PCs, and Apple/Motorola G-4 machines. In this chapter, we
will cover both old and new and find that the old paradigms for programming
were simpler because CMOS or ECL memories permitted easy non-unit stride
memory access. Most of the ideas are the same, so the simpler programming
methodology makes it easy to understand the concepts. As PC and Mac compilers improve, perhaps automatic vectorization will become as effective as on
the older non-cache machines. In the meantime, on PCs and Macs we will often
need to use **intrinsics** ([23, 22, 51]).

It seems at first that the intrinsics keep a programmer close to the hardware,
which is not a bad thing, but this is somewhat misleading. Hardware control
in this method of programming is only indirect. Actual register assignments
are made by the compiler and may not be quite what the programmer wants.
The SSE2 or Altivec programming serves to illustrate a form of instruction level
parallelism we wish to emphasize. This form, SIMD or vectorization, has single
instructions which operate on multiple data. There are variants on this theme
which use templates or macros which consist of multiple instructions carefully
scheduled to accomplish the same objective, but are not strictly speaking SIMD,
for example see Section 1.2.2.1. Intrinsics are C macros which contain one or
more SIMD instructions to execute certain operations on multiple data, usually
4-words/time in our case. Data are explicitly declared __mm128 datatypes in the
Intel SSE case and `vector` variables using the G-4 Altivec. Our examples will
show you how this works.

Four basic concepts are important:

- Memory access
- data dependencies: Sections 3.2, 3.2.2, 3.5.1, and 3.5.2
- pipelining and unrolling loops: Sections 3.2, 3.2.1, and 1.2.2
- branch execution: Section 3.2.8
- reduction operations: Section 3.3

Consistent with our notion that examples are the best way to learn, several will be illustrated:

- from linear algebra, the Level 1 basic linear algebra subprograms (BLAS)

— vector updates (-*axpy*)
— reduction operations and linear searches

- recurrence formulae and polynomial evaluations
- uniform random number generation.
- FFT

First we review the notation and conventions of Chapter 1, p. 11. Generic segments of size VL data are accumulated and processed in multi-word registers. Some typical operations are denoted:

$V_1 \leftarrow M$:   loads VL data from memory M into register V_1,
$M \leftarrow V_1$:   stores contents of register V_1 into memory M,
$V_3 \leftarrow V_1 + V_2$: adds contents of V_1 and V_2 and store results into V_3, and
$V_3 \leftarrow V_1 * V_2$: multiplies contents of V_1 by V_2, and stores these into V_3.

3.2 Data dependencies and loop unrolling

We first illustrate some basic notions of **data independence**. Look at the following loop in which $f(x)$ is some arbitrary function (see Section 3.5 to see more such recurrences),

```
for(i=m;i<n;i++){
    x[i]=f(x[i-k]);
}
```

If the order of execution follows **C** rules, x[i-k] must be computed before x[i] when $k > 0$. We will see that the maximum number that may be computed in parallel is

number of x[i]'s computed in parallel $\leq k$.

For example, for $k = 2$ the order of execution goes

```
x[m  ]=f(x[m-2]);
x[m+1]=f(x[m-1]);
```

```
x[m+2]=f(x[m  ]);   /* x[m] is new data! */
x[m+3]=f(x[m+1]);   /* likewise x[m+1]    */
x[m+4]=f(x[m+2]);   /* etc. */
        . . .
```

By line three, $x[m]$ must have been properly updated from the first line or $x[m]$ will be an **old** value, not the updated value **C** language rules prescribe. This **data dependency** in the loop is what makes it complicated for a compiler or the programmer to vectorize. This would not be the case if the output values were stored into a different array y, for example:

```
for(i=m;i<n;i++){
    y[i]=f(x[i-k]);
}
```

There is no overlap in values read in segments (groups) and those stored in that situation. Since none of the values of x would be modified in the loop, either we or the compiler can **unroll** the loop in any way desired. If $n - m$ were divisible by 4, consider unrolling the loop above with a dependency into groups of 2,

```
for(i=m;i<n;i+=2){
    x[i  ]=f(x[i-k  ]);
    x[i+1]=f(x[i-k+1]);
}
```

or groups of 4,

```
for(i=m;i<n;i+=4){
    x[i  ]=f(x[i-k  ]);
    x[i+1]=f(x[i-k+1]);
    x[i+2]=f(x[i-k+2]);
    x[i+3]=f(x[i-k+3]);
}
```

If $k = 2$, unrolling the loop to a depth of 2 to do two elements at a time would have no read/write overlap. For the same value of k, however, unrolling to depth 4 would not permit doing all 4 values independently of each other: The first pair must be finished before the second can proceed.

Conversely, according to the **C** ordering rules,

```
for(i=m;i<n;i++){
    x[i]=f(x[i+k]);
}
```

when $k > 0$ all $n - m$ could be computed as vectors as long as the sequential i ordering is preserved. Let us see what sort of instructions a vectorizing compiler would generate to do VL operands.

$$V_1 \leftarrow [x_{m+k}, x_{m+k+1}, x_{m+k+2}, ...] \quad // \text{ VL of these}$$
$$V_2 \leftarrow f(V_1) \quad // \text{ vector of results}$$
$$[x_m, x_{m+1}, ...] \leftarrow V_2 \quad // \text{ store VL results,}$$

Registers V_r are purely symbolic and may be one of

(1) V_r is a vector register (Cray, NEC, Fujitsu); or Motorola/Apple G-4 **Altivec** register; SSE2 register, Appendix B; AMD **3DNow** technology [1]; or

(2) V_r is a collection of registers, say $R_1, R_7, R_3, R_5...$ where each R_j stores only one word. This would be the type of optimization a compiler would generate for **superscalar** chips. The term superscalar applies to single word register machines which permit concurrent execution of instructions. Hence, several single word registers can be used to form multi-word operations, see Section 1.2.2.1. Although this mode is instruction level parallelism, it is not SIMD because multiple data are processed each by individual instructions.

Although the segments $[x_{m+k}, x_{m+k+1}, ...]$ and $[x_m, x_{m+1}, ...]$ overlap, V_1 has a copy of the old data, so no x[i] is ever written onto before its value is copied, then used. At issue are the **C** (or Fortran) execution order rules of the expressions. Such recurrences and short vector dependencies will be discussed further in Section 3.5. In sequential fashion, for the pair

```
x[1]=f(x[0]);
x[2]=f(x[1]);   /* x[1] must be new data */
```

the value of $x[1]$ must be computed in the first expression before its new value is used in the second. Its old value is lost forever. Whereas, in

```
x[0]=f(x[1]);   /* x[1] is old data */
x[1]=f(x[2]);   /* x[1] may now be clobbered */
```

the old value of x[1] has already been copied into a register and used, so what happens to it afterward no longer matters.

An example. In the applications provided in Chapter 2, we pointed out that the lagged Fibonacci sequence (2.60)

$$x_n = x_{n-p} + x_{n-q} \mod 1.0.$$

can be SIMD parallelized with a vector length $VL \le \min(p, q)$. According to the discussion given there, the larger $\min(p, q)$ is, the better the quality of the generator. On p. 61, we showed code which uses a circular buffer (buff) of length $\max(p, q)$ to compute this long recurrence formula. In that case, better performance and higher quality go together.

The basic procedure of **unrolling** loops is the same: A loop is broken into segments. For a loop of n iterations, one unrolls the loop into segments of length VL by

$$n = q \cdot VL + r$$

where q = the number of full segments, and $0 \leq r < VL$ is a residual. The total number of segments processed is q if $r = 0$, otherwise $q + 1$ when $r > 0$. To return to a basic example, the loop

```
for(i=p;i<n;i++){
    y[i]=f(x[i]);
}
```

may be unrolled into groups of 4. Let $p = n$ **mod** 4; either we programmers, or better, the compiler, unrolls this loop into:

```
y[0]=f(x[0]); ... y[p-1]=f(x[p-1]);  /* p<4 */
for(i=p;i<n;i+=4){
    y[i  ]=f(x[i]);
    y[i+1]=f(x[i+1]);
    y[i+2]=f(x[i+2]);
    y[i+3]=f(x[i+3]);
}
```

These groups (vectors) are four at a time. The generalization to say m at a time is obvious. It must be remarked that sometimes the residual segment is processed first, but sometimes after all the q full VL segments. In either case, **why would we do this, or why would a compiler do it?** The following section explains.

3.2.1 *Pipelining and segmentation*

The following analysis, and its subsequent generalization in Section 3.2.3, is very simplified. Where it may differ significantly from real machines is where there is out-of-order execution, for example, on Intel Pentium III and Pentium 4 machines. On out-of-order execution machines, a general analysis of speedup becomes difficult. The terminology "pipeline" is easy enough to understand: One imagines a small pipe to be filled with balls of slightly smaller diameter. The overhead (same as latency in this case) is how many balls will fit into the pipe before it is full, Figure 3.1. Subsequently, pushing more balls into the pipe causes balls to emerge from the other end at the same rate they are pushed in. Today nearly all functional units are pipelined, the idea apparently having originated in 1962 with the University of Manchester's **Atlas** project [91]. Hardware rarely does any single operation in one clock tick. For example, imagine we wish to multiply an array of integers **A** times **B** to get array **C**: for $i \geq 0$, $C_i = A_i * B_i$. This is sometimes called a Hadamard or element by element product. A special notation is used in MatLab for these products: A.*B. We indicate the successive bytes of each element by numbering them 3,2,1,0, that is, little-endian,

$$A_i = [A_{i3}, A_{i2}, A_{i1}, A_{i0}],$$
$$B_i = [B_{i3}, B_{i2}, B_{i1}, B_{i0}],$$
$$C_i = [C_{i3}, C_{i2}, C_{i1}, C_{i0}].$$

Byte numbered j must wait until byte $j-1$ is computed via

$$C_{ij} = A_{ij} * B_{ij} + \text{carry from } A_{i,j-1} * B_{i,j-1}. \tag{3.1}$$

When stage j is done with $A_{i,j} * B_{i,j}$, it (stage j) can be used for $A_{i+1,j} * B_{i+1,j}$, until reaching the last i. After four cycles the pipeline is full. Look at the time flow in Figure 3.1 to see how it works. Subsequently, we get one result/clock-cycle. It takes 4 clock ticks to do one multiply, while in the pipelined case it takes $4 + n$ to do n, the speedup is thus

$$\text{speedup} = \frac{4n}{4+n} \tag{3.2}$$

which for large number of elements $n \leq VL$ is the pipeline length ($=4$ in this case).

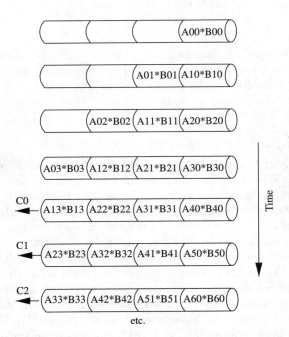

FIG. 3.1. *Four-stage multiply pipeline:* $\mathbf{C} = \mathbf{A} * \mathbf{B}$. *In this simplified example, four cycles (the pipeline latency) are needed to fill the pipeline after which one result is produced per cycle.*

3.2.2   *More about dependencies, scatter/gather operations*

From our examples above, it is hopefully clear that reading data from one portion of an array and storing updated versions of it back into different locations of the same array may lead to dependencies which must be resolved by the programmer, or by the compiler, perhaps with help from the programmer. In the latter case, certain **compiler directives** are available. These directives, `pragma`'s in **C** and their Fortran (e.g. `cdir$`) equivalents, treated in more detail in Chapter 4 on shared memory parallelism, are instructions whose syntax looks like code comments but give guidance to compilers for optimization within a restricted scope. Look at the simple example in Figure 3.3. One special class of these dependencies garnered a special name—scatter/gather operations. To illustrate, let `index` be an array of integer indices whose values do not exceed the array bounds of our arrays. In their simplest form, the two operations are in Figure 3.2. It is not hard to understand the terminology: `scatter` takes a segment of elements (e.g. the contiguous x_i above) and scatters them into random locations; `gather` collects elements from random locations. In the `scatter` case, the difficulty for a compiler is that it is impossible to know at compile time that all the indices (`index`) are unique. If they are unique, all n may be processed in any order, regardless of how the loop count n is segmented (unrolled). The `gather` operation has a similar problem, and another when **w** and **z** overlap, which is frequently the case. Let us beat this to death so that there is no confusion. Take the case that two of the indices are not unique:

$$index[1]=3$$
$$index[2]=1$$
$$index[3]=1$$

For $n = 3$, after the loop in Figure 3.3 is executed, we should have array **y** with the values

```
for(i=0;i<n;i++){
    y[index[i]] = x[i];        /* scatter */
    w[i]        = z[index[i]];  /* gather  */
}
```

FIG. 3.2. *Scatter and gather operations.*

```
#pragma ivdep
    for(i=0;i<n;i++){
        y[index[i]) = x[i];
    }
```

FIG. 3.3. *Scatter operation with a directive telling the* **C** *compiler to ignore any apparent* **v***ector* **dep***endencies. If any two array elements of* `index` *have the same value, there would be such a dependency.*

```
y[1]=x[3]
y[2]=unchanged
y[3]=x[1]
```

where perhaps $y[1]$ was set to $x[2]$, then reset to $x[1]$. If all n calculations were done asynchronously, $y[1]$ might end up containing $x[2]$, an incorrect value according to the **C** execution rules. What is the unfortunate compiler to do? Obviously, it has to be conservative and generates only one/time code. There could be no parallel execution in that case. Not only must the results be those specified by the one after another **C** execution rules, but the compiler cannot assume that all the indices (**index**) are unique. After all, maybe there is something subtle going on here that the compiler cannot know about. Beginning in the late 1970s, Cray Research invented **compiler directives** to help the frustrated compiler when it is confused by its task. The syntax is shown in Figure 3.3.

The **pragma** tells the compiler that indeed Ms. Programmer knows what she is doing and to **ignore** the **vector dep**endency. Now everybody is happy: The programmer gets her vectorized code and the compiler does the right optimization it was designed to do. And as icing on the cake, the resultant code is approximately portable. The worst that could happen is that another compiler may complain that it does not understand the **pragma** and either ignore it, or (rarely) give up compiling. If done in purely sequential order, the results should agree with SIMD parallelized results.

In **C** and Fortran where pointers are permitted, the gather operation in Figure 3.2 can be problematic, too. Namely if **w** and **z** are pointers to a memory region where gathered data (**w**) are stored into parts of **z**, again the compiler must be conservative and generate only one/time code. In the event that out-of-sequence execution would effect the results, the dependencies are called antidependencies [146]. For example, if a loop index $i + 1$ were executed before the i-th, this would be contrary to the order of execution rules. As an asynchronous parallel operation, the order might be arbitrary. There are many compiler directives to aid compilation; we will illustrate some of them and enumerate the others.

3.2.3 Cray SV-1 hardware

To better understand these ideas about pipelining and vectors, some illustration about the hardware should be helpful. Bear in mind that the analysis only roughly applies to in-order execution with fixed starting overhead (latencies). Out-of-order execution [23] can hide latencies, thus speedups may be higher than (3.5). Conversely, since memory architectures on Pentiums and Motorola G-4s have multiple layers of cache, speedups may also be lower than our analysis. Figure 3.4 shows the block diagram for the Cray SV-1 central processing unit. This machine has fixed overheads (latencies) for the functional units, although the processing rate may differ when confronted with

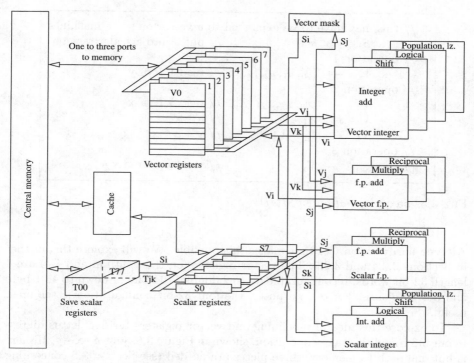

FIG. 3.4. *Cray SV-1 CPU diagram.*

memory bank conflicts. These conflicts occur when bulk memory is laid
out in banks (typically up to 1024 of these) and when successive requests to
the same bank happen faster than the request/refresh cycle of the bank. The
only parts of interest to us here are the eight 64-word floating point vector
registers and eight 64-bit scalar registers. The eight vector registers, numbered
$V_0, \ldots, V_7$, are shown in the upper middle portion. The pipelines of the arithmetic units appear in the upper right—add, multiply, reciprocal approximation,
logical.

There are many variants on this theme. NEC SX-4, SX-5, and SX-6 machines
have reconfigurable blocks of vector registers. Cray C-90 has registers with
128, not 64, floating point words and so forth. Intel began with the Pentium
featuring MMX integer SIMD technology. Later, the Pentium III featured similar vector registers called XMM (floating point) and again included the integer
MMX hardware. The three letter acronym SSE refers to this technology and
means **streaming SIMD extensions**; its successor SSE2 includes double precision (64 bit) operations. Not surprisingly, the "MM" stands for multimedia.
Furthermore, if you, gentle reader, wonder how any of the **Jaguar** swoosh-
ing windows can happen in Macintosh OS-X, some of it is the power of the

```
// this may have to be expanded to a vector on some machines
     S₁   ←   a              // put a into a scalar register
// operation 1
     V₁   ←   [y₀, y₁, y₂, ...]   // read VL of y
// operation 2
     V₂   ←   [x₀, x₁, x₂, ...]   // read VL of x
     V₃   ←   S₁ * V₂         // a * x
     V₄   ←   V₁ + V₃         // y + a * x
// operation 3
[y₀, y₁, ...]   ←   V₄        // store updated y's
```

FIG. 3.5. saxpy *operation by SIMD.*

Altivec hardware on G-4 that makes this possible. We will explore this further in Sections 3.2.4 and 3.2.5. The vector registers on the Pentium and G-4 are 4 length 32-bit words, reconfigurable up to 2 doubles (64-bit) or down to 16 1-byte and 8 2-byte sizes. For our purposes, the four 32-bit configuration is the most useful.

To explore this idea of pipelining and vector registers further, let us digress to our old friend the saxpy operation, shown in Figure 3.5, $y \leftarrow a \cdot x + y$. If there is but one path to memory, three pieces are needed (see Section 3.6 concerning the first comment in the pseudo-code):

Why are the three parts of *operation 2* in Figure 3.5 considered only one operation? Because the functional units used are all independent of each other: as soon as the first word (containing y_0) arrives in V_2 after π_{memory} cycles, the multiply operation can start, similar to Figure 3.1. **Memory is also a pipelined functional unit**, see for example [23]. As soon as the first result $(a \cdot x_0)$ of the $a \cdot x$ operation arrives (π_{multiply} cycles later) in V_3, the add operation with the y elements already in V_1 may begin. Hence, the read of x, multiplication by a, and subsequent add to y may all run concurrently as soon as the respective operations' pipelines are full. **Subsequently, (one result)/(clock tick) is the computational rate**. Since there is only one port to memory, however, the final results now in V_4 cannot be stored until all of V_4 is filled. This is because memory is busy streaming data into V_2 and is not available to stream the results into V_4. Thus, with only one port to memory, the processing rate is approximately (1 saxpy result)/(3 clock ticks).

However, if as in Figure 3.4, there are three ports to memory, the three operations of Figure 3.1 collapse into only one: read, read, multiply, add, and store—all running concurrently [80, 122].

To be more general than the simple speedup formula 3.2, a **segmented vector timing formula** can be written for a segment length $n \leq VL$, where for each pipe of length π_i it takes $\pi_i + n$ cycles to do n operandpairs. With the notation,

$$n = \text{number of independent data}$$
$$\pi_i = \text{pipeline overhead for linked operation } i$$
$$\alpha = \text{number of linked operations}$$
$$R_{\text{vector}} = \text{processing rate (data/clock period)}$$

we get the following processing rate which applies when π_{memory} is not longer than the computation,

$$R_{\text{vector}} = \frac{n}{\sum_{i=1}^{\alpha}\{\pi_i + n\}}. \qquad (3.3)$$

In one/time mode, the number cycles to compute one result is,

$$\frac{1}{R_{\text{scalar}}} = \sum_{i=1}^{\alpha} \pi_i.$$

The speedup, comparing the vector (R_{vector}) to scalar (R_{scalar}) processing rates, is

$$\text{speedup} = \frac{R_{\text{vector}}}{R_{\text{scalar}}} = \frac{n \sum_{i=1}^{\alpha} \pi_i}{\sum_{i=1}^{\alpha}\{\pi_i + n\}}. \qquad (3.4)$$

If $n \leq VL$ is small, the speedup ratio is roughly 1; if n is large compared to the overheads π_i, however, this ratio becomes (as n gets large)

$$\text{speedup} \approx \frac{\sum_{i=1}^{\alpha} \pi_i}{\alpha} = \langle \pi \rangle,$$

that is, the average pipeline overhead (latency). It may seem curious at first, but the larger the overhead, the higher the speedup is. Typically, these startup latency counts are 3 to 15 cycles for arithmetic operations, which is similar to π_{memory} when CMOS or ECL memory is used. On machines with cache memories, it may be hard to determine a priori how long is π_{memory}, the pipeline length for memory, because of multiple cache levels (up to three). In that case, the next Section 3.2.4 applies. Hardware reference manuals and experimentation are the ultimate sources of information on these quantities. The number of linked operations is usually much easier to determine:

> The number α of linked operations is determined by the number of independent functional units or the number of registers. When an instruction sequence exhausts the number of resources, α must be increased. Such a resource might be the number of memory ports or the number of add or multiply units. No linked operation can exist if the number of functional units of one category is exceeded. For example, two multiplies if there is only one multiply unit mean two separate operations.

3.2.4 *Long memory latencies and short vector lengths*

On systems with cache, the most important latency to be reckoned with is waiting to fetch data from bulk memory. Typical memory latencies may be 10 times that of a relatively simple computation, for example `saxpy`. This can be longer than the inner portion of a loop. Thus, unrolling loops by using the vector hardware to compute

$$\mathbf{B} = f(\mathbf{A})$$

takes on forms shown in Figure 3.6. There are two variants which loop through the computation 4/time. In the first, without any prefetch, the vector register V_0 (size four here) is loaded with $A_i, A_{i+1}, A_{i+2}, A_{i+3}$ and after the time needed for these data to arrive, $f(\mathbf{A})$ for these four elements can be computed. These data are then stored in a segment $(B_i, B_{i+1}, B_{i+2}, B_{i+3})$ of $\mathbf{B}$. In the second variant, $A_i, A_{i+1}, A_{i+2}, A_{i+3}$ are prefetched into V_0 before entering the loop, these data saved in V_1 as the first instruction of the loop, then the next segment fetch $(A_{i+4}, A_{i+5}, A_{i+6}, A_{i+7})$ is begun before the $i, i+1, i+2, i+3$ elements of $f(\mathbf{A})$ are computed. The advantage of this prefetching strategy is that part of the memory latency may be hidden behind the computation f, $VL = 4$ times for the current segment. That is, instead of a delay of $T_{wait\ memory}$, the latency is reduced to $T_{wait\ memory} - T_f - T_j$ where T_f is the time for the $VL = 4$ computations of $f()$ for the current segment, and T_j is the cost of the jump back to the beginning of the loop. It is hard to imagine how to prefetch more than one segment ahead, that is, more than one $i, i+1, i+2, i+3$ loop count because the prefetch is pipelined and not readily influenced by software control. How does

for $i = 0, n-1$ **by** 4 {	$V_0 \leftarrow A_0, \ldots, A_3$
	for $i = 0, n-5$ **by** 4 {
$\qquad V_0 \leftarrow A_i, \ldots, A_{i+3}$	
$\qquad$ wait memory	$\qquad V_1 \leftarrow V_0$
$\qquad .$	$\qquad V_0 \leftarrow A_{i+4}, \ldots, A_{i+7}$
$\qquad .$	$\qquad$ (wait memory) $- T_f - T_j$
$\qquad .$	$\qquad V_2 \leftarrow f(V_1)$
$\qquad V_1 \leftarrow f(V_0)$	$\qquad B_i, \ldots, B_{i+3} \leftarrow V_2$
$\qquad B_i, \ldots, B_{i+3} \leftarrow V_1$	}
	$V_2 \qquad\qquad\qquad \leftarrow f(V_0)$
}	$B_{i+4}, \ldots, B_{i+7} \leftarrow V_2$

FIG. 3.6. *Long memory latency vector computation, without prefetch on left, with prefetch on the right: T_f is the time for function f and T_j is the cost of the jump to the top of the loop.*

one save data that have not yet arrived? It is possible to unroll the loop to do $2 \cdot VL$ or $3 \cdot VL$, etc., at a time in some situations, but not more than one loop iteration ahead. However, since higher levels of cache typically have larger block sizes (see Table 1.1) than L1, fetching $A_i, A_{i+1}, A_{i+2}, A_{i+3}$ into L1 also brings $A_{i+4}, A_{i+5}, A_{i+6}, \ldots, A_{i+\text{L2B}}$ into L2, where L2B is the L2 cache block size. This foreshortens the next memory fetch latency for successive $VL = 4$ segments. The result is, in effect, the same as aligning four templates as in Figures 1.9, 1.10 from Chapter 1. In both cases of Figure 3.6, we get the following speedup from unrolling the loop into segments of size VL:

$$\text{speedup} = \frac{R_{\text{vector}}}{R_{\text{scalar}}} \leq VL \qquad (3.5)$$

In summary, then, on SSE2 and Altivec hardware, one can expect speedup ≤ 4 (single precision) or speedup ≤ 2 (double precision). Experimentally, these inequalities are fairly sharp, namely speedups of 4 (or 2 in double) are often closely reached. To be clear: **unrolling with this mechanism is powerful because of the principle of data locality** from Chapter 1, Section 1.1. Namely, once datum A_i is fetched, the other date $A_{i+1}, A_{i+2}, A_{i+3}$ are in the same cacheline and come almost gratis.

3.2.5 *Pentium 4 and Motorola G-4 architectures*

In this book, we can only give a very superficial overview of the architectural features of both Intel Pentium 4 and Motorola G-4 chips. This overview will be limited to those features which pertain to the SIMD hardware available (SSE on the Pentium, and Altivec on G-4). In this regard, we will rely on diagrams to give a flavor of the appropriate features. Both machines permit modes of out-of-order execution. On the Pentium, the *out of order core* can actually reorder instructions, whereas on the G-4 this does not happen. Instructions may issue before others are completed, however, thus permitting arithmetic pipeline filling before all the results are stored, as in Figures 3.7 and 3.8. For our purposes, this overlap of partially completed instructions is enough to outline the SIMD behavior.

3.2.6 *Pentium 4 architecture*

Instruction execution on the Pentium 4 (and on the Pentium III, it must be remarked) is deeply pipelined. On a Pentium 4, an instruction cache (*Trace cache*) of 12k µops (micro-operations) provides instructions to an out-of-order core (previously *Dispatch/execute* unit on Pentium III) from a pool of machine instructions which may be reordered according to available resources. The general case of reordering is beyond the scope of this text, so we will only be concerned with instruction issues which proceed before previous instructions have finished. See our example in Figures 3.7 and 3.8. Figure 3.9 shows a block diagram of the instruction pipeline. The *out of order core* has four ports to

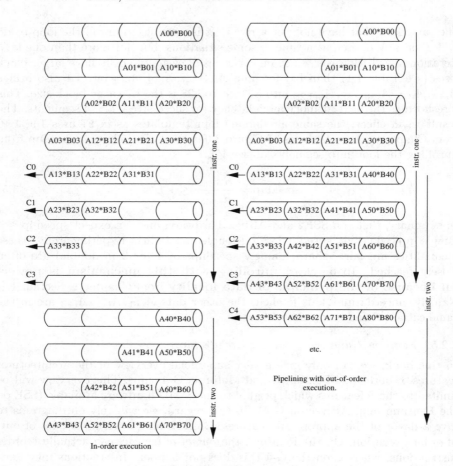

FIG. 3.7. *Four-stage multiply pipeline:* $\mathbf{C} = \mathbf{A} * \mathbf{B}$ *with out-of-order instruction issue. The left side of the figure shows in-order pipelined execution for* $VL = 4$. *On the right, pipelined execution (out-of-order) shows that the next segment of* $VL = 4$ *can begin filling the arithmetic pipeline without flushing, see Figures 3.1 and 3.3.*

various functional units—integer, floating point, logical, etc. These are shown in Figure 3.10. In brief, then, the various parts of the *NetBurst* architecture are:

1. **Out-of-order** core can dispatch up to 6 μops/cycle. There are four ports (0,1,2,3) to the execution core: see Figure 3.10.
2. **Retirement unit** receives results from the execution unit and updates the system state in proper program order.
3. **Execution trace cache** is the primary instruction cache. This cache can hold up to 12k μops and can deliver up to 3 μops/cycle.

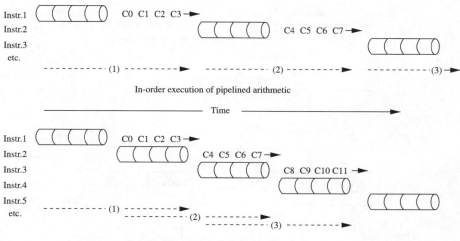

In-order execution of pipelined arithmetic

Out-of-order execution of pipelined arithmetic

FIG. 3.8. *Another way of looking at Figure 3.7: since instruction (2) may begin before (1) is finished, (2) can start filling the pipeline as soon as the first result from instruction (1) C_0 emerges. In consequence, there is an overlap of instruction execution. In this instance, out-of-order means that (2), subsequently (3) and (4), can begin before earlier issues have completed all their results.*

4. **Branch prediction** permits beginning execution of instructions before the actual branch information is available. There is a delay for failed prediction: typically this delay is at least the pipeline length π_i as in (3.5) plus a penalty for any instruction cache flushing. A history of previous branches taken is kept to predict the next branch. This history is updated and the order of execution adjusted accordingly, see Figure 3.9. Intel's branch prediction algorithm is heuristic but they claim it is more than 95 percent correct.

Instruction fetches (see *Fetch/decode* unit in Figure 3.9) are always in-order and likewise retirement and result storage. In between, however, the instructions are in a *pool* of concurrent instructions and may be reordered by the *Execution* unit. Other important architectural features are the register sets. On the Pentium 4, there are

1. Eight scalar floating point registers (80 bits).
2. Eight 128-bit floating point vector registers. Each may be partitioned in various ways: 16 bytes/register, 4 single precision 32-bit words, or 2 double precision 64-bit words, for example. Our principle interest here will be in the 32-bit single precision partitioning. These registers are called **XMM** registers: and are numbered XMM0, XMM1, ..., XMM7.

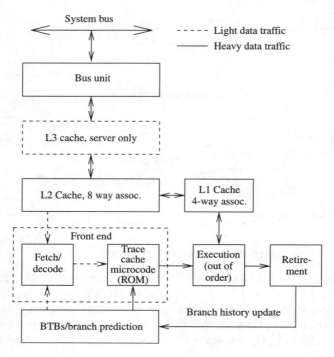

FIG. 3.9. *Block diagram of Intel Pentium 4 pipelined instruction execution unit. Intel calls this system the* NetBurst *Micro-architecture. Loads may be speculative, but stores are in-order. The trace cache replaced the older P-3 instruction cache and has a 12k μops capacity, see: [23].*

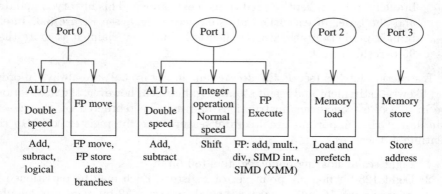

FIG. 3.10. *Port structure of Intel Pentium 4 out-of-order instruction core. Port 1 handles the SIMD instructions, see: [23].*

3. Eight 64-bit integer vector registers. These are the integer counterpart to the XMM registers, called **MMX**, and numbered MM0, MM1, ..., MM7. Originally, these labels meant "multimedia," but because of their great flexibility Intel no longer refers to them in this way.

3.2.7   Motorola G-4 architecture

The joint Motorola/IBM/Apple G-4 chip is a sophisticated RISC processor. Its instruction issue is always in-order, but instruction execution may begin prior to the completion of earlier ones. For our examples here, it is similar to the more deeply pipelined Intel Pentium 4 chip. The G-4 chip has a rich set of registers (see Figure 3.11):

1. Thirty-two *general purpose registers* (GPUs), of 64-bit length.
2. Thirty-two *floating point registers* (FPRs), of 64-bit length. Floating point arithmetic is generally done in 80-bit precision on G-4 [48], [25].

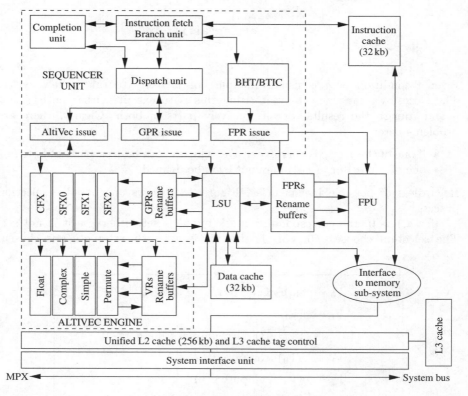

FIG. 3.11. *High level overview of the Motorola G-4 structure, including the Altivec technology, see: [29].*

3. Thirty-two *Altivec* registers, each of 128-bit length. These may be partitioned in various ways: 16 bytes/register, 4 single precision 32-bit floating point words/register, or 2 double precision 64-bit words/register, for example.

3.2.8 *Branching and conditional execution*

Using the SIMD paradigm for loops with if statements or other forms of branching is tricky. Branch prediction has become an important part of hardware design (e.g. see [23] and [71]). It is impossible, almost by definition, to compute if's or branches in SIMD efficiently. Indeed, a conditional execution with even two choices (f or g) cannot be done directly with one instruction on multiple data. Look at the following example.

```
for(i=0;i<n;i++){
    if(e(a[i])>0.0){
        c[i]=f(a[i]);
    } else {
        c[i]=g(a[i]);
    }
}
```

Branch condition $e(x)$ is usually simple but is likely to take a few cycles. The closest we can come to vectorizing this is to execute either both f and g and **merge** the results, or alternatively parts of both. Clearly, there are problems here:

- if one of the f or g is very expensive, why do both or even parts of both?
- one of $f(a[i])$ or $g(a[i])$ may not even be defined.

Regardless of possible inefficiencies, Figure 3.12 shows one possible selection process.

If $e(a_i) > 0$, the corresponding mask bit 'i' is set, otherwise it is not set. The selection chooses $f(a_i)$ if the ith bit is set, otherwise $g(a_i)$ is chosen.

$$V_0 \leftarrow [a_0, a_1, \ldots]$$
$$V_7 \leftarrow e(V_0)$$
$$VM \leftarrow (V_7 > 0?) \text{ forms a mask if } e(a_i) > 0$$
$$V_1 \leftarrow f(V_0) \text{ compute f(a)}$$
$$V_2 \leftarrow g(V_0) \text{ compute g(a)}$$
$$V_3 \leftarrow VM?V_1 : V_2 \text{ selects } f \text{ if VM bit set}$$

FIG. 3.12. *Branch processing by merging results.*

The following is another example of such a branching, but is efficient in this case,

```
d[i]=(e(a[i])>0.0)?b[i]:c[i];
```

because b_i and c_i require no calculation—only selection. An alternative to possible inefficient procedures is to use **scatter/gather**:

```
npicka=0; npickb=0;
for(i=0;i<n;i++){
    if(e(a[i])>0.0){
        picka[npicka++]=i;
    } else {
        pickb[npickb++]=i;
    }
}
for(k=0;k<npicka;k++) c(picka[k])=f(a[picka[k]]);
for(k=0;k<npickb;k++) c(pickb[k])=g(b[pickb[k]]);
```

Either way, you will probably have to work to optimize (vectorize) such branching loops. In the example of **isamax** later in Section 3.5.7, we will see how we effect a merge operation on Intel Pentium's SSE hardware.

Branch prediction is now a staple feature of modern hardware. A simplified illustration can be shown when the operations, $f(x), g(x)$, in the computation of the loop on p. 102 take multiple steps. Imagine that at least two operations are necessary to compute these functions:

$$f(x) = f_2(f_1(x)),$$
$$g(x) = g_2(g_1(x)).$$

If $e(x) > 0$ is more probable, the following branch prediction sequence (Figure 3.13) will be efficient (see p. 86 for register conventions). Conversely, what if the branch $e(x) \leq 0$ were more probable? In that case, a more efficient branch prediction would be Figure 3.14. Since the computation of f_1 in Figure 3.13 (or $g_1(x)$ in the case shown in Figure 3.14) is a pipelined operation, it may run concurrently with the steps needed to determine the if$(e(R_0) > 0)$ test. In Figure 3.13, if it turns out $R_7 \leq 0$, the prediction fails and there will be penalties, obviously at least the cost of computing $R_1 = f_1(R_0)$ because it is not used. Instruction reordering is done for optimization, so a missed branch prediction also forces an instruction cache flush—roughly 10 clock cycles on Pentium III and 20 cycles on Pentium 4. As many as 126 instructions can be in the instruction pipe on P-4. In Figure 3.14, if $R_7 > 0$ the prediction likewise fails and penalties will be exacted. Regardless of these penalties, branch prediction failure penalties are almost always far less costly than the merging results procedure illustrated in Figure 3.12.

Now imagine that the hardware keeps a history which records the last selection of this branch. If it turns out that $R_7 \leq 0$ seems more likely, according

$$
\begin{aligned}
&R_0 &\leftarrow&\quad x \\
&R_7 &\leftarrow&\quad e(x) \\
&R_1 &\leftarrow&\quad f_1(R_0) &&\text{// compute part of } f(x) \\
&\text{if } (R_7 > 0) \ \{ \\
&\quad\quad R_3 \leftarrow f_2(R_1) &&&&\text{// predicted } f \text{ if } e(x) > 0 \\
&\} \text{ else } \{ \\
&\quad\quad R_4 \leftarrow g_1(R_0) &&&&\text{// picks } g \text{ otherwise} \\
&\quad\quad R_3 \leftarrow g_2(R_4) \\
&\}
\end{aligned}
$$

FIG. 3.13. *Branch prediction best when $e(x) > 0$.*

$$
\begin{aligned}
&R_0 &\leftarrow&\quad x \\
&R_7 &\leftarrow&\quad e(x) \\
&R_1 &\leftarrow&\quad g_1(R_0) &&\text{// compute part of } g(x) \\
&\text{if } (R_7 > 0) \ \{ \\
&\quad\quad R_4 \leftarrow f_1(R_0) &&&&\text{// picks } f \text{ if } e(x) > 0 \\
&\quad\quad R_3 \leftarrow f_2(R_4) \\
&\} \text{ else } \{ \\
&\quad\quad R_3 \leftarrow g_2(R_1) &&&&\text{// predicted } g \\
&\}
\end{aligned}
$$

FIG. 3.14. *Branch prediction best if $e(x) \le 0$.*

to that history, then the second sequence Figure 3.14 should be used. With out-of-order execution possible, the instruction sequence could be reordered such that the $g(x)$ path is the most likely branch. With some examination, it is not hard to convince yourself that the second expression (Figure 3.14) is just a reordering of the first (Figure 3.13); particularly if the registers can be renamed. The Pentium 4 allows both reordering (see Figure 3.9) and renaming of registers [23, 131]. Likewise, Power-PC (Motorola G-4) allows renaming registers [131].

Thus, in loops, the history of the previously chosen branches is used to predict which branch to choose the next time, usually when the loop is unrolled (see Section 3.2). Solid advice is given on p. 12 of reference [23] about branch prediction and elimination of branches, when the latter is possible. A great deal of thought has been given to robust hardware determination of branch prediction: again, see [23] or [71]. The isamax0 example given on p. 125 is more appropriate for our SIMD discussion and the decision about which branch to choose is done by the programmer, not by hardware.

3.3   Reduction operations, searching

The astute reader will have noticed that only vector → vector operations have been discussed above. Operations which reduce the number of elements of operands to a scalar or an index of a scalar are usually not vector operations in the same sense. In SIMD, shared memory parallelism, and distributed memory parallelism, reduction operations can be painful. For example, unless a machine has special purpose hardware for an inner product, that operation requires clever programming to be efficient. Let us consider the usual inner product operation. The calculation is

$$\text{dot} = (\mathbf{x}, \mathbf{y}) = \sum_{i=1}^{n} x_i y_i$$

where the result `dot` is a simple scalar element. It is easy enough to do a partial reduction to VL elements. Assume for simplicity that the number n of elements is a multiple of VL (the segment length): $n = q \cdot VL$,

$$
\begin{array}{llll}
V_1 & \leftarrow & [0,0,0,\ldots] & \text{// initialize } V_0 \text{ to zero} \\
\multicolumn{4}{l}{\text{// loop over segments: m += VL each time}} \\
V_1 & \leftarrow & [x_m, x_{m+1}, x_{m+2}, \ldots] & \text{// read } VL \text{ of } \mathbf{x} \\
V_2 & \leftarrow & [y_m, y_{m+1}, y_{m+2}, \ldots] & \text{// read } VL \text{ of } \mathbf{y} \\
V_3 & \leftarrow & V_1 * V_2 & \text{// segment of } \mathbf{x}^*\mathbf{y} \\
V_0 & \leftarrow & V_0 + V_3 & \text{// accumulate partial result}
\end{array}
$$

which yields a segment of length VL of partial sums in V_0:

$$\text{partial}_i = \sum_{k=0}^{q-1} x_{i+k \cdot VL} \cdot y_{i+k \cdot VL},$$

which must be further reduced to get the final result,

$$\text{dot} = \sum_{i=1}^{VL} \text{partial}_i.$$

Not surprisingly, the last reduction of VL partial sums may be expensive and given all the special cases which have to be treated (e.g. $n \neq q \cdot VL$), it is likely less efficient than using pure vector operations. Fortunately for the programmer, many compilers look for such obvious constructions and insert optimized routines to do reduction operations such as inner products, for example, the BLAS routine `sdot`. Obviously, no matter how clever the compiler is, there will be reduction operations it cannot recognize and the resultant code will not parallelize well. Another important operation is a maximum element search. We only illustrate a unit stride version. The BLAS version of `isamax` has an arbitrary but fixed stride, ours is

$$\text{isamax0} = \inf_i \{ i \mid |x_i| \geq |x_k|, \forall k \}$$

that is, the first index i for which $|x_i| \geq |x_k|$ for all $1 \leq k \leq n$. The Linpack benchmark uses gefa to factor a matrix $A = LU$ by partial pivoting Gaussian elimination, and requires such a search for the element of maximum absolute value. In examples later in this chapter, we will show how to use the SSE (Pentium III and 4) and Altivec (Apple G-4) hardware to efficiently do both sdot and the isamax operations (see p. 124, 125). Meanwhile we will show that it is sometimes possible to avoid some reductions.

3.4   Some basic linear algebra examples

We have repeatedly flogged the saxpy operation because it is important in several important tasks. We will now illustrate two: matrix × matrix multiply and Gaussian elimination. In the first case, we show that a loop interchange can be helpful.

3.4.1   *Matrix multiply*

In this example, we want the matrix product $C = AB$, where matrices A, B, C are assumed to be square and of size $n \times n$. Here is the usual textbook way of writing the operation (e.g. [89], section 7.3). We use the **C** ordering wherein columns of B are assumed stored consecutively and that successive rows of A are stored n floating point words apart in memory:

```
for (i=0;i<n;i++){  /* mxm by dot product */
    for (j=0;j<n;j++){
        c[i][j]=0.;
        for (k=0;k<n;k++){
            c[i][j] += a[i][k]*b[k][j];
        }
    }
}
```

It is important to observe that the inner loop counter k does not index elements of the result (c[i][j]): that is, $C_{i,j}$ is a fixed location with respect to the index k. We could as well write this as

```
for (i=0;i<n;i++){ /* mxm by expl. dot product */
    for (j=0;j<n;j++){
        c[i][j]=sdot(n,&a[i][0],1,&b[0][j],n);
    }
}
```

An especially good compiler might recognize the situation and insert a high-performance sdot routine in place of the inner loop in our first way of expressing the matrix multiply. Alternatively, we might turn the two inner loops inside out to get

```
for (i=0;i<n;i++){ /* mxm by outer product */
   for (j=0;j<n;j++){
      c[i][j]=0.;
   }
   for (k=0;k<n;k++){
      for (j=0;j<n;j++){
         c[i][j] += a[i][k]*b[k][j];
      }
   }
}
```

The astute reader will readily observe that we could be more effective by initializing the i-th row, $C_{i,*}$ with the first $a_{i,0}b_{0,*}$ rather than zero. However, the important thing here is that the inner loop is now a saxpy operation, namely, repeatedly for $k \rightarrow k + 1$,

$$C_{i,*} \leftarrow C_{i,*} + a_{i,k} \cdot b_{k,*}.$$

Here, the '$*$' means all $j = 0, \ldots, n - 1$ elements in the row i. This trick of **inverting loops** can be quite effective [80] and is often the essence of shared memory parallelism. Similar examples can be found in digital filtering [122]. In a further example, that of Gaussian elimination, the order of the two inner loops is entirely arbitrary. We will use this arbitrariness to introduce shared memory parallelism.

3.4.2 *SGEFA: The Linpack benchmark*

It is certain that the Linpack [37] benchmark is the most famous computer floating point performance test. Based on J. Dongarra's version of SGEFA [53] which appeared in **Linpack** [38], this test has been run on every computer supporting a Fortran compiler and in **C** versions [143] on countless others. The core operation is an LU factorization

$$A \rightarrow PLU$$

where L is lower triangular with unit diagonals (these are not stored), U is upper triangular (diagonals stored), and P is a permutation matrix which permits the factorization to be done in-place but nevertheless using partial pivoting. Since the permutation P involves row exchanges, only a vector (ip on p. 108) is necessary for the permutation information. Our version is readily adapted to shared memory parallelism. That is, either of the inner loops (i, j) may be chosen for vectorization. In this example, we assume Fortran ordering (column major order, where elements are stored in sequential words, see Appendix E)to be consistent with the Linpack benchmark. A reformulation of Gaussian elimination as matrix–vector and matrix–matrix multiplications was given in Section 2.2.2.1.

Heretofore, we have not discussed two simple BLAS operations: `sswap`, a simple vector swap ($\mathbf{y} \leftrightarrow \mathbf{x}$), and `sscal`, which simply scales a vector ($\mathbf{x} \leftarrow a \cdot \mathbf{x}$). These may be fetched from [111]. Here is the classical algorithm:

```
for 0 ≤ k ≤ n − 1 {
    l      ←           max_l |a_kl|
    p      ←           a_kl
    ip_k   ←           l
    if(l ≠ k) a_kk    ↔ a_lk
    for(i = k ... n − 1) a_ik ← −a_ik/p
    if(l ≠ k) for(j = k + 1 ... n − 1) a_kj ↔ a_lj
// a_kj independent of i, or a_ik indep. of j
    for(k + 1 ≤ i, j ≤ n − 1){
        a_ij ← a_ij + a_ik · a_kj
    }
}
```

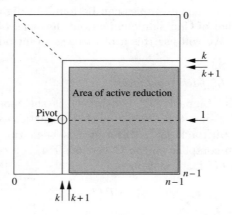

FIG. 3.15. *Simple parallel version of SGEFA.*

To hopefully clarify the structure, Figure 3.15 shows a diagram which indicates that the lower shaded portion (pushed down as k increases) is the active portion of the reduction. Here is the code for the *PLU* reduction. Vector `ip` contains pivot information: the permutation matrix P is computed from this vector [38]. Macro `am` is used for Fortran or column major ordering, see Appendix E.

```
#define am(p,q) (a+p*la+q)
void sgefa(float *a,int la,int n,int *ip,int info)
{
/* parallel C version of SGEFA: wpp 18/4/2000 */
    int j,k,kp1,l,nm1,isamax();
    float *pa1,*pa2,t;
    void saxpy(),sscal(),sswap();
    *info=0;
    nm1  =n-1;
    for(k=0;k<nm1;k++){
       kp1=k+1; pa1=am(k,k);
       l  =isamax(n-k,pa1,1)+k; ip[k]=l;
       if((*am(l,k))==0.0){*info=k; return;}
       if(l!=k){
          t       =*am(k,l);
          *am(k,l)=*am(k,k);
          *am(k,k)=t;
       }
       t  =-1.0/(*am(k,k));  pa1=am(k,kp1);
       sscal(n-k-1,t,pa1,1);
       if(l!=k){
          pa1=am(kp1,l); pa2=am(kp1,k);
          sswap(n-k-1,pa1,la,pa2,la);
       }
       for(j=kp1;j<n;j++){  /* msaxpy, sger */
          pa1=am(k,kp1);
          pa2=am(j,kp1);
          t  =*am(j,k);
          saxpy(n-k-1,t,pa1,1,pa2,1);
       }                    /* end msaxpy, sger */
    }
}
#undef am
```

A variant may be effected by replacing the lines between and including msaxpy
and end msaxpy with saxpy

```
msaxpy(n-k-1,n-k-1,am(k,kp1),n,am(kp1,k),am(kp1,kp1));
```

where msaxpy is shown below (also see Appendix E for a review of column major ordering). We will review this update again in Chapter 4, Section 4.8.2 but note in passing that it is equivalent to the Level 2 BLAS routine sger, a rank-1 update.

```
#define ym(p,q) (y+p+q*n)
void msaxpy(nr,nc,a,n,x,y)
int nr,nc,n;
float *a,*x,*y;
{
/* multiple SAXY: y(*,j) <- a(j)*x[*]+y(*,j)
   wpp 29/01/2003 */
   int i,j,ka;
   ka=0;
   for(j=0;j<nc;j++){
       for(i=0;i<nr;i++){
           *ym(i,j) += a[ka]*x[i];
       }
       ka += n;
   }
}
#undef ym
```

3.5   Recurrence formulae, polynomial evaluation

In the previous Sections 3.4.1, 3.4.2, we have shown how relatively simple loop interchanges can facilitate vectorizing loops by avoiding reductions. Usually, however, we are not so lucky and must use more sophisticated algorithms. We now show two examples: (1) Polynomial evaluation ($P_n(x) = \sum_{k=0}^{n} a_k x^k$), and (2) cyclic reduction for the solution of tridiagonal linear systems.

Polynomial evaluations are usually evaluated by Horner's rule (initially, $p^{(0)} = a_n$) as a recurrence formula

$$p^{(k)} = a_{n-k} + p^{(k-1)} \cdot x, \tag{3.6}$$

where the result is $P_n = p^{(n)}$. For a single polynomial of one argument x, Horner's rule is strictly recursive and not vectorizable. Instead, for long polynomials, we evaluate the polynomial by **recursive doubling**.

3.5.1   *Polynomial evaluation*

From the recurrence (3.6), it is clear that $p^{(k-1)}$ must be available before the computation of $p^{(k)}$ by (3.6) begins. The following is not usually an effective way to compute $P_n(x)$, but may be useful in instances when n is large.

One scheme for $x, x^2, x^3, x^4, \ldots$, uses recursive doubling, with the first step,

$$\begin{bmatrix} v_1 \\ v_2 \end{bmatrix} \leftarrow \begin{bmatrix} x \\ x^2 \end{bmatrix}.$$

The next two are

$$\begin{bmatrix} v_3 \\ v_4 \end{bmatrix} \leftarrow v_2 \begin{bmatrix} v_1 \\ v_2 \end{bmatrix},$$

and the next four,

$$\begin{bmatrix} v_5 \\ v_6 \\ v_7 \\ v_8 \end{bmatrix} \leftarrow v_4 \begin{bmatrix} v_1 \\ v_2 \\ v_3 \\ v_4 \end{bmatrix}.$$

The general scheme is

$$\begin{bmatrix} v_{2^k+1} \\ v_{2^k+2} \\ \cdot \\ \cdot \\ v_{2^{k+1}} \end{bmatrix} \leftarrow v_{2^k} \begin{bmatrix} v_1 \\ v_2 \\ \cdot \\ \cdot \\ v_{2^k} \end{bmatrix}.$$

The polynomial evaluation may now be written as a dot product.

```
float poly(int n,float *a,float *v,float x)
{
    int i,one,id,nd,itd;
    fortran float SDOT();
    float xi,p;
    v[0]=1; v[1] =x; v[2] =x*x;
    id =2;   one =1; nd   =id;
    while(nd<n){
        itd=(id <= n)?id:(n-nd);
        xi =v[id];
#pragma ivdep
        for (i=1;i<=itd;i++) v[id+i]=xi*v[i];
        id=id+id; nd=nd+itd;
    }
    nd=n+1;
    p =SDOT(&nd,a,&one,v,&one);
    return(p);
}
```

Obviously, n must be fairly large for all this to be efficient. In most instances, the actual problem at hand will be to evaluate the same polynomial for multiple arguments. In that case, the problem may be stated as

$$\text{for } i = 1, \ldots, m, \ P_n(x_i) = \sum_{k=0}^{n} a_k x_i^k,$$

that is, $i = 1, \ldots, m$ independent evaluations of $P_n(x_i)$. For this situation, it is more efficient to again use Horner's rule, but for m independent $x_i, i = 1, \ldots, m$, and we get

```
void multihorner(float *a,int m,int n,float *x,float *p)
{  /* multiple (m) polynomial evaluations */
    int i,j;
    for (j=0;j<=m;j++){
        p[j] =a[n];
    }
    for (i=n-1;i>=0;i--){
        for (j=0;j<=m;j++){
            p[j]=p[j]*x[j]+a[i];
        }
    }
    return;
}
```

3.5.2 *A single tridiagonal system*

In this example, we illustrate using non-unit stride algorithms to permit parallelism. The solution to be solved is $T\mathbf{x} = \mathbf{b}$, where T is a tridiagonal matrix. For the purpose of illustration we consider a matrix of order $n = 7$,

$$
T = \begin{bmatrix}
d_0 & f_0 & & & & & \\
e_1 & d_1 & f_1 & & & & \\
 & e_2 & d_2 & f_2 & & & \\
 & & e_3 & d_3 & f_3 & & \\
 & & & e_4 & d_4 & f_4 & \\
 & & & & e_5 & d_5 & f_5 \\
 & & & & & e_6 & f_6
\end{bmatrix},
\tag{3.7}
$$

For bookkeeping convenience we define $e_0 = 0$ and $f_{n-1} = 0$. If T is diagonally dominant, that is, if $|d_i| > |e_i| + |f_i|$ holds for all i, then Gaussian elimination *without* pivoting provides a stable triangular decomposition,

$$
T = LU \equiv \begin{bmatrix}
1 & & & & & & \\
\ell_1 & 1 & & & & & \\
 & \ell_2 & 1 & & & & \\
 & & \ell_3 & 1 & & & \\
 & & & \ell_4 & 1 & & \\
 & & & & \ell_5 & 1 & \\
 & & & & & \ell_6 & 1
\end{bmatrix}
\begin{bmatrix}
c_0 & f_0 & & & & & \\
 & c_1 & f_1 & & & & \\
 & & c_2 & f_2 & & & \\
 & & & c_3 & f_3 & & \\
 & & & & c_4 & f_4 & \\
 & & & & & c_5 & f_5 \\
 & & & & & & c_6
\end{bmatrix}.
\tag{3.8}
$$

Notice that the ones on the diagonal of L imply that the upper off-diagonal elements of U are equal to those of T. Comparing element—wise the two representations of T in (3.7) and (3.8) yields the usual recursive algorithm for determining the unknown entries of L and U [54]. The factorization portion could be made *in-place*, that is, the vectors l and c could overwrite e and d such that there would be no workspace needed. The following version saves the input and computes l and c as separate arrays, however. After having computing the LU

```
void tridiag(int n,float *d,float *e,float *f,
         float *x,float *b,float *l,float *c)
{
/* solves a single tridiagonal system Tx=b.
   l=lower, c=diagonal */
   int i;
   c[0]    =e[0];  /* factorization */
   for(i=1;i<n;i++){
       l[i]=d[i]/c[i-1];
       c[i]=e[i] - l[i]*f[i-1];
   }
   x[0]    =b[0];  /*forward to solve: Ly=b */
   for(i=1;i<n;i++){
       x[i]=b[i]-l[i]*x[i-1];
   }
   x[n-1]   =x[n-1]/c[n-1]; /* back: Ux=y */
   for(i=n-2;i>=0;i--){
       x[i]=(x[i]-f[i]*x[i+1])/c[i];
   }
}
```

factorization, the tridiagonal system $Tx = LUx = b$ is solved by first finding y from $Ly = b$ going forward, then computing x from $Ux = y$ by going backward. By Gaussian elimination, diagonally dominant tridiagonal systems can be solved stably in as few as $8n$ floating point operations. The LU factorization is not parallelizable because the computation of c requires that c_{i-1} is updated before c_i can be computed. Likewise, in the following steps, x_{i-1} has to have been computed in the previous iteration of the loop before x_i. Finally, in the back solve x_{i+1} must be computed before x_i. For all three tasks, in each loop iteration array elements are needed from the previous iteration.

Because of its importance, many attempts have been made to devise parallel tridiagonal system solvers [3, 13, 45, 69, 70, 81, 137, 147]. The algorithm that is closest in operation count to the original LU factorization is the so-called twisted factorization [144], where the factorization is started at both ends of the diagonal. In that approach, only two elements can be computed in parallel. Other approaches provide parallelism but require more work. The best known of these is cyclic reduction, which we now discuss.

3.5.3 *Solving tridiagonal systems by cyclic reduction.*

Cyclic reduction is an algorithm for solving tridiagonal systems that is parallelizable albeit at the expense of some redundant work. It was apparently first presented by Hockney [74]. We show the classical cyclic reduction for diagonally dominant systems. For a cyclic reduction for arbitrary tridiagonal systems see [5]. Let us return to the system of equations $T\mathbf{x} = \mathbf{b}$ with the system matrix T given in (3.7). We rearrange $\mathbf{x}$ and $\mathbf{b}$ such that first the even and then the odd elements appear. In this process, T is permuted to become

$$
T' = \left[
\begin{array}{cccc|ccc}
d_0 & & & & f_0 & & \\
& d_2 & & & e_2 & f_2 & \\
& & d_4 & & & e_4 & f_4 \\
& & & d_6 & & & e_6 \\
\hline
e_1 & f_1 & & & d_1 & & \\
& e_3 & f_3 & & & d_3 & \\
& & e_5 & f_5 & & & d_5
\end{array}
\right].
\tag{3.9}
$$

T' is still diagonally dominant. It can be factored stably in the form

$$
T' = \left[
\begin{array}{cccc|ccc}
1 & & & & & & \\
& 1 & & & & & \\
& & 1 & & & & \\
& & & 1 & & & \\
\hline
\ell_1 & m_1 & & & 1 & & \\
& \ell_3 & m_3 & & & 1 & \\
& & \ell_5 & m_5 & & & 1
\end{array}
\right]
\left[
\begin{array}{cccc|ccc}
d_0 & & & & f_0 & & \\
& d_2 & & & e_2 & f_2 & \\
& & d_4 & & & e_4 & f_4 \\
& & & d_6 & & & e_6 \\
\hline
& & & & d_1' & f_1' & \\
& & & & e_3' & d_3' & f_3' \\
& & & & & e_5' & d_5'
\end{array}
\right].
$$

$$\tag{3.10}$$

This is usually called a 2×2 block LU factorization. The diagonal blocks differ in their order by one if T has odd order. Otherwise, they have the same order. More precisely, the lower left block of L is $\lfloor n/2 \rfloor \times \lceil n/2 \rceil$. The elements of L and U are given by

$$
\begin{array}{lll}
\ell_{2k+1} & = e_{2k+1}/d_{2k}, & 0 \le k < \lfloor n/2 \rfloor, \\
m_{2k+1} & = f_{2k+1}/d_{2k+2}, & 0 \le k < \lceil n/2 \rceil, \\
d_k' & = d_{2k+1} - l_{2k+1}f_{2k} - m_{2k+1}e_{2k+2}, & 0 \le k < \lfloor n/2 \rfloor, \\
e_{2k+1}' & = -l_{2k+1}e_{2k}, & 1 \le k < \lfloor n/2 \rfloor, \\
d_{2k+1}' & = -m_{2k+1}d_{2k+2}, & 0 \le k < \lfloor n/2 \rfloor - 1,
\end{array}
$$

where we used the conventions $e_0 = 0$ and $f_{n-1} = 0$. It is important to observe the ranges of k defined by the *floor* $\lfloor n/2 \rfloor$ and *ceiling* $\lceil n/2 \rceil$ brackets: the greatest integer less than or equal to $n/2$ and least integer greater than or equal to $n/2$, respectively (e.g. the standard **C** functions, `floor` and `ceil`, may be used [84]).

The *reduced system* in the (2,2) block of U made up of the element d_i', e_i', and f_i' is again a diagonally dominant tridiagonal matrix. Therefore the previous procedure can be repeated until a 1×1 system of equations remains.

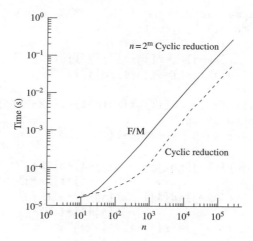

FIG. 3.16. *Times for cyclic reduction vs. the recursive procedure of Gaussian Elimination (GE) on pages 112, 113. Machine is Athos, a Cray SV-1. Speedup is about five for large n.*

Cyclic reduction needs two additional vectors **l** and **m**. The reduced matrix containing d'_i, e'_i, and f'_i can be stored in place of the original matrix T, that is, in the vectors **d**, **e**, and **f**. This classical way of implementing cyclic reduction evidently saves memory but it has the disadvantage that the memory is accessed in large *strides*. In the first step of cyclic reduction, the indices of the entries of the reduced system are two apart. Applied recursively, the strides in cyclic reduction get larger by powers of two. This inevitably means cache misses on machines with memory hierarchies. Already on the Cray vector machines, large tridiagonal systems caused memory bank conflicts. Another way of storing the reduced system is by *appending* the d'_i, e'_i, and f'_i to the original elements d_i, e_i, and f_i. In the following C code, cyclic reduction is implemented in this way.

Solving tridiagonal systems of equations by cyclic reduction costs $19n$ floating point operations, $10n$ for the factorization and $9n$ for forward and backward substitution. Thus the work redundancy of the cyclic reduction algorithm is 2.5 because the Gaussian of the previous section elimination only needs $8n$ flops: see Figures 3.15, 3.16.

```
void fcr(int n,double *d,double *e,
    double *f,double *x,double *b)
{
  int k,kk,i,j,jj,m,nn[21];
/* Initializations */
  m=n; nn[0]=n; i=0; kk=0; e[0]=0.0; f[n-1]=0.0;
  while (m>1){           /* Gaussian elimination */
    k=kk; kk=k+m; nn[++i]=m-m/2; m=m/2;
    e[kk]=e[k+1]/d[k];
```

```
#pragma ivdep
    for (j=0; j<m-1; j++){
        jj        =2*j+k+2;
        f[kk+j]   =f[jj-1]/d[jj];
        e[kk+j+1]=e[jj+1]/d[jj];
    }
    if (m != nn[i]) f[kk+m-1]=f[kk-2]/d[kk-1];
#pragma ivdep
    for (j=0; j<m; j++){
        jj=k+2*j+1;
        b[kk+j]=b[jj]  - b[jj-1]*e[kk+j]
                       - b[jj+1]*f[kk+j];
        d[kk+j]=d[jj]  - f[jj-1]*e[kk+j]
                       - e[jj+1]*f[kk+j];
        f[kk+j]=-f[jj+1]*f[kk+j];
        e[kk+j]=-e[jj-1]*e[kk+j];
    }
}
x[kk]=b[kk]/d[kk]; /* Back substitution */
while (i>0){
#pragma ivdep
    for (j=0; j<m; j++){
        jj        =k+2*j;
        x[jj]     =(b[jj]  - e[jj]*x[kk+j-1]
                   - f[jj]*x[kk+j])/d[jj];
        x[jj+1]=x[kk+j];
    }
    if (m != nn[i])
        x[kk-1]=(b[kk-1]-e[kk-1]*x[kk+m-1])/d[kk-1];
    m=m+nn[i]; kk=k; k -= (nn[--i]+m);
}
}
```

A superior parallelization is effected in the case of multiple right-hand sides. Namely, if X and B consists of L columns,

$$T \underbrace{X}_{L \text{ columns}} = \underbrace{B}_{L \text{ columns}}$$

then we can use the recursive method on pages 112, 113. In this situation, there is an inner loop, which counts the L columns of X: $x_i, b_i, i = 0, \ldots, L-1$ systems. Again, the xm and bm macros are for Fortran ordering.

```
#define xm(p,q) *(x+q+p*n)
#define bm(p,q) *(b+q+p*n)
void multidiag(int n,int L,float *d,float *e,
    float *f,float *m,float *u,float *x,float *b)
{
/* solves tridiagonal system with multiple
   right hand sides: one T matrix, L solutions X */
   int i,j;
   u[0]=e[0];
   for(j=0;j<L;j++) xm(0,j)=bm(0,j);
   for(i=1;i<n;i++){
       m[i]=d[i]/u[i-1];
       u[i]=e[i] - m[i]*f[i-1];
       for(j=0;j<L;j++){
           xm(i,j)=bm(i,j) - m[i]*xm(i-1,j);
       }
   }
   for(j=1;j<L;j++) xm(n-1,j)=xm(n-1,j)/u[n-1];
   for(i=n-2;i>=0;i--){
       for(j=0;j<L;j++){
           xm(i,j)=(xm(i,j)-f[i]*xm(i+1,j))/u[i];
       }
   }
}
#undef xm
#undef bm
```

3.5.4   *Another example of non-unit strides to achieve parallelism*

From the above tridiagonal system solution, we saw that doubling strides may be used to achieve SIMD parallelism. On most machines, it is less efficient to use some non-unit strides: for example, there may be memory bank conflicts on cacheless machines [122], or cache misses for memory systems with cache. Memory bank conflicts may also occur in cache memory architectures and result from the organization of memory into **banks** wherein successive elements are stored in successive banks. For example, a[i] and a[i+1] will be stored in successive banks (or columns). Upon accessing these data, a bank requires a certain time to read (or store) them and refresh itself for subsequent reads (or stores). Requesting data from the same bank successively forces a delay until the read/refresh cycle is completed. Memory hardware often has mechanisms to anticipate constant stride memory references, once they have been previously used (locally). Intel features a hardware prefetcher: When a cache miss occurs twice for regularly ordered data, this prefetcher is started. Even so, basic cache structure assumes locality: if a word is fetched from memory, the safest assumption is that other words nearby will also be used. Hence an associated cache line is loaded from memory, even though parts of the line might not be used. Cray, Fujitsu, and NEC vector hardware does not use caches for their vector memory references. Thus, non-unit stride does not carry the same penalty as its cache-miss equivalents on cache memory machines.

In this section, another example of doubling stride memory access is shown: an in-place, in-order binary radix FFT. The algorithm is most appropriate for cacheless machines like the Cray SV-1 or NEC SX-5, although the performance on Pentium 4 is quite respectable due to the anticipation of non-unit stride memory hardware. The point of using non-unit strides is to avoid data dependencies wherein memory locations could be written over before the previous (old) data are used. To look a few pages ahead, examine the signal flow diagrams in Figures 3.20 and 3.21 (which defines the **a**, **b**, **c**, and **d** variables). Notice that if the **d** result of the first ($k = 0$) computational box is written before the first $k = 1$ **a** input for the second box is used, the previous value of that **a** will be lost forever and the final results will be incorrect. Likewise for the **c** result of the second box ($k = 1$), which will be written onto the **a** input for the third box ($k = 2$), and so on. The algorithm of Figure 3.20 cannot be done **in-place**. That is, the intermediate stages cannot write to the same memory locations as their inputs. An astute observer will notice that the last stage can be done in-place, however, since the input locations are exactly the same as the outputs and do not use **w**. One step does not an algorithm make, however, so one has to be clever to design a strategy, which will group the "boxes" (as in Figure 3.20) so there are no data dependencies.

Fortunately, there are such clever strategies and here we illustrate one— Temperton's in-place, in-order procedure. It turns out that there are in-place, in-order algorithms, with unit stride, but these procedures are more appropriate for large n ($n = 2^m$ is the dimension of the transform) and more complicated than we have space for here ([96]). Figure 3.17 shows the signal flow diagram for $n = 16$. The general strategy is as follows.

- The first "half" of the m steps (recall $n = 2^m$) are from Cooley and Tukey [21]. There are two loops: one over the number of twiddle factors ω^k, and a second over the number of "boxes" that use any one particular twiddle factor, indexed by k in Figures 3.17 and 3.20.
- The second "half" of the m steps also re-order the storage by using three loops instead of two.
- The final $m/2$ steps ($(m-1)/2$ if m is odd) group the "boxes" in pairs so that storing results does not write onto inputs still to be used. Figure 3.18 shows the double boxes.

Finally, here is the code for the driver (cfft_2) showing the order in which step1 (Cooley–Tukey step) and step2 (step plus ordering) are referenced. Array **w** contains the pre-computed twiddle factors: $w_k = exp(2\pi i k/n)$ for $k = 0, \ldots, n/2 - 1$,

```
void cfft2(n,x,w,iw,sign)
int n,iw,int sign;
float x[][2],w[][2];
{
/*
  n=2**m FFT from C. Temperton, SIAM J. on Sci.
  and Stat. Computing, 1991. WPP: 25/8/1999, ETHZ
*/
    int n2,m,j,mj,p2,p3,p4,BK;
    void step1(), step2();
    m  = (int) (log((float) n)/log(1.999));
    mj = 1; n2 = n/2;
    for(j=0;j<m;j++){
      if(j < (m+1)/2){ p2 = n2/mj;
         step1(n,mj,&x[0][0],&x[p2][0],w,iw,sign);
      } else{ p2 = n2/mj; p3 = mj; p4 = p2+mj;
         step2(n,mj,&x[0][0],&x[p2][0],
         &x[p3][0],&x[p4][0],w,iw,sign);
      }
      mj = 2*mj;
    }
}
```

Here is the Cooley–Tukey step (step1):

```
void step1(n,mj,a,b,w,iw,sign)
int iw,n,mj,sign;
float a[][2],b[][2],w[][2];
{
   float wkr,wku,wambr,wambu;
   int i,k,ks,kw,lj,ii,ij;
   lj = n/(2*mj); ij = n/mj; ks = iw*mj;
   for(i=0;i<mj;i++){
      ii = i*ij;
      if(sign > 0){
#pragma ivdep
         for(k=0;k<lj;k++){
            kw=k*ks; wkr=w[kw][0]; wku=w[kw][1];
            wambr = wkr*(a[ii+k][0]-b[ii+k][0])
                  - wku*(a[ii+k][1]-b[ii+k][1]);
            wambu = wku*(a[ii+k][0]-b[ii+k][0])
                  + wkr*(a[ii+k][1]-b[ii+k][1]);
            a[ii+k][0] = a[ii+k][0]+b[ii+k][0];
```

```
            a[ii+k][1] = a[ii+k][1]+b[ii+k][1];
            b[ii+k][0] = wambr; b[ii+k][1] = wambu;
        }
      } else {
#pragma ivdep
        for(k=0;k<lj;k++){
            kw=k*ks; wkr=w[kw][0]; wku=-w[kw][1];
            wambr = wkr*(a[ii+k][0]-b[ii+k][0])
                    - wku*(a[ii+k][1]-b[ii+k][1]);
            wambu = wku*(a[ii+k][0]-b[ii+k][0])
                    + wkr*(a[ii+k][1]-b[ii+k][1]);
            a[ii+k][0] = a[ii+k][0]+b[ii+k][0];
            a[ii+k][1] = a[ii+k][1]+b[ii+k][1];
            b[ii+k][0] = wambr; b[ii+k][1] = wambu;
        }
      }
    }
}
```

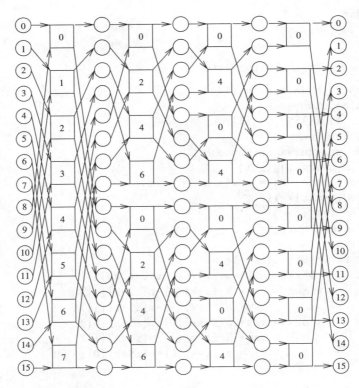

FIG. 3.17. *In-place, self-sorting FFT. Also see Fig. 3.20.*

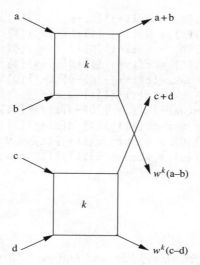

FIG. 3.18. *Double "bug" for in-place, self-sorting FFT. Also see Fig. 3.21.*

Next we have the routine for the last $m/2$ steps, which permutes everything so that the final result comes out in the proper order. Notice that there are three loops and not two. Not surprisingly, the k loop which indexes the twiddle factors (**w**) may be made into an outer loop with the same j, i loop structure (see also Chapter 4).

```
void step2(n,mj,a,b,c,d,w,iw,sign)
int iw,n,mj;
float a[][2],b[][2],c[][2],d[][2],w[][2];
int sign;
{
    float wkr,wku,wambr,wambu,wcmdr,wcmdu;
    int mj2,i,j,k,ks,kw,lj,ii;
    mj2=2*mj; lj=n/mj2; ks=iw*mj;
    for(k=0;k<lj;k++){
        kw = k*ks; wkr = w[kw][0];
        wku=(sign>0)?w[kw][1]:(-w[kw][1]);
        for(i=0;i<lj;i++){
            ii = i*mj2;
#pragma ivdep
            for(j=k;j<mj;j+=n/mj){
                wambr = wkr*(a[ii+j][0]-b[ii+j][0])
                      - wku*(a[ii+j][1]-b[ii+j][1]);
                wambu = wku*(a[ii+j][0]-b[ii+j][0])
                      + wkr*(a[ii+j][1]-b[ii+j][1]);
```

```
            a[ii+j][0] = a[ii+j][0]+b[ii+j][0];
            a[ii+j][1] = a[ii+j][1]+b[ii+j][1];
            b[ii+j][0] = c[ii+j][0]+d[ii+j][0];
            b[ii+j][1] = c[ii+j][1]+d[ii+j][1];
            wcmdr = wkr*(c[ii+j][0]-d[ii+j][0])
                  - wku*(c[ii+j][1]-d[ii+j][1]);
            wcmdu = wku*(c[ii+j][0]-d[ii+j][0])
                  + wkr*(c[ii+j][1]-d[ii+j][1]);
            c[ii+j][0] = wambr; c[ii+j][1] = wambu;
            d[ii+j][0] = wcmdr; d[ii+j][1] = wcmdu;
          }
        }
      }
    }
```

3.5.5 *Some examples from Intel SSE and Motorola Altivec*

In what follows, we proceed a little deeper into vector processing. The Intel
Pentium III, and Pentium 4 chips have a set of eight vector registers called
XMM, from Section 3.2.5. Under the generic title **SSE** (for Streaming SIMD
Extensions), these eight 4-word registers (of 32 bits) are well adapted to vector
processing scientific computations. Similarly, the Apple/Motorola modification
of the IBM G-4 chip has additional hardware called **Altivec**: thirty-two 4-word
registers, see Section 3.2.7. Because the saxpy operation is so simple and is part of
an exercise, we examine sdot and isamax on these two platforms. Subsequently,
in Section 3.6 we will cover FFT on Intel P-4 and Apple G4.

One **extremely important** consideration in using the Altivec and SSE
hardware is **data alignment**. As we showed in Section 1.2, cache loadings are
associative. Namely, an address in memory is loaded into cache modulo cache
associativity: that is, in the case of 4-way associativity, a cacheline is 16 bytes
long (4 words) and the associated memory loaded on 4-word boundaries. When
loading a scalar word from memory at address m, this address is taken modulo
16 (bytes) and loading begins at address $(m/16) \cdot 16$. As in Figure 3.19, if we
wish to load a 4-word segment beginning at A_3, two cachelines (cache blocks)
must be loaded to get the complete 4-word segment. When using the 4-word
(128 bit) vector registers, in this example a misalignment occurs: the data are
not on 16-byte boundaries. This misalignment must be handled by the program;
it is not automatically done properly by the hardware as it is in the case of
simple scalar (integer or floating point) data. Possible misalignment may occur
for both loads and stores. The vector data are loaded (stored) from (into) cache
when using vector registers (V_i in our examples) on these cacheline boundaries. In our BLAS examples below, therefore, we assume the data are properly
4-word aligned. Our website BLAS code examples do not assume proper alignment but rather treat 1–3 word initial and end misalignments as special cases.

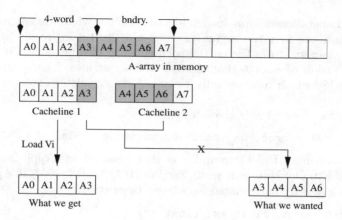

FIG. 3.19. *Data misalignment in vector reads.*

See [20], or section 2.22 in [23]. Our FFT examples use 4-word alignment memory allocation—_mm_malloc or `valloc` for SSE and Altivec, respectively. One should note that `valloc` is a Posix standard and could be used for either machine, that is, instead of _mm_malloc on Pentium 4.

3.5.6   *SDOT on G-4*

The basic procedure has been outlined in Section 3.3. There, only the reduction from the partial accumulation of VL (= 4 in the present case, see page 87) remains to be described. We only do a simple obvious variant. Both Intel and Apple have chosen **intrinsics** for their programming paradigm on these platforms. Somewhat abbreviated summaries of these intrinsics are given in Appendix A and Appendix B, respectively. Assembly language programming provides much more precise access to this hardware, but using intrinsics is easier and allows comparison between the machines. Furthermore, in-line assembly language segments in the code cause the **C** optimizer serious problems. In what follows, keep in mind that the "variables" V_i are only symbolic and actual register assignments are determined by the compiler. Hence, V_i does not refer directly to any actual hardware assignments. One considers what one wants the compiler to do and hope it actually does something similar.

Our web-server contains the complete code for both systems including simple test programs. Hopefully edifying explanations for the central ideas are given here. An important difference between the intrinsics versions and their assembler counterparts is that many details may be omitted in the **C** intrinsics. In particular, register management and indexing are handled by the **C** compiler when using intrinsics. For purposes of exposition, we make the simplifying assumption that the number of elements in `sdot` n is a multiple of 4 (i.e. $4|n$),

$$n = q \cdot 4.$$

The vec_ld operations simply load a 4-word segment, while the vec_madd operations multiply the first two arguments and add the 4-word result to the third. Conversely, vec_st stores the partial accumulation into memory. First we show a Altivec version of sdot0, that is sdot without strides. The accumulation is in variable V_7, which may actually be any Altivec register chosen by the **gcc** compiler.

The choice of switches is given by

$$\text{gcc -03 -faltivec sdottest.c -lm}$$

The **gcc** version of the **C** compiler is that released by Apple in their free Developers' Kit. Our tests used **gcc3**, version 1161, April 4, 2003. In Appendix B, we include a slightly abbreviated list of **vec_operation**s.

```
float sdot0(int n, float *x, float *y)
{                      /* no x,y strides */
  float *xp,*yp,sum=0.0;
  int i,ii,nres,nsegs;   /* nsegs = q */
  vector float V7 = (vector float)(0.0,0.0,0.0,0.0);
  vector float V0,V1;
  float psum[4];
  xp = x; yp = y;
  V0    = vec_ld(0,xp); xp += 4; /* load x */
  V1    = vec_ld(0,yp); yp += 4; /* load y */
  nsegs = (n >> 2) - 1;
  nres  = n - ((nsegs+1) << 2);  /* nres=n mod 4 */
  for(i=0;i<nsegs;i++){
     V7 = vec_madd(V0,V1,V7); /* part sum  of 4 */
     V0 = vec_ld(0,xp); xp += 4; /* load next 4 x */
     V1 = vec_ld(0,yp); yp += 4; /* load next 4 y */
  }
  V7 = vec_madd(V0,V1,V7); /* final part sum */
/* Now finish up: v7 contains partials */
  vec_st(V7,0,psum); /* store partials to memory */
  for(i=0;i<4;i++){
     sum += psum[i];
  }
  return(sum);
}
```

3.5.7   *ISAMAX on Intel using SSE*

The index of maximum element search is somewhat trickier. Namely, the merge operation referenced in Section 3.2.8 can be implemented in various ways on different machines, or a well scheduled branch prediction scheme is required. We show here how it works in both the Pentium III and Pentium 4 machines.

Our website has code for the Apple G-4. The appropriate compiler, which supports this hardware on Pentium III or Pentium 4 is **icc** (Intel also provides a Fortran [24]):

```
icc -O3 -axK -vec_report3 isamaxtest.c -lm
```

On the Pentium, the 4-word SSE arrays are declared by _m128 declarations. Other XMM (SSE) instructions in the `isamax` routine are described in reference [27] and in slightly abbreviated form in Appendix A.

- _mm_set_ps sets the result array to the contents of the parenthetical constants.
- _mm_set_ps1 sets entire array to content of parenthetical constant.
- _mm_load_ps loads 4 words beginning at its pointer argument.
- _mm_andnot_ps is used to compute the absolute values of the first argument by $abs(a) = a$ and $not(-0.0)$. This is a mask of all bits except the sign.
- _mm_cmpnle_ps compares the first argument with the second, to form a mask (in V_3 here) if it is larger.
- _mm_movemask_ps counts the number which are larger, if any.
- _mm_add_ps in this instance increments the index count by 4.
- _mm_max_ps selects the larger of the two arguments.
- _mm_and_ps performs an **and** operation.
- _mm_store_ps stores 4 words beginning at the location specified by the first argument.

In this example, we have assumed the x data are aligned on 4-word boundaries and that $n = q \cdot 4$ (i.e. $4|n$). Data loads of x are performed for a segment (of 4) ahead. This routine is a stripped-down variant of that given in an Intel report [26].

```
int isamax0(int n, float *x) /* no stride for x */
{
  float ebig,*xp;
  int i,ibig,nsegs,mb,nn;   /* nsegs = q */
  _m128 offset4,V0,V1,V2,V3,V6,V7;
  _declspec (align(16)) float xbig[4],indx[4];
  V7       = _mm_set_ps(3.0,2.0,1.0,0.0);
  V2       = _mm_set_ps(3.0,2.0,1.0,0.0);
  V6       = _mm_set_ps1(-0.0);
  offset4 = _mm_set_ps1(4.0);
  xp = x; nsegs = (nn >> 2) - 2;
  V0 = _mm_load_ps(xp); xp += 4; /* 1st 4  */
  V1 = _mm_load_ps(xp); xp += 4; /* next 4 */
  V0 = _mm_andnot_ps(V6,V0);       /* abs. value */
  for(i=0;i<nsegs;i++){
      V1 = _mm_andnot_ps(V6,V1);   /* abs. value */
      V3 = _mm_cmpnle_ps(V1,V0);   /* old vs new */
```

```
    mb = _mm_movemask_ps(V3);    /* any bigger */
    V2 = _mm_add_ps(V2,offset4); /* add offset */
    if(mb > 0){V0 = _mm_max_ps(V0,V1); /* BRANCH */
       V3=_mm_and_ps(V2,V3); V7=_mm_max_ps(V7,V3);}
    V1 = _mm_load_ps(xp); xp += 4; /* load new 4 */
  }
/* process last segment of 4 */
  V1 = _mm_andnot_ps(V6,V1);    /* abs. value */
  V3 = _mm_cmpnle_ps(V1,V0);    /* old vs new */
  mb = _mm_movemask_ps(V3);     /* any bigger */
  V2 = _mm_add_ps(V2,offset4);  /* add offset */
  if(mb > 0){V0 = _mm_max_ps(V0,V1);
     V3=_mm_and_ps(V2,V3); V7=_mm_max_ps(V7,V3);}
/* Finish up: maxima are in V0, indices in V7 */
  _mm_store_ps(xbig,V0); _mm_store_ps(indx,V7);
  big  = 0.0; ibig = 0;
  for(i=0;i<4;i++){
    if(xbig[i]>big){big=xbig[i]; ibig=(int)indx[i];}
  }
  return(ibig);
}
```

3.6   FFT on SSE and Altivec

For our last two examples of SIMD programming, we turn again to Fast Fourier Transform, this time using the Intel SSE and Apple/Motorola Altivec hardware. For faster but more complicated variants, see references [28, 30, 31, 108]. Because these machines favor unit stride memory access, we chose a form which restricts the inner loop access to stride one in memory. However, because our preference has been for self-sorting methods we chose an algorithm, which uses a workspace. In Figure 3.20, one can see the signal flow diagram for $n = 8$. If you look carefully, it is apparent why a workspace is needed. Output from the **bugs** (Figure 3.21) will write into areas where the next elements are read—a dependency situation if the output array is the same as the input. As in Section 3.2, if the output array is different, this data dependency goes away. An obvious question is whether there is an in-place and self-sorting method. The answer is yes, but it is complicated to do with unit stride. Hence, for reasons of simplicity of exposition, we use a self-sorting algorithm with unit stride but this uses a workspace [140, 122].

The workspace version simply toggles back and forth between the input (**x**) and the workspace/output (**y**), with some logic to assign the result to the output **y**. In fact, the ccopy (copies one n–dimensional complex array into another, see: Section 2.2) is not needed except to adhere to the **C** language rules. Without it, some compiler optimizations could cause trouble. A careful examination of Figure 3.20 shows that the last pass could in principle be done in-place. The following code is the driver routine, a complex binary radix ($n = 2^m$) FFT.

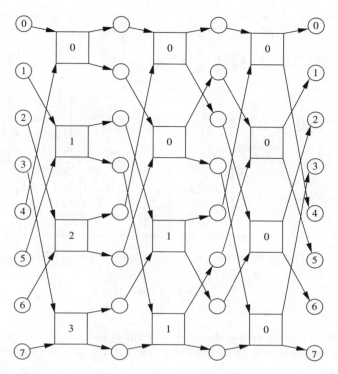

FIG. 3.20. *Workspace version of self-sorting FFT.*

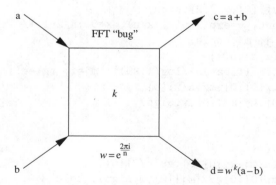

FIG. 3.21. *Decimation in time computational "bug."*

One step through the data is represented in Figure 3.20 by a column of boxes (**bugs**) shown in Figure 3.21. Each "bug" computes: $c = a + b$ and $d = w^k(a-b)$, where $w =$ the nth root of unity. Since complex data in Fortran and similar variants of **C** supporting `complex` data type are stored $Re\ x_0,\ Im\ x_0,\ Re\ x_1, \ldots$, the

$$V_3 = \begin{bmatrix} (a-b)_r \\ (a-b)_i \\ (a-b)_r \\ (a-b)_i \end{bmatrix}, \quad V_6 = \begin{bmatrix} \omega_r \\ \omega_r \\ \omega_r \\ \omega_r \end{bmatrix}, \quad V_7 = \begin{bmatrix} -\omega_i \\ \omega_i \\ -\omega_i \\ \omega_i \end{bmatrix},$$

$$V_3 \xrightarrow{shuffle} V_4 = \begin{bmatrix} (a-b)_i \\ (a-b)_r \\ (a-b)_i \\ (a-b)_r \end{bmatrix}, \quad V_0 = V_6 \cdot V_3 = \begin{bmatrix} \omega_r(a-b)_r \\ \omega_r(a-b)_i \\ \omega_r(a-b)_r \\ \omega_r(a-b)_i \end{bmatrix},$$

$$V_1 = V_7 \cdot V_4 = \begin{bmatrix} -\omega_i(a-b)_i \\ \omega_i(a-b)_r \\ -\omega_i(a-b)_i \\ \omega_i(a-b)_r \end{bmatrix}, \quad \begin{matrix} \mathbf{d} = V_2 = V_0 + V_1. \\ (result) \end{matrix}$$

FIG. 3.22. *Complex arithmetic for* $\mathbf{d} = w^k(\mathbf{a} - \mathbf{b})$ *on SSE and Altivec. In Figure 3.21,* $\mathbf{c}$ *is easy.*

arithmetic for d (now a vector $\mathbf{d}$ with two complex elements) is slightly involved. Figure 3.22 indicates how `_mm_shuffle_ps` is used for this calculation.

```
void cfft2(n,x,y,w,sign)
int n;
float x[][2],y[][2],w[][2],sign;
{ /* x=in, y=out, w=exp(2*pi*i*k/n), k=0..n/2-1 */
   int jb, m, j, mj, tgle;
   void ccopy(),step();
   m = (int)(log((float)n)/log(1.99)); mj=1; tgle=1;
   step(n,mj,&x[0][0],&x[n/2][0],
       &y[0][0],&y[mj][0],w,sign);
   for(j=0;j<m-2;j++){
      mj *= 2;
      if(tgle){
         step(n,mj,&y[0][0],&y[n/2][0],
             &x[0][0],&x[mj][0],w,sign); tgle = 0;
      } else {
         step(n,mj,&x[0][0],&x[n/2][0],
             &y[0][0],&y[mj][0],w,sign); tgle = 1;
      }
   }
   if(tgle){ccopy(n,y,x);} /* if tgle: y -> x */
   mj   = n/2;
```

```
        step(n,mj,&x[0][0],&x[n/2][0],
             &y[0][0],&y[mj][0],w,sign);
}
```

The next code is the Intel SSE version of `step` [27]. Examining the driver (`cfft2`, above), the locations of half-arrays $(\mathbf{a}, \mathbf{b}, \mathbf{c}, \mathbf{d})$ are easy to determine: $\mathbf{b}$ is located $n/2$ complex elements from $\mathbf{a}$, while the output $\mathbf{d}$ is $m_j = 2^j$ complex locations from $\mathbf{c}$ where $j = 0, \ldots, \log_2(n) - 1$ is the step number.

```
void step(n,mj,a,b,c,d,w,sign)
int n, mj;
float a[][2],b[][2],c[][2],d[][2],w[][2],sign;
{
    int j,k,jc,jw,l,lj,mj2,mseg;
    float rp,up;
    _declspec (align(16)) float wr[4],wu[4];
    _m128 V0,V1,V2,V3,V4,V6,V7;
    mj2 = 2*mj; lj  = n/mj2;
    for(j=0; j<lj; j++){
        jw  = j*mj;     jc = j*mj2;
        rp  = w[jw][0]; up = w[jw][1];
        if(sign<0.0) up = -up;
        if(mj<2){   /* special case mj=1 */
            d[jc][0] = rp*(a[jw][0] - b[jw][0])
                     - up*(a[jw][1] - b[jw][1]);
            d[jc][1] = up*(a[jw][0] - b[jw][0])
                     + rp*(a[jw][1] - b[jw][1]);
            c[jc][0] = a[jw][0] + b[jw][0];
            c[jc][1] = a[jw][1] + b[jw][1];
        } else {    /* mj > 1 cases */
            wr[0] =  rp; wr[1] = rp;
            wr[2] =  rp; wr[3] = rp;
            wu[0] = -up; wu[1] = up;
            wu[2] = -up; wu[3] = up;
            V6 = _mm_load_ps(wr);
            V7 = _mm_load_ps(wu);
            for(k=0; k<mj; k+=2){
                V0 = _mm_load_ps(&a[jw+k][0]);
                V1 = _mm_load_ps(&b[jw+k][0]);
                V2 = _mm_add_ps(V0,V1); /* a+b */
                _mm_store_ps(&c[jc+k][0],V2); /* c to M */
                V3 = _mm_sub_ps(V0,V1);   /* a-b */
                V4 = _mm_shuffle_ps(V3,V3,
                        _MM_SHUFFLE(2,3,0,1));
                V0 = _mm_mul_ps(V6,V3);
```

```
            V1 = _mm_mul_ps(V7,V4);
            V2 = _mm_add_ps(V0,V1);    /* w*(a-b) */
            _mm_store_ps(&d[jc+k][0],V2); /* d to M */
          }
        }
      }
    }
```

In Figure 3.23, we show the performance of three FFT variants: the in-place (Section 3.5.4), the SSE intrinsics (Section 3.6), and a generic version of the same workspace algorithm on a 1.7 GHz Pentium 4 running Linux version 2.4.18. There are many possible improvements: both split-radix [44] and radix 4 are faster than radix 2. Because of symmetries in the twiddle factors, fewer need to be accessed from memory. Also, competing with professionals is always hard. However, notice that the improvement using SSE is a factor of 2.35 faster than the generic version, which uses the same algorithm. In our Chapter 4 (Section 4.8.3) on shared memory parallelism we show a variant of **step** used here. In that case, the work of the outer loop (over twiddle factors, the **w** array elements) may be distributed over multiple processors. The work done by each computation box, labeled k in Figure 3.21, is independent of every other k. Thus, these tasks may be distributed over multiple CPUs. Multiple processors may be used when available, and MKL [28] uses the **pthreads** library to facilitate this.

Here is **step** for the G-4 Altivec. Older versions of Apple Developers' kit C compiler, gcc, supported complex arithmetic, **cplx** data type, but we do not

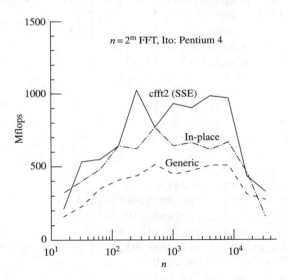

FIG. 3.23. *Intrinsics, in-place (non-unit stride), and generic FFT. Ito: 1.7 GHz Pentium 4.*

use this typing here. Newer versions apparently do not encourage this `complex` typing.

```
#define _cvf constant vector float
#define _cvuc constant vector unsigned char
void step(int n,int mj, float a[][2], float b[][2],
float c[][2], float d[][2],float w[][2], float sign)
{
   int j,k,jc,jw,l,lj,mj2;
   float rp,up;
   float wr[4], wu[4];
   _cvf vminus = (vector float)(-0.,0.,-0.,0.);
   _cvf vzero  = (vector float)(0.,0.,0.,0.);
   _cvuc pv3201 = (vector unsigned char)
      (4,5,6,7,0,1,2,3,12,13,14,15,8,9,10,11);
   vector float V0,V1,V2,V3,V4,V5,V6,V7;

   mj2 = 2*mj;
   lj  = n/mj2;

   for(j=0; j<lj; j++){
      jw  = j*mj; jc  = j*mj2;
      rp = w[jw][0];
      up = w[jw][1];
      if(sign<0.0) up = -up;
      if(mj<2){
/* special case mj=1 */
         d[jc][0] = rp*(a[jw][0] - b[jw][0])
                  - up*(a[jw][1] - b[jw][1]);
         d[jc][1] = up*(a[jw][0] - b[jw][0])
                  + rp*(a[jw][1] - b[jw][1]);
         c[jc][0] = a[jw][0] + b[jw][0];
         c[jc][1] = a[jw][1] + b[jw][1];
      } else {
/* mj>=2 case */
         wr[0]=rp; wr[1]=rp; wr[2]=rp; wr[3]=rp;
         wu[0]=up; wu[1]=up; wu[2]=up; wu[3]=up;
         V6 = vec_ld(0,wr);
         V7 = vec_ld(0,wu);
         V7 = vec_xor(V7,vminus);
         for(k=0; k<mj; k+=2){   /* read a,b */
            V0 = vec_ld(0,(vector float *)&a[jw+k][0]);
            V1 = vec_ld(0,(vector float *)&b[jw+k][0]);
            V2 = vec_add(V0, V1); /* c=a-b */
```

```
            vec_st(V2,0,(vector float *)&c[jc+k][0]);
            V3 = vec_sub(V0, V1);
            V4 = vec_perm(V3,V3,pv3201); /* shuffle */
            V0 = vec_madd(V6,V3,vzero);
            V1 = vec_madd(V7,V4,vzero);
            V2 = vec_add(V0,V1);   /* d=w*(a-b) */
            vec_st(v2,0,(vector float *)&d[jc+k][0]);
         }
      }
   }
}
```

Although the Altivec instructions used here are similar to the SSE variant, here is a brief summary of their functionality 30. A summary is also given in Appendix B.

- V0 = vec_ld(0,ptr) loads its result V0 with four floating point words beginning at pointer ptr and block offset 0.
- V2 = vec_add(V0, V1) performs an element by element floating point add of V0 and V1 to yield result vector V2.
- vec_st(V2,0,ptr) stores the four word contents of vector V2 beginning at pointer ptr with block offset 0.
- V3 = vec_sub(V0, V1) subtracts the four floating point elements of V1 from V0 to yield result V3.
- V2 = vec_perm(V0,V1,pv) selects bytes from V0 or V1 according to the permutation vector pv to yield a permuted vector V2. These are arranged in *little endian* fashion [30].
- V3 = vec_madd(V0,V1,V2) is a multiply–add operation: V3 = V0*V1+V2, where the multiply is element by element, and likewise the add.

In Figure 3.24, we show our results on a Power Mac G-4. This is a 1.25 GHz machine running OS-X (version 10.2) and the Developers' kit gcc compiler (version 1161, April 4, 2003). The Altivec version using intrinsics is three times faster than the generic one using the same algorithm.

Exercise 3.1 Variants of matrix–matrix multiply In Section 3.4.1 are descriptions of two variations of matrix–matrix multiply: $C = AB$. The two are (1) the text book method which computes $c_{ij} = \sum_k a_{ik}b_{kj}$, and (2) the outer product variant $c_{*j} = \sum_k a_{*k}b_{kj}$, which processes whole columns/time. The first variant is a dot-product (sdot), while the second uses repeated saxpy operations.

What is to be done?
The task here is to code these two variants in several ways:

1. First, program the dot-product variant using three nested loops, then instead of the inner-most loop, substitute sdot.

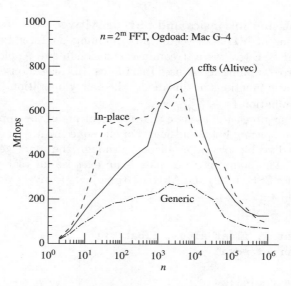

FIG. 3.24. *Intrinsics, in-place (non-unit stride), and generic FFT. Tests are from a machine named Ogdoad: 1.25 GHz Power Mac G-4.*

2. Next, program the outer-product variant using three nested loops, then replace the inner-most loop with `saxpy`.

3. Using large enough matrices to get good timing results, compare the performances of these variants. Again, we recommend using the `clock` function, except on Cray platforms where `second` gives better resolution.

4. By using multiple repetitions of the calculations with BLAS routines `sdot` and `saxpy`, see if you can estimate the function call overhead. That is, how long does it take to call either `sdot` or `saxpy` even if $n = 0$? This is trickier than it seems: some timers only have 1/60 second resolution, so many repetitions may be required.

5. Finally, using the outer-product method (without substituting `saxpy`), see if you can unroll the first outer loop to a depth of 2—hence using two columns of B as operands at a time (Section 3.2). To make your life simpler, choose the leading dimension of C (also A) to be even. Do you see any cache effects for large n (the leading dimension of A and C)?

Helpful hints: Look in `/usr/local/lib` for the BLAS: for example, `libblas.a` or as a shared object `libblas.so`. The utilities `nm` or `ar` (plus `grep`) may make it easier to find the BLAS routines you want: `ar t libblas.a |grep -i dot`, or `nm libblas.so |grep -i axpy`. These are likely to be FORTRAN routines, so consult Appendix E to get the FORTRAN-C communication correct and the proper libraries loaded.

Exercise 3.2 Using intrinsics and SSE or Altivec In Section 3.5.5 we gave descriptions of **VL** = 4-vector programming on Intel Pentium III and Pentium 4 using SSE (software streaming extensions), and Apple/Motorola G-4 Altivec. The programming mode uses **intrinsics**. In this exercise, we ask you to program two basic functions in this mode: the **saxpy** operation ($\mathbf{y} \leftarrow \alpha \cdot \mathbf{x} + \mathbf{y}$), and **ssum** a summation ($s \leftarrow \sum_{i=0}^{n-1} x_i$).

To make your job easier, assume that the elements of the appropriate arrays ($\mathbf{x}$, $\mathbf{y}$) have unit spacing between them. For the squeemish, you can also assume that $4|n$ (n is divisible by 4), as below, although the more general case is a useful exercise. The non-unit stride case is an exercise for real gurus. Here are two examples, for SSE (Intel) and Altivec (Apple), respectively, doing the simpler sscal problem ($\mathbf{x} \leftarrow \alpha \cdot \mathbf{x}$).

SSE version:

```
void sscal(int n, float alpha, float *x) {
/* SSE version of sscal */
  int i,ns;
  float alpha_vec[4];
  _m128 tmm0,tmm1;

  for (i = 0; i < 4; i ++){
    alpha_vec[i] = alpha; /* 4 copies of alpha */
  }
  tmm0 = _mm_load_ps(alpha_vec); /* alphas in tmm0 */

  ns = n/4;
  for (i = 0; i < ns; i ++) {
    tmm1 = _mm_load_ps(&x[4*i]);   /* load 4 x's */
    tmm1 = _mm_mul_ps(tmm1, tmm0); /* alpha*x's  */
    _mm_store_ps(&x[4*i],tmm1);    /* store x's  */
  }
}
```

Altivec version:

```
void sscal(int n, float alpha, float *x) {
/* Altivec version of sscal */
  int i,ns;
  float alpha_vec[4];
  const vector float vzero =
            (vector float)(0.,0.,0.,0.);
  vector float V0,V1;

  for (i = 0; i < 4; i ++){
    alpha_vec[i] = alpha;    /* 4 copies of alpha */
```

```
}
VO = vec_ld(0,alpha_vec);  /* copies into VO */

ns = n/4;
for (i = 0; i < ns; i ++) {
  V1 = vec_ld(0,(vector float *)&x[4*i]); /* load  */
  V1 = vec_madd(VO,V1,vzero);              /* a*x   */
  vec_st(V1,0,(vector float *)&x[4*i]);    /* store */
}
}
```

What is to be done?
Using one/other of the above sscal routines as examples, program both saxpy and ssum using either the SSE or Altivec intrinsics. You may choose one machine or the other. The examples isamax from Section 3.5.7 or sdot from Section 3.5.6 may be helpful for coding the reduction operation ssum.

1. Write test programs for these routines—with a large number of iterations and/or big vectors—to get good timings for your results. Use the system timer time = (double) clock(); and scale your timings by CLOCKS_PER_SEC defined in <time.h>.
2. Modify your code to use a pre-fetch strategy to load the next segment to be used while computing the current segment.
3. Compare the pre-fetch strategy to the vanilla version.

If your local machines do not have the appropriate compilers, they are available (free, without support) from

- The gcc Apple compiler is available from the Apple developer web-site

  http://developer.apple.com/.

- The Intel icc compiler is available from

  http://developer.intel.com/.

Our Beowulf machine *Asgard* has an up-to-date version of this compiler.

References: Technical report [26] and website www.simdtech.org.

4

SHARED MEMORY PARALLELISM

I think there's a world market for about five computers.

Th. J. Watson (1943)

4.1 Introduction

Shared memory machines typically have relatively few processors, say 2–128. An intrinsic characteristic of these machines is a strategy for memory coherence and a fast tightly coupled network for distributing data from a commonly accessible memory system. Our test examples were run on two HP Superdome clusters: *Stardust* is a production machine with 64 PA-8700 processors, and *Pegasus* is a 32 CPU machine with the same kind of processors.

4.2 HP9000 Superdome machine

The HP9000 is grouped into **cells** (Figure 4.1), each with 4 CPUs, a common memory/cell, and connected to a CCNUMA crossbar network. The network consists of sets of 4×4 crossbars and is shown in Figure 4.2. An effective bandwidth test, the EFF_BW benchmark [116], groups processors into two equally sized sets.

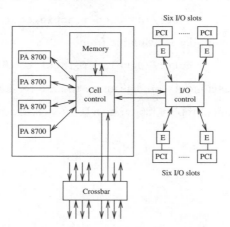

FIG. 4.1. *One* **cell** *of the HP9000 Superdome. Each cell has 4 PA-8700 CPUs and a common memory. See Figure 4.2.*

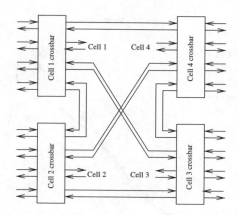

FIG. 4.2. *Crossbar interconnect architecture of the HP9000 Superdome.*

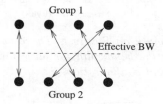

FIG. 4.3. *Pallas EFF_BW benchmark. The processors are divided into two equally sized groups and arbitrary pairwise connections are made between processors from each group: simultaneous messages from each pair are sent and received.*

Arbitrary pairings are made between elements from each group, Figure 4.3, and the cross-sectional bandwidth of the network is measured for a fixed number of processors and varying message sizes. The results from the HP9000 machine **Stardust** are shown in Figure 4.4. It is clear from this figure that the cross-sectional bandwidth of the network is quite high. Although not apparent from Figure 4.4, the latency for this test (the intercept near Message Size = 0) is not high. Due to the low incremental resolution of MPI_Wtime (see p. 234), multiple test runs must be done to quantify the latency. Dr Byrde's tests show that minimum latency is $\gtrsim 1.5 \,\mu$s.

4.3 Cray X1 machine

A clearer example of a shared memory architecture is the Cray X1 machine, shown in Figures 4.5 and 4.6. In Figure 4.6, the shared memory design is obvious. Each multi-streaming processor (MSP) shown in Figure 4.5 has 4 processors (custom designed processor chips forged by IBM), and 4 corresponding caches.

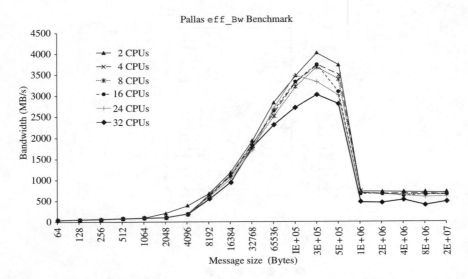

FIG. 4.4. *EFF_BW benchmark on Stardust. These data are courtesy of Olivier Byrde. The collapse of the bandwidth for large message lengths seems to be cache/buffer management configuration.*

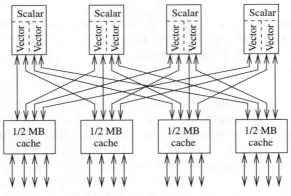

FIG. 4.5. *Cray X1 MSP. The only memory in each of these MSPs consists of four sets of 1/2 MB caches (called Ecache). There are four of these MSPs per node, Figure 4.6.*

Although not clear from available diagrams, vector memory access apparently permits cache by-pass; hence the term *streaming* in MSP. That is, vector registers are loaded directly from memory: see, for example, Figure 3.4. On each board (called nodes) are 4 such MSPs and 16 memory modules which share a common

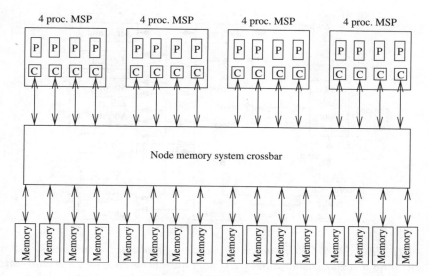

FIG. 4.6. *Cray X1 node (board): each board has 4 groups of 4 MSPs (Figure 4.5),*
16 processors total. Cache coherency is maintained only within one node.
Between nodes, MPI is used.

(coherent) memory view. Coherence is only maintained on each board, but not
across multiple board systems. The processors have 2 complete sets of vector
units, each containing 32 vector registers of 64 words/each (each word is 64-bits),
and attendant arithmetic/logical/shift functional units. Message passing is used
between nodes: see Chapter 5.

4.4 NEC SX-6 machine

Another example of vector CPUs tightly coupled to a common memory system is
the Nippon Electric Company (NEC) SX-6 series (Figure 4.7). The evolution of
this vector processing line follows from earlier Watanabe designed SX-2 through
SX-5 machines, and recent versions are extremely powerful. Our experience
has shown that NEC's fast clocks, made possible by CMOS technology, and
multiple vector functional unit sets per CPU make these machines formidable.
The Yokohama *Earth Simulator* is a particularly large version (5120 nodes) from
this line of NEC distributed node vector machines. At least two features distin-
guish it from Cray designs: (1) reconfigurable vector register files, and (2) there
are up to 8 vector units/CPU [139]. Reconfigurable vector registers means that
the 144 kB register file may be partitioned into a number of fixed sized vector
registers whose total size remains 144 kB. Up to 128 nodes (each with 8 CPUs)
are available in the SX-6/128M models (Figure 4.8). Between nodes, message
passing is used, as described in Chapter 5.

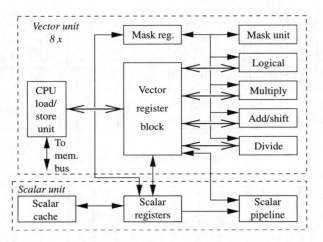

FIG. 4.7. *NEC SX-6 CPU: each node contains multiple vector units, a scalar unit, and a scalar cache. Each CPU may have between 4 and 8 vector register sets and corresponding vector functional units sets. Vector registers are 144 kB register files of 64-bit words. These vector registers are reconfigurable with different numbers of words/vector. See Figure 4.8.*

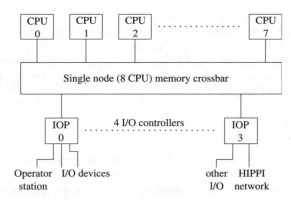

FIG. 4.8. *NEC SX-6 node: each contains multiple vector CPUs. Each node may have between 4 and 8 CPUs which are connected to a common memory system. Up to 16 such nodes may be connected to each other by a Internode crossbar switch: up to 128 CPUs total, see Figure 4.7.*

4.5 OpenMP standard

In this book, we use OpenMP [17] because it seems to have become a **standard** shared memory programming paradigm. Appendix C gives a summary of its functionality. A Posix standard, **pthreads**, allows tighter control of shared memory parallelism but is more painful to program. Namely, because it allows so much user control, more work is required for the programmer. In our examples from the Hewlett-Packard *Superdome* machine at ETH Zürich, OpenMP is implemented using **pthreads**. This is also true on many Intel PC clusters. From p. 108, we saw a straightforward parallelized version of the Linpack benchmark `sgefa`. In this section, we explore the outer-loop parallelism of this straightforward implementation and find its efficiency limited by poor scaling: it works well on a few processors, but scaling degrades when the number of CPUs exceeds eight. The speedup is 7.4 on 8 CPUs, but flattens to 10 on 16. Similar scaling to 8 CPUs was reported by Röllin and Fichtner [126], but they do not show data for any larger number of CPUs.

4.6   Shared memory versions of the BLAS and LAPACK

Loop structures of linear algebra tasks are the first places to look for parallelism. Time critical tasks—matrix–vector multiplication, matrix–matrix multiplication, and *LU* factorization—have nested loop structures. In a shared memory environment, it is usually straightforward to parallelize these loop-based algorithms by means of compiler directives from OpenMP. As the important basic tasks are embedded in basic linear algebra subroutines (BLAS) it often suffices to parallelize these in order to get good parallel performance. Looking at the triangular factorization in Figure 2.3, one can see that in `dgetrf` the routines to parallelize are `dtrsm` and `dgemm` (see Table 2.2).   The mathematical library MLIB from Hewlett-Packard [73] conforms to the public domain version 3.0 of LAPACK in all user-visible usage conventions. But the internal workings of some subprograms have been tuned and optimized for HP computers. In Table 4.1 we list execution times for solving systems of equations of orders from $n = 500$–5000. For problem sizes up to 1000, it evidently does not make sense to employ more

Table 4.1   *Times t in seconds (s) and speedups $S(p)$ for various problem sizes n and processor numbers p for solving a random system of equations with the general solver* **dgesv** *of LAPACK on the HP Superdome. The execution times are the best of three measurements.*

p	$n = 500$		$n = 1000$		$n = 2000$		$n = 5000$	
	$t(s)$	$S(p)$	$t(s)$	$S(p)$	$t(s)$	$S(p)$	$t(s)$	$S(p)$
1	0.08	1	0.66	1	4.62	1	72.3	1
2	0.05	1.6	0.30	2.2	2.15	2.2	32.3	2.2
4	0.03	2.7	0.16	4.1	1.09	4.2	16.4	4.4
8	0.02	4.0	0.09	7.3	0.61	7.6	8.3	8.7
12	0.02	4.0	0.08	8.3	0.45	10.3	5.9	12.3
16	0.02	4.0	0.08	8.3	0.37	12.5	4.6	15.7
24			0.08	8.3	0.32	14.4	3.3	21.9
32					0.29	15.9	3.0	24.1

than a very few processors. The overhead for the management of the various threads (startup, synchronization) soon outweighs the gain from splitting the work among processors. The execution times and speedups for these small problems level off so quickly that it appears the operating system makes available only a limited number of processors. This is not the case for $n = 2000$. The speedup is very good up to 8 processors and good up to 16 processors. Beyond this number, the speedup again deteriorates. Also, the execution times are no longer reproducible. The operating system apparently finds it hard to allocate threads to equally (un)loaded processors. This effect is not so evident in our largest problem size tests.

Performance of the BLAS routines largely depend on the right choices of block (or panel) sizes. These depend on the algorithm but even more on the cache and memory sizes. The authors of LAPACK and previously of LINPACK initially hoped that independent computer vendors would provide high performing BLAS. Quickly changing hardware, however, made this approach less than satisfactory. Often, only the fraction of the BLAS used in the LINPACK benchmark were properly tuned. Faced with this misery, an ambitious project was started in the late 1990s with the aim of letting the computer do this tedious work. In the ATLAS project [149, 150], a methodology was developed for the automatic generation of efficient basic linear algebra routines for computers with hierarchical memories. The idea in principle is fairly simple. One just measures the execution times of the building blocks of the BLAS with varying parameters and chooses those settings that provide the fastest results. This approach was successful for the matrix–matrix multiplication [149]. On many platforms, the automated tuning of Level 3 BLAS dgemm outperformed the hand-tuned version from computer vendors. Tuning all of the BLAS takes hours, but the benefit remains as long as the hardware is not modified.

4.7   Basic operations with vectors

In Sections 2.1 and 3.2.3, we discussed both the saxpy operation (2.3)

$$\mathbf{y} = \alpha\mathbf{x} + \mathbf{y},$$

and inner product sdot (2.4)

$$s = \mathbf{x} \cdot \mathbf{y}.$$

In the following, these operations are reprogrammed for shared memory machines using OpenMP. In coding such shared memory routines, the programmer's first task is **data scoping**. Within an OpenMP parallel region, data are either **private** (meaning local to the processor computing the inner portion of the parallel region) or **shared** (meaning data shared between processors). Loop variables and temporary variables are local to a processor and should be declared **private**, which means their values may be changed without modifying other private copies. Even though **shared** data may be modified by any processor, the computation is not parallel unless only independent regions are modified. Otherwise, there will be a data dependency, see Section 3.2. There are ways to control such dependencies: locks and synchronization barriers are necessary. In that case, the parallel regions are not really parallel, see Appendix C. Hence, **private** data may be modified only locally by one processor (or group of processors working on a common task), while **shared** data are globally accessible but each region to be modified should be independent of other processors working on the same shared data. Several examples of this **scoping** will be given below.

4.7.1 *Basic vector operations with OpenMP*

4.7.1.1 *SAXPY*

The parallelization of the `saxpy` operation is simple. An OpenMP `for` directive generates a parallel region and assigns the vectors to the p processors in blocks (or chunks) of size N/p.

```
#pragma omp parallel for
    for (i=0; i< N; i++){
       y[i] += alpha*x[i];
    }
```

When we want the processors to get blocks of smaller sizes we can do this by the `schedule` option. If a block size of 100 is desired, we can change the above code fragment by adding a `schedule` qualifier:

```
#pragma omp parallel for schedule(static,100)
    for (i=0; i< N; i++){
       y[i] += alpha*x[i];
    }
```

Now chunks of size 100 are cyclically assigned to each processor. In Table 4.2, timings on the HP Superdome are shown for $N = 10^6$ and chunks of size N/p, 100, 4, and 1. It is evident that large chunk sizes are to be preferred for vector operations. Both chunk sizes N/p and 100 give good timings and speedups. The latter causes more overhead of OpenMP's thread management. This overhead becomes quite overwhelming for the block size 4. Here $2.5 \cdot 10^5$ loops of only

Table 4.2 *Some execution times in microseconds for the* `saxpy` *operation.*

Chunk size	$p = 1$	2	4	6	8	12	16
N/p	1674	854	449	317	239	176	59
100	1694	1089	601	405	317	239	166
4	1934	2139	1606	1294	850	742	483
1	2593	2993	3159	2553	2334	2329	2129

length 4 are to be issued. The block size 1 is of course ridiculous. Here, the memory traffic is the bottleneck. Each of the four `double` words of a cacheline are handled by a different processor (if $p \geq 4$). The speed of the computation is determined by the memory bandwidth. There is no speedup at all.

4.7.1.2 *Dot product*

OpenMP implements a fork-join parallelism on a shared memory multicomputer. Therefore the result of the dot product will be stored in a single variable in the master thread. In a first approach we proceed in a similar fashion to `saxpy`, see Figure 4.9. By running this code segment on multiple processors, we see that the result is only correct using one processor. In fact, the results are not even reproducible when $p > 1$. To understand this we have to remember that *all* variables except the loop counter are shared among the processors. Here, the variable `dot` is read and updated in an asynchronous way by all the processors. This phenomenon is known as a *race condition* in which the precise timing of instruction execution effects the results [125]. In order to prevent untimely accesses of `dot` we have to protect reading and storing it. This can be done by protecting the statement that modifies `dot` from being executed by multiple threads at the same time. This mutual exclusion synchronization is enforced by the `critical` construct in OpenMP, Figure 4.10: While this solution is correct, it is intolerably slow because it is really serial execution. To show this, we list the execution times for various numbers of processors in row II of Table 4.3. There is a barrier in each iteration that serializes the access to the memory cell that stores `dot`. In this implementation of the dot product, the variable `dot` is written N times. To prevent data dependencies among threads, we introduce a *local* variable

```
dot = 0.0;
#pragma omp parallel for
for (i=0; i< N; i++){
  dot += x[i]*y[i];
}
```

FIG. 4.9. *Global variable* `dot` *unprotected, and thus giving incorrect results (version I).*

```
dot = 0.0;
#pragma omp parallel for
  for (i=0; i< N; i++){
#pragma omp critical
    { dot += x[i]*y[i]; }
}
```

FIG. 4.10. *OpenMP* `critical` *region protection for global variable* `dot` *(version II).*

Table 4.3 *Execution times in microseconds for our dot product, using the* **C** *compiler* `guidec`. *Line I means no protection for global variable* `dot`, *from Figure 4.9; line II means the* `critical` *region for global variable variant* `dot` *from Figure 4.10; line III means* `critical` *region for local variable* `local_dot` *from Figure 4.11; and line IV means* `parallel reduction for` *from Figure 4.12.*

Version	$p = 1$	2	4	6	8	12	16
I	1875	4321	8799	8105	6348	7339	6538
II	155,547	121,387	139,795	140,576	171,973	1,052,832	3,541,113
III	1387	728	381	264	225	176	93
IV	1392	732	381	269	220	176	88

```
        dot = 0.0;
#pragma omp parallel shared(dot,p,N,x,y) \
                private(local_dot,i,k,offset)
#pragma omp for
        for(k=0;k<p;k++){
           offset    = k*(N/p);
           local_dot = 0.0;
           for (i=offset; i< offset+(N/p); i++){
              local_dot += x[i]*y[i];
           }
#pragma omp critical
           { dot += local_dot; }
        }
```

FIG. 4.11. *OpenMP* critical *region protection only for local accumulations* `local_dot` *(version III).*

`local_dot` for each thread which keeps a partial result (Figure 4.11). To get the full result, we form

$$\texttt{dot} = \sum_{k=0}^{p-1} \texttt{local\_dot}_k,$$

where $\texttt{local\_dot}_k$ is the portion of the inner product that is computed by processor k. Each $\texttt{local\_dot}_k$ can be computed independently of every other. Each thread has its own instance of `private` variable `local_dot`. Only at the end are the p individual local results added. These are just p accesses to the global variable `dot`. Row III in Table 4.3 shows that this local accumulation reduces the execution time significantly.

In Chapter 3, we distinguished between vector operations whose results were either the same size as an input vector, or those reductions which typically yield a single element. For example, inner products and maximum element searches,

```
        dot = 0.0;
#pragma omp parallel for reduction(+ : dot)
        for (i=0; i< N; i++){
           dot += x[i]*y[i];
        }
```

FIG. 4.12. *OpenMP reduction syntax for* dot *(version IV).*

Section 3.3, are reductions. OpenMP has built-in mechanisms for certain reduction operations. Figure 4.12 is an inner product example. Here, dot is the reduction variable and the plus sign "+" is the reduction operation. There are a number of other reduction operations besides addition. The OpenMP standard does not specify how a reduction has to be implemented. Actual implementations can be adapted to the underlying hardware.

4.8 OpenMP matrix vector multiplication

As we discussed in Chapter 3 regarding matrix multiplication, there are at least two distinct ways to effect this operation, particularly Section 3.4.1. Likewise, its sub-operation, matrix–vector multiplication, can be arranged as the textbook method, which uses an inner product; or alternatively as an outer product which preserves vector length. If A is an $m \times n$ matrix and $\mathbf{x}$ a vector of length n, then A times the vector $\mathbf{x}$ is a vector of length m, and with indices written out

$$\mathbf{y} = A\mathbf{x} \quad \text{or} \quad y_k = \sum_{i=0}^{n-1} a_{k,i} x_i, \ 0 \le k < m.$$

A **C** code fragment for the matrix–vector multiplication can be written as a reduction

```
/* dot product variant of matrix-vector product */
for (k=0; k<m; k++){
  y[k] = 0.0;
  for (i=0; i<n; i++)
    y[k] += A[k+i*m]*x[i];
}
```

Here again, we assume that the matrix is stored in column (Fortran, or column major) order. In this code fragment, each y_k is computed as the dot product of the kth row of A with the vector $\mathbf{x}$. Alternatively, an outer product loop ordering is based on the saxpy operation (Section 3.4.1)

```
/* saxpy variant of matrix-vector product */
  for (k=0; k<m; k++) y[k] = 0.0;
  for (i=0; i<n; i++)
  for (k=0; k<m; k++)
    y[k] += a[k+i*m]*x[i];
```

Here, the ith column of A takes the role of $\mathbf{x}$ in (2.3) while x_i takes the role of the scalar α and $\mathbf{y}$ is the $\mathbf{y}$ in saxpy, as usual (2.3).

4.8.1 *The matrix–vector multiplication with OpenMP*

In OpenMP the goal is usually to parallelize loops. There are four options to parallelize the matrix–vector multiplication. We can parallelize either the inner or the outer loop of one of the two variants given above. The outer loop in the dot product variant can be parallelized without problem by just prepending an omp parallel for compiler directive to the outer for loop. It is important not to forget to declare shared the loop counter i of the inner loop! Likewise, parallelization of the inner loop in the saxpy variant of the matrix–vector product is straightforward.

The other two parallelization possibilities are more difficult because they involve reductions. The parallelization of the inner loop of the dot product variant can be as a simple dot product

```
for (k=0; k<m; k++){
    tmp = 0.0;
#pragma omp parallel for reduction(+ : tmp)
    for (i=0; i<n; i++){
        tmp += A[k+i*m]*x[i];
    }
    y[k] = tmp;
}
```

Parallelization of the outer loop of the saxpy variant is a reduction operation to compute the variable y[k] = tmp. As OpenMP does not permit reduction variables to be of pointer type, we have to resort to the approach of code fragment Figure 4.12 and insert a critical section into the parallel region

```
#pragma omp parallel  private(j,z)
    {
        for (j=0; j<M; j++) z[j] = 0.0;
#pragma omp for
        for (i=0; i<N; i++){
            for (j=0; j<M; j++){
                z[j] += A[j+i*M]*x[i];
            }
        }
#pragma omp critical
        for (j=0; j<M; j++) y[j] += z[j];
    }
```

We compared the four approaches. Execution times obtained on the HP Superdome are listed in Table 4.4. First of all the execution times show that parallelizing the inner loop is obviously a bad idea. OpenMP implicitly sets a

Table 4.4 *Some execution times in microseconds for the matrix–vector multiplication with OpenMP on the HP superdome.*

Variant	Loop parallelized	P					
		1	2	4	8	16	32
n = 100							
dot	Outer	19.5	9.76	9.76	39.1	78.1	146
dot	Inner	273	420	2256	6064	13,711	33,056
saxpy	Outer	9.76	9.76	19.5	68.4	146	342
saxpy	Inner	244	322	420	3574	7128	14,912
n = 500							
dot	Outer	732	293	146	97.7	146	196
dot	Inner	1660	2197	12,109	31,689	68,261	165,185
saxpy	Outer	732	146	48.8	97.7	195	488
saxpy	Inner	2050	1904	2539	17,725	35,498	72,656
n = 500							
dot	Outer	2734	1367	684	293	196	293
dot	Inner	4199	4785	23,046	61,914	138,379	319,531
saxpy	Outer	2930	1464	781	195	391	977
saxpy	Inner	6055	4883	5078	36,328	71,777	146,484

synchronization point at the end of each parallel region. Therefore, the parallel threads are synchronized for each iteration step of the outer loop. Evidently, this produces a large overhead.

Table 4.4 shows that parallelizing the outer loop gives good performance and satisfactory speedups as long as the processor number is not large. There is no clear winner among the dot product and saxpy variant. A slightly faster alternative to the dot product variant is the following code segment where the dot product of a single thread is collapsed into one call to the Level 2 BLAS subroutine for matrix–vector multiplication dgemv.

```
        n0 = (m - 1)/p + 1;
#pragma omp parallel for private(blksize)
    for (i=0; i<p; i++){
        blksize = min(n0, m-i*n0);
        if (blksize > 0)
        dgemv_("N", &blksize, &n, &DONE, &A[i*n0],
               &m, x, &ONE, &DZERO, &y[i*n0], &ONE);
    }
```

The variable blksize holds the number of *A*'s rows that are computed by the respective threads. The variables ONE, DONE, and DZERO are used to pass by address the integer value 1, and the double values 1.0 and 0.0 to the Fortran subroutine dgemv (see Appendix E).

4.8.2 Shared memory version of SGEFA

The basic coding below is a variant from Section 3.4.2. Again, we have used the Fortran or column major storage convention wherein columns are stored in sequential memory locations, not by the C row-wise convention. Array y is the active portion of the reduction in Figure 3.15. The layout for the multiple saxpy operation (msaxpy) is

$$
\begin{array}{cccccc}
& a_0 & a_1 & a_2 & \cdots & a_{m-1} \\
x_0 & y_{0,0} & y_{0,1} & y_{0,2} & \cdots & y_{0,m-1} \\
x_1 & y_{1,0} & y_{1,1} & y_{1,2} & \cdots & y_{1,m-1} \\
\vdots & \vdots & \vdots & & \vdots & \vdots \\
x_{m-1} & y_{m-1,0} & y_{m-1,1} & y_{m-1,2} & \cdots & y_{m-1,m-1}
\end{array}
$$

And the calculation is, for $j = 0, \ldots, m-1$

$$
\mathbf{y}_j \leftarrow a_j \mathbf{x} + \mathbf{y}_j, \tag{4.1}
$$

where $\mathbf{y}_j$ is the jth column in the region of active reduction in Figure 3.15. Column $\mathbf{x}$ is the first column of the augmented system, and $\mathbf{a}$ is the first row of that system. Neither $\mathbf{a}$ nor $\mathbf{x}$ are modified by msaxpy. Column $\mathbf{y}_j$ in msaxpy (4.1) is modified only by the processor which reduces this jth column and no other. In BLAS language, the msaxpy computation is a rank-1 update [135, section 4.9]

$$
Y \leftarrow \mathbf{x}\,\mathbf{a}^{\mathrm{T}} + Y. \tag{4.2}
$$

Revisit Figure 2.1 to see the Level 2 BLAS variant.

```
#define ym(p,q) (y+p+q*n)
void msaxpy(nr,nc,a,n,x,y)
int nr,nc,n;
float *a,*x,*y;
{
/* multiple SAXPY operation, wpp 29/01/2003 */
    int i,j;
#pragma omp parallel shared(nr,nc,a,x,y) private(i,j)
#pragma omp for schedule(static,10) nowait
    for(j=0;j<nc;j++){
        for(i=0;i<nr;i++){
            *ym(i,j) += a[j*n]*x[i];
        }
    }
}
#undef ym
```

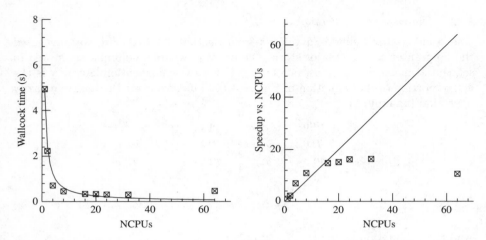

FIG. 4.13. *Times and speedups for parallel version of classical Gaussian elimination, SGEFA, on p. 108, [37]. The machine is Stardust, an HP 9000
Superdome cluster with 64 CPUs. Data is from a problem matrix of size
1000×1000. Chunk size specification of the* for *loop is* (static,32), *and
shows how scaling is satisfactory only to about NCPUs ≤ 16, after which
system parameters discourage more NCPUs. The compiler was* cc.

In preparing the data for Figure 4.13, several variants of the OpenMP
parameters were tested. These variants were all modifications of the

```
#pragma omp for schedule(static,10) nowait
```

line. The choice shown, schedule(static,10) nowait, gave the best results of
several experiments. The so-called **chunksize** numerical argument to schedule
refers to the depth of unrolling of the outer j-loop, in this case the unrolling is to
10 j-values/loop; for example, see Section 3.2. The following compiler switches
and environmental variables were used. Our best results used HP's compiler **cc**

```
cc +O4 +Oparallel +Oopenmp filename.c -lcl -lm -lomp
            -lcps -lpthread
```

with guidec giving much less satisfactory results. An environmental variable
specifying the maximum number of processors must be set:

```
setenv OMP_NUM_THREADS 8
```

In this expression, OMP_NUM_THREADS is set to eight, whereas any number larger
than zero but no more than the total number of processors could be specified.

4.8.3 Shared memory version of FFT

Another recurring example in this book, the binary radix FFT, shows a less desirable property of this architecture or of the OpenMP implementation. Here is an OpenMP version of step used in Section 3.6, specifically the driver given on p. 128. Several variants of the omp for loop were tried and the schedule(static,16) nowait worked better than the others.

```
void step(n,mj,a,b,c,d,w,sign)
int n,mj;
float a[][2],b[][2],c[][2],d[][2],w[][2];
float sign;
{
    float ambr, ambu, wjw[2];
    int j, k, ja, jb, jc, jd, jw, lj, mj2;
/* one step of workspace version of CFFT2 */
    mj2 = 2*mj; lj  = n/mj2;
#pragma omp parallel shared(w,a,b,c,d,lj,mj,mj2,sign) \
 private(j,k,jw,ja,jb,jc,jd,ambr,ambu,wjw)
#pragma omp for schedule(static,16) nowait
    for(j=0;j<lj;j++){
        jw=j*mj; ja=jw; jb=ja; jc=j*mj2; jd=jc;
        wjw[0] = w[jw][0]; wjw[1] = w[jw][1];
        if(sign<0) wjw[1]=-wjw[1];
        for(k=0; k<mj; k++){
            c[jc + k][0] = a[ja + k][0] + b[jb + k][0];
            c[jc + k][1] = a[ja + k][1] + b[jb + k][1];
            ambr = a[ja + k][0] - b[jb + k][0];
            ambu = a[ja + k][1] - b[jb + k][1];
            d[jd + k][0] = wjw[0]*ambr - wjw[1]*ambu;
            d[jd + k][1] = wjw[1]*ambr + wjw[0]*ambu;
        }
    }
}
```

An examination of Figure 3.20 shows that the computation of all the computation boxes (Figure 3.21) using each *twiddle factor* are independent—at an inner loop level. Furthermore, each set of computations using *twiddle factor* $\omega^k = \exp(2\pi i k/n)$ is also independent of every other k—at an outer loop level counted by $k = 0, \ldots$. Hence, the computation of step may be parallelized at an outer loop level (over the *twiddle factors*) and vectorized at the inner loop level (the number of independent boxes using ω^k). The results are not so satisfying, as we see in Figure 4.14. There is considerable improvement in the processing rate for large n, which falls dramatically on one CPU when L1 cache is exhausted. However, there is no significant improvement near the peak rate as NCPU increases and worse, the small n rates are significantly worse. These odd

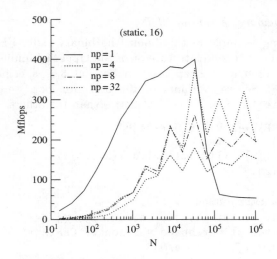

FIG. 4.14. *Simple minded approach to parallelizing one* $n = 2^m$ *FFT using OpenMP on Stardust. The algorithm is the generic one from Figure 3.20 parallelized using OpenMP for the outer loop on the twiddle factors* ω^k. *The compiler was* **cc.** *np = number of CPUs.*

results seem to be a result of cache coherency enforcement of the memory image over the whole machine. An examination of Figures 4.1 and 4.2 shows that when data are local to a **cell**, memory access is fast: each memory module is local to the cell. Conversely, when data are not local to a cell, the **ccnuma** architecture seems to exact a penalty to maintain the cache coherency of blocks on other cells. Writes on these machines are write-through (see Section 1.2.1.1), which means that the cache blocks corresponding to these new data must be marked invalid on every processor but the one writing these updates. It seems, therefore, that the overhead for parallelizing at an outer loop level when the inner loop does so little computation is simply too high. The independent tasks are assigned to an independent CPU, they should be large enough to amortize this latency.

4.9 Overview of OpenMP commands

The OpenMP standard is gratefully a relatively limited set. It is designed for shared memory parallelism, but lacks any vectorization features. On many machines (e.g. Intel Pentium, Crays, SGIs), the `pragma` directives in **C**, or functionally similar directives (`cdir$`, `*vdir`, etc.) in Fortran can be used to control vectorization: see Section 3.2.2. OpenMP is a relatively sparse set of commands (see Appendix C) and unfortunately has no SIMDvector control structures. Alas, this means no non-vendor specific vectorization standard exists at all. For the purposes of our examples, `#pragma ivdep` are satisfactory, but more general structures are not standard. A summary of these commands is given in Appendix C.

4.10   Using Libraries

Classical Gaussian elimination is inferior to a blocked procedure as we indicated in Sections 2.2.2.1 and 2.2.2.2 because matrix multiplication is an accumulation of vectors (see Section 3.4.1). Hence, `dgemm`, Section 2.2.2.2, should be superior to variants of `saxpy`. This is indeed the case as we now show. The test results are from HP's MLIB, which contains LAPACK. Our numbers are from a Fortran version

```
f90 +O3 +Oparallel filename.f -llapack
```

and the LAPACK library on our system is to be found in

$$-\texttt{llapack} \rightarrow \texttt{/opt/mlib/lib/pa2.0/liblapack.a.}$$

This specific path to LAPACK may well be different on another machine. To specify the maximum number of CPUs you might want for your job, the following permits you to control this

```
setenv MLIB_NUMBER_OF_THREADS ncpus
```

where **ncpus** (say eight) is the maximum number. On a loaded machine, you can expect less than optimal performance from your job when **ncpus** becomes comparable to total number of processors on the system. The ETH Superdome has 64 processors and when **ncpus** is larger than about 1/4 of this number, scaling suffers. Both Figures 4.13 and 4.15 show that when **ncpus** > 8, performance no longer scales linearly with **ncpus**.

We feel there are some important lessons to be learned from these examples.

- Whenever possible, use high quality library routines: reinventing the wheel rarely produces a better one. In the case of LAPACK, an enormous amount of work has produced a high performance and well-documented collection of the best algorithms.
- A good algorithm is better than a mediocre one. `sgetrf` uses a blocked algorithm for Gaussian elimination, while the classical method `sgefa` involves too much data traffic.
- Even though OpenMP can be used effectively for parallelization, its indirectness makes tuning necessary. Table 4.2 shows that codes can be sensitive to chunk sizes and types of scheduling.

Exercise 4.1 Parallelize the Linpack benchmark. The task here is to parallelize the Linpack benchmark described in Section 3.4.2, p. 108, and Section 4.8.2. Start with Bonnie Toy's **C** version of the benchmark which you

154 SHARED MEMORY PARALLELISM

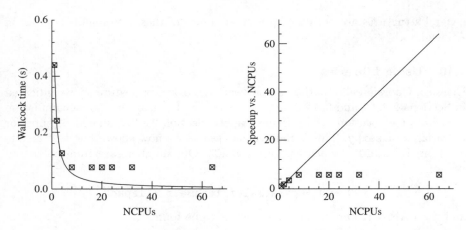

FIG. 4.15. *Times and speedups for the Hewlett-Packard MLIB version LAPACK routine* sgetrf. *The test was in Fortran, compiled with* **f90**. *Scaling is adequate for NCPUs < 8, but is less than satisfactory for larger NCPUs. However, the performance of the MLIB version of* sgetrf *is clearly superior to classical Gaussian elimination* sgefa *shown in Figure 4.13. The problem size is* 1000 × 1000.

can download from NETLIB [111]:

http://www.netlib.org/benchmark/linpackc

The complete source code we will call clinpack.c. In Section 4.8.2, we saw a version of **sgefa.c** which used the OpenMP "omp for" construct. In clinpack.c, the relevant section is in the **double** version dgefa (an int procedure there). Beginning with the comment row elimination with column indexing, you can see two code fragments in the for (j = kp1; j < n; j++) loop. The first swaps row elements a(k+1+i,l) for a(k+1+i,k) for i=0..n-k-1. In fact, as we noted on p. 108, this can be pulled out of the loop. Look at the if(l!=k) section of p. 108 before the corresponding for(j=kp1;k<n;k++) loop. Your task, after moving out this swap, is to parallelize the remaining for loop. One way to do this is by using the OMP **parallel for** directive to parallelize the corresponding daxpy call in Toy's version.

What is to be done?

1. From the NETLIB site (above), download the clinpack.c version of the Linpack benchmark.
2. With some effort, port this code to the shared memory machine of your choice. The only real porting problem here is likely to be the timer— **second**. We recommend replacing **second** with the **walltime** routine (returns a **double**) given below. On Cray hardware, use **timef** instead of **walltime** for multi-CPU tests.

3. Once you get the code ported and the `walltime` clock installed, then proceed to run the code to get initial 1-CPU timing(s).

4. Now modify the `dgefa` routine in the way described above to use the OpenMP "`omp parallel for`" directive to call `daxpy` independently for each processor available. You need to be careful about the data scoping rules.

5. Run your modified version, with various chunksizes if need be and plot the multiple-CPU timing results compared to the initial 1-CPU value(s). Be sure that the numerical solutions are correct. Vary the number of CPUs by using the `setenv OMP_NUM_THREADS` settings from Section 4.8.2. Also compare your initial 1-CPU result(s) to `setenv OMP_NUM_THREADS 1` values. Also, try different matrix sizes other than the original 200×200.

For the wallclock timing, use the following (t0 = 0.0 initially),

```
tw = walltime(&t0);        /* start timer   */
sgefa(a,n,n,ipvt,&info);   /* factor A -> LU */
t0 = walltime(&tw);        /* time for sgefa */
```

where variables `tw,t0` start the timer and return the difference between the start and end. `walltime` is

```
#include <sys/time.h>
double walltime(double *t0)
{
    double mic, time, mega=0.000001;
    struct timeval tp;
    struct timezone tzp;
    static long base_sec = 0, base_usec = 0;

    (void) gettimeofday(&tp, &tzp);
    if (base_sec == 0) {
      base_sec  = tp.tv_sec; base_usec = tp.tv_usec;
    }
    time = (double)(tp.tv_sec - base_sec);
    mic = (double)(tp.tv_usec - base_usec);
    time = (time + mic * mega) - *t0;
    return(time);
}
```

Benchmark report: from the NETLIB server [111], download the latest version of `performance.ps` just to see how you are doing. Do not expect your results to be as fast as those listed in this report. Rather, the exercise is just to parallelize `dgefa`. Any ideas how to modify Toy's loop unrolling of **daxpy**?

5

MIMD, MULTIPLE INSTRUCTION, MULTIPLE DATA

Never trust a computer you can't throw out a window.

S. Wozniak

The **Multiple instruction, multiple data** (MIMD) programming model usually refers to computing on distributed memory machines with multiple independent processors. Although processors may run independent instruction streams, we are interested in streams that are always portions of a single program. Between processors which share a coherent memory view (within a node), data access is immediate, whereas between nodes data access is effected by **message passing**. In this book, we use **MPI** for such message passing. **MPI** has emerged as a more/less standard message passing system used on both shared memory and distributed memory machines.

It is often the case that although the system consists of multiple independent instruction streams, the programming model is not too different from SIMD. Namely, the totality of a program is logically split into many independent tasks each processed by a **group** (see Appendix D) of processes—but the overall program is effectively single threaded at the beginning, and likewise at the end. The MIMD model, however, is extremely flexible in that no one process is always **master** and the other processes **slaves**. A communicator **group** of processes performs certain tasks, usually with an arbitrary master/slave relationship. One process may be assigned to be **master** (or **root**) and coordinates the tasks of others in the group. We emphasize that the assignments of which is **root** is arbitrary—any processor may be chosen. Frequently, however, this choice is one of convenience—a file server node, for example.

Processors and memory are connected by a network, for example, Figure 5.1. In this form, each processor has its own local memory. This is not always the case: The Cray X1 (Figures 4.5 and 4.6), and NEC SX-6 through SX-8 series machines (Figures 4.7 and 4.8), have common memory within nodes. Within a node, memory coherency is maintained within local caches. Between nodes, it remains the programmer's responsibility to assure a proper read–update relationship in the shared data. Data updated by one set of processes should not be clobbered by another set until the data are properly used.

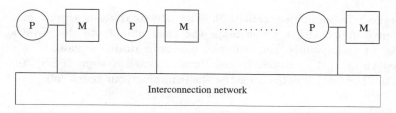

FIG. 5.1. *Generic MIMD distributed-memory computer (multiprocessor).*

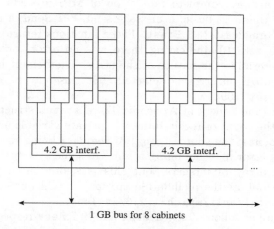

FIG. 5.2. *Network connection for ETH Beowulf cluster.*

Although a much more comprehensive review of the plethora of networks in use is given in section 2.4.2. of Hwang [75], we note here several types of networks used on distributed memory machines:

1. **Bus**: a congestion-bound, but cheap, and scalable with respect to cost network (like on our Beowulf cluster, *Asgard*, Figure 5.2).
2. **Dynamic networks**: for example, a *crossbar* which is hard to scale and has very many switches, is expensive, and typically used for only limited number of processors.
3. **Static networks**: for example, Ω-networks, arrays, rings, meshes, tori, *hypercubes*. In Chapter 1, we showed an Ω-network in Figures 1.11 and 1.12. That example used 2×2 switches, but we also noted in Chapter 4 regarding the HP9000 machine that higher order switches (e.g. 4×4) are also used.
4. **Combinations**: for example, a bus connecting clusters which are connected by a static network: see Section 5.2.

An arbitrarily selected node, **node**$_i$, is chosen to coordinate the others. In **MPI**, the numbering of each node is called its `rank`. In many situations, a selected master node is numbered rank= 0. The **physical assignment** of nodes is in an environmental list which maps the rank number to the physical nodes the system understands. For example, processor **node**$_i$ = rank = 0 might be mapped **rank** = 0 → **n038**. In the Parallel Batch System (PBS), this list is PBS_NODEFILE, and is defined for the shell running your batch job.

5.1   MPI commands and examples

Before we do an example, we need to show the basic forms of MPI commands. In Appendix D, a more complete tabulation of MPI procedures is given, but here are three of the most basic: a message send, MPI_Send; a message receive, MPI_Recv; and a broadcast, MPI_Bcast. These functions return an integer value which is either a zero (0) indicating there was no error, or a nonzero from which one can determine the nature of the error. The default behavior of MPI is to abort the job if an error is detected, but this may be controlled using MPI_Errhandler_set [109].

For MPI_Recv (and others in Appendix D), a status structure, Figure 5.3, is used to check the count of received data (a private variable accessible only by using MPI_Get_count), the source (rank) of the data being received, the message tag, and any error message information. On some systems, private_count is an integer or array of integers, but this is seldom used. For your local implementation, look at the include file mpidefs.h. On our system, this is in directory /usr/local/apli/mpich-1.2.3/include.

These fields are as follows for MPI_Send and MPI_Recv respectively [115].

1. send_data is a pointer to the data to be sent; recv_data is the pointer to where the received data are to be stored.
2. count is the number of items to send, or expected, respectively.
3. datatype is the type of each item in the message; for example, type MPI_FLOAT which means a single precision floating point datum.
4. dest_rank is the rank of the node to which the data are to be sent; source_rank is the rank of the node which is expected to be sending data. Frequently, MPI_Recv will accept data from any source and uses MPI_ANY_SOURCE to do so. This variable is defined in the mpi.h include file.
5. tag_ident is a tag or label on the message. Often the MPI_Recv procedure would use MPI_ANY_TAG to accept a message with any tag. This is defined in mpi.h.
6. comm defines a set allowed to send/receive data. When communicating between all parts of your code, this is usually MPI_COMM_WORLD, meaning any source or destination. When using libraries, parts of code which were written by someone else, or even parts of your own code which do distinctly different calculations, this mechanism can be useful. Distinct portions of code may send the same tag, and must be classified into **communicators** to control their passing messages to each other.

7. `status` is a structure (see Figure 5.3) used in `MPI_Recv` that contains information from the source about how many elements were send, the source's rank, the tag of the message, and any error information. The count is accessible only through `MPI_Get_count`. On some systems, more information is returned in `private_count`. See the `MPI_status` struct above.

Commands `MPI_Send` and `MPI_Recv` are said to be *blocking*. This means the functions do not return to the routine which called them until the messages are sent or received, respectively [115]. There are also non-blocking equivalents of these send/receive commands. For example, the pair `MPI_Isend` or `MPI_Irecv` initiate sending a message and receive it, respectively, but `MPI_Isend` immediately

```
int MPI_Send(     /* returns 0 if success */
    void*         send_data,   /* message to send */
    int           count,       /* input */
    MPI_Datatype  datatype,    /* input */
    int           dest_rank,   /* input */
    int           tag_ident,   /* input */
    MPI_Comm      comm)        /* input */

typedef struct {
    int count;
    int MPI_SOURCE;
    int MPI_TAG;
    int MPI_ERROR;
/*  int private_count; */
} MPI_Status;

int MPI_Recv(     /* returns 0 if success */
    void*         recv_data,   /* message to receive */
    int           count,       /* input */
    MPI_Datatype  datatype,    /* input */
    int           source_rank, /* input */
    int           tag_ident,   /* input */
    MPI_Comm      comm,        /* input */
    MPI_Status*   status)      /* struct */

int MPI_Bcast(    /* returns 0 if success */
    void*         message,     /* output/input */
    int           count,       /* input */
    MPI_Datatype  datatype,    /* input */
    int           root,        /* input */
    MPI_Comm      comm)        /* input */
```

FIG. 5.3. *MPI status* struct *for* **send** *and* **receive** *functions.*

returns to the calling procedure once the transmission is initialized—irrespective of whether the transmission actually occurred. The danger is that the associated send/receive buffers might be modified before either operation is explicitly completed. We do not illustrate these non-blocking commands here because on our Beowulf system they are effectively blocking anyway since all data traffic share the same memory channel. In addition, they can be dangerous: The buffers may be modified and thus updated information lost. Both forms (non-blocking and blocking) of these commands are *point to point*. This means data are transmitted only from one node to another.

Another commonly used command involves a *point-to-many* broadcast. For example, in our $y = Ax$ matrix–vector multiply example discussed later, it is convenient to distribute vector x to every processor available. Vector x is unmodified by these processors, but is needed in its entirety to compute the segment of the result y computed on each node. This broadcast command, however, has the peculiarity that it is both a send and receive: From the initiator (say root= 0), it is a broadcast; while for a slave = rank $\neq$ root, it is a receive function. The parameters in MPI_Bcast, as typed in the template above, are as follows.

1. message is a pointer to the data to be sent to all elements in the communicator comm (as input) if the node processing the MPI_Bcast command has rank = root. If rank $\neq$ root, then the command is processed as a receive and message (output) is a pointer to where the received data broadcast from root are to be stored.
2. count is the integer number of elements of type datatype to be broadcast (input), or the number received (output).
3. datatype specifies the datatype of the received message. These may be one of the usual MPI datatypes, for example, MPI_FLOAT (see Table D.1).
4. root is an integer parameter specifying the rank of the initiator of the broadcast. If the rank of the node is not root, MPI_Bcast is a command to receive data sent by root.
5. comm is of MPI_Comm type and specifies the communicator group to which the broadcast is to be distributed. Other communicators are not affected.

A more complete explanation of MPI functions and procedures is given in Peter Pacheco's book [115], and the definitive reference is from Argonne [110]. In Fortran, an important reference is Gropp *et al.* [64]. Otherwise, download the MPI-2 standard reference guide from NETLIB [111]. In order to supplement our less complete treatment, Appendix D contains a useful subset of MPI functionality.

Before we proceed to some examples, we would like to show the way to compile and execute MPI programs. Included are compile and PBS scripts. You may have to modify some details for your local environment, but the general features are hopefully correct.

To submit a batch job, you will need PBS commands. Many operations are better done in command line mode, however: for example, compilations and small jobs. Since compilers are frequently unavailable on every node, batch jobs for compilation may fail. At your discretion are the number of nodes and wallclock time limit.

1. PBS = "parallel batch system" commands:

   - **qsub** submits your job script:

     ```
     qsub qjob
     ```

   - **qstat** gets the status of the previously submitted qjob (designated, say, 123456.gate01 by PBS):

     ```
     qstat 123456.gate01
     ```

   - **qdel** deletes a job from PBS queue:

     ```
     qdel 123456
     ```

2. An available nodefile, PBS_NODEFILE, is assigned to the job **qjob** you submit. This nodefile mapping can be useful for other purposes. For example, to get the number of nodes available to your job **qjob**:

   ```
   nnodes=`wc $PBS_NODEFILE|awk '{print $1}'`
   ```

3. **mpicc** = C compiler for MPICH/LAM version of MPI:

   ```
   mpicc -O3 yourcode.c -lm -lblas -lf2c
   ```

   the compile includes a load of the BLAS library and libf2c.a for Fortran–**C** communication.

4. **mpirun** = run command MPICH/LAM with options for NCPUs:

   ```
   mpirun -machinefile $PBS_NODEFILE -np $nnodes a.out
   ```

Next, you will likely need a batch script to submit your job. On our systems, two choices are available: MPICH [109] and LAM [90]. The following scripts will be subject to some modifications for your local system: in particular, the pathname $MPICHBIN, which is the directory where the compiler mpicc and supervisory execution program mpirun are located. On our systems, the compiler runs only on the service nodes (three of these)—so you need a **compile script** to generate the desired four executables (run128, run256, run512, run1024). Figure 5.4 shows the compile script which prepares run128,..., run1024 and runs interactively (not through PBS).

And Figure 5.5 is the PBS batch script (submitted by qsub) to run the run128,..., run1024 executables.

The **compile script** Figure 5.4 is easily modified for LAM by changing the MPICH path to the "commented out" LAM path (remove the # character). A PBS script for LAM is similar to modify and is shown in Figure 5.6.

5.2 Matrix and vector operations with PBLAS and BLACS

Operations as simple as $y = Ax$ for distributed memory computers have obviously been written into libraries, and not surprisingly a lot more.

```
#!/bin/bash

# LAM path
# inc=/usr/local/apli/lam-6.5.6/include
# MPICC=/usr/local/apli/lam-6.5.6/mpicc

# MPICH path
inc=/usr/local/apli/mpich-1.2.3/include
MPICC=/usr/local/apli/mpich-1.2.3/bin/mpicc

echo "$inc files" >comp.out

for sz in 128 256 512 1024
do
    echo "${sz} executable"
    which $MPICC
    sed "s/MAX_X=64/MAX_X=$sz/" <time3D.c >timeit.c
    $MPICC -I${inc} -O3 -o run${sz} timeit.c -lm
done
```

FIG. 5.4. MPICH *compile script.*

```
#!/bin/bash
#                   MPICH batch script
#
#PBS -l nodes=64,walltime=200
set echo
date
MRUN = /usr/local/apli/mpich-1.2.3/bin/mpirun
nnodes='`wc $PBS_NODEFILE|awk '{print $1}'`'

echo "=== QJOB submitted via MPICH ==="
for sz in 128 256 512 1024
do
    echo "=======N=$sz timings======"
    $MRUN -machinefile $PBS_NODEFILE -np $nnodes run${sz}
    echo "=========================="
done
```

FIG. 5.5. MPICH *(PBS) batch run script.*

```
#!/bin/bash
#                   LAM batch script
#
LAMBIN = /usr/local/apli/lam-6.5.6/bin
machinefile='basename $PBS_NODEFILE.tmp'
uniq $PBS_NODEFILE > $machinefile
nnodes='wc $machinefile|awk '{print $1}''
nnodes=$(( nnodes - 1 ))
$LAMBIN/lamboot -v $machinefile
echo "=== QJOB submitted via LAM ==="
# yourcode is your sourcefile
$LAMBIN/mpicc -O3 yourcode.c -lm
$LAMBIN/mpirun n0-$nnodes -v a.out
$LAMBIN/lamwipe -v $machinefile
rm -f $machinefile
```

FIG. 5.6. LAM *(PBS) run script.*

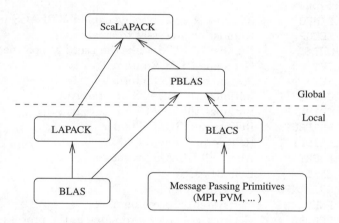

FIG. 5.7. *The ScaLAPACK software hierarchy.*

ScaLAPACK [12] is the standard library for the basic algorithms from linear algebra on MIMD distributed memory parallel machines. It builds on the algorithms implemented in LAPACK that are available on virtually all shared memory computers. The algorithms in LAPACK are designed to provide accurate results and high performance. High performance is obtained through the three levels of basic linear algebra subroutines (BLAS), which are discussed in Section 2.2. Level 3 BLAS routines make it possible to exploit the hierarchical memories partly described in Chapter 1. LAPACK and the BLAS are used in ScaLAPACK for the local computations, that is, computations that are bound to one processor, see Figure 5.7. Global aspects are dealt with by using the Parallel Basic Linear Algebra Subroutines (PBLAS), see Table 5.2, that are an extension of the BLAS for distributed memories [19]. In Section 5.4 we show how the PBLAS access matrices are distributed among the processors in a two-dimensional block cyclic data layout. Recall that vectors and scalars are considered special cases of matrices. The actual communication is implemented in the Basic Linear Algebra Communication Subprograms (BLACS) [149]. The BLACS are high level communication functions that provide primitives for transferring matrices that are distributed on the process grid according to the two-dimensional block cyclic data layout of Section 5.4, see Table 5.1. Besides general rectangular matrices, the BLACS also provide communication routines for trapezoidal and triangular matrices. In particular, they provide the so-called **scoped operations**, that is, collective communication routines that apply only to process columns or rows.

Table 5.1 *Summary of the BLACS. The context of many of these routines can be a column, a row, or the whole process grid.*

Support routines	
BLACS_PINFO	Number of processes available for BLACS use
BLACS_SETUP	Number of processes to create
SETPVMTIDS	Number of PVM tasks the user has spawned
BLACS_GET	Get some BLACS internals
BLACS_SET	Set some BLACS internals
BLACS_GRIDINIT	Initialize the BLACS process grid
BLACS_GRIDMAP	Initialize the BLACS process grid
BLACS_FREEBUF	Release the BLACS buffer
BLACS_GRIDEXIT	Release process grid
BLACS_ABORT	Abort all BLACS processes
BLACS_EXIT	Exit BLACS
BLACS_GRIDINFO	Get grid information
BLACS_PNUM	Get system process number
BLACS_PCOORD	Get row/column coordinates in the process grid
BLACS_BARRIER	Set a synchronization point
Point-to-point communication	
_GESD2D, _TRSD2D	General/trapezoidal matrix send
_GERV2D, _TRRV2D	General/trapezoidal matrix receive
Broadcasts	
_GEBS2D, _TRBS2D	General/trapezoidal matrix broadcast (sending)
_GEBR2D, _TRBR2D	General/trapezoidal matrix broadcast (receiving)
Reduction (combine) operations	
_GSUM2D, _GAMX2D, _GAMN2D	Reduction with sum/max/min operator

The BLACS are implemented by some lower level message passing interface. Figure 5.7 indicates that the BLACS are built on top of MPI. The BLACS have synchronous **send** and **receive** routines to communicate matrices or submatrices from one process to another; functions to **broadcast** submatrices to many processes; and others to compute global reductions. The PBLAS and the BLACS relieve the application programmer from the writing of functions for moving matrices and vectors. Because of the standardized conventions, code becomes more portable and is easier to write. As with the BLAS, the basic operations are defined for a relatively few basic functions that can be optimized for all computing platforms. The PBLAS provide most of the functionality of the BLAS for two-dimensional block cyclically distributed matrices shown in Section 5.4. Matrix transposition is also available.

Besides its communication functions, the BLACS have features to initialize, change, and query process grids. An application programmer will usually directly use the BLACS only by these routines. In the code fragment in Figure 5.8, it is shown how a process grid is initialized after MPI has been started. The invocation of `Cblacs_get` returns a *handle* (`ctxt`) to a process grid, called **context**. A context is analogous to an MPI communicator, that is, it is the "world" in which communication takes place. The grid is initialized by the call to `Cblacs_gridinit`, which determines the size of the process grid and the numbering order of process rows or columns. Figure 5.9 shows the grid that is obtained by this code when $p = 8$. The eight processes are numbered row by row, that is, in *row-major ordering*. Finally, the call to `Cblacs_pcoord` in Figure 5.8 returns the row and column indices of the actual process `myid` in the process grid, $0 \leq$ `myrow` $<$ `pr` and $0 \leq$ `mycol` $<$ `pc`. If the number of processors available is larger than the number of processes in the process grid, then `mycol = myrow = -1` for the superfluous processes.

After the completion of the parallel computation, the allocated memory space needs to be freed, the process grid released, and MPI should be shut down, see Figure 5.10.

After having initialized the process grid, the arrays are to be allocated and initialized. The initialization of matrices and vectors is the responsibility of the application programmer. This can be a tedious and error-prone task, and there are many ways to proceed.

5.3   Distribution of vectors

To be more specific about arrangements of array distributions, let us first ponder the problem of distributing a vector **x** with n elements $x_0, x_1, \ldots, x_{n-1}$ on p processors.

5.3.1   *Cyclic vector distribution*

A straightforward distribution is obtained in a manner similar to dealing a deck of cards: The first number x_0 is stored on processor 0, the second number x_1

Table 5.2 *Summary of the PBLAS.*

Level 1 PBLAS

P_SWAP	Swap two vectors: $\mathbf{x} \leftrightarrow \mathbf{y}$
P_SCAL	Scale a vector: $\mathbf{x} \leftarrow \alpha\mathbf{x}$
P_COPY	Copy a vector: $\mathbf{x} \leftarrow \mathbf{y}$
P_AXPY	_axpy operation: $\mathbf{y} \leftarrow \mathbf{y} + \alpha\mathbf{x}$
P_DOT, P_DOTU, P_DOTC	Dot product: $s \leftarrow \mathbf{x} \cdot \mathbf{y} = \mathbf{x}^*\mathbf{y}$
P_NRM2	2-norm: $s \leftarrow \|\mathbf{x}\|_2$
P_ASUM	1-norm: $s \leftarrow \|\mathbf{x}\|_1$
P_AMAX	Index of largest vector element: first i such $|x_i| \geq |x_k|$ for all k

Level 2 PBLAS

P_GEMV	General matrix–vector multiply: $\mathbf{y} \leftarrow \alpha A\mathbf{x} + \beta\mathbf{y}$
P_HEMV	Hermitian matrix–vector multiply: $\mathbf{y} \leftarrow \alpha A\mathbf{x} + \beta\mathbf{y}$
P_SYMV	Symmetric matrix–vector multiply: $\mathbf{y} \leftarrow \alpha A\mathbf{x} + \beta\mathbf{y}$
P_TRMV	Triangular matrix–vector multiply: $\mathbf{x} \leftarrow A\mathbf{x}$
P_TRSV	Triangular system solves (forward/backward substitution): $\mathbf{x} \leftarrow A^{-1}\mathbf{x}$
P_GER, P_GERU, P_GERC	Rank-1 updates: $A \leftarrow \alpha\mathbf{x}\mathbf{y}^* + A$
P_HER, P_SYR	Hermitian/symmetric rank-1 updates: $A \leftarrow \alpha\mathbf{x}\mathbf{x}^* + A$
P_HER2, P_SYR2	Hermitian/symmetric rank-2 updates: $A \leftarrow \alpha\mathbf{x}\mathbf{y}^* + \alpha^*\mathbf{y}\mathbf{x}^* + A$

Level 3 PBLAS

P_GEMM, P_SYMM, P_HEMM	General/symmetric/Hermitian matrix–matrix multiply: $C \leftarrow \alpha AB + \beta C$
P_SYRK, P_HERK	Symmetric/Hermitian rank-k update: $C \leftarrow \alpha AA^* + \beta C$
P_SYR2K, P_HER2K	Symmetric/Hermitian rank-k update: $C \leftarrow \alpha AB^* + \alpha^* BA^* + \beta C$
P_TRAN, P_TRANU, P_TRANC	Matrix transposition: $C \leftarrow \beta C + \alpha A^*$
P_TRMM	Multiple triangular matrix–vector multiplies: $B \leftarrow \alpha AB$
P_TRSM	Multiple triangular system solves: $B \leftarrow \alpha A^{-1}B$

```
/* Start the MPI engine */
MPI_Init(&argc, &argv);

/* Find out number of processes */
MPI_Comm_size(MPI_COMM_WORLD, &p);

/* Find out process rank */
MPI_Comm_rank(MPI_COMM_WORLD, &myid);

/* Get a BLACS context */
Cblacs_get(0, 0, &ctxt);

/* Determine pr and pc for the pr x pc grid */
for (pc=p/2; p%pc; pc--);
pr = p/pc;
if (pr > pc){pc = pr; pr = p/pc;}

/* Initialize the pr x pc process grid */
Cblacs_gridinit(&ctxt, "Row-major", pr, pc);
Cblacs_pcoord(ctxt, myid, &myrow, &mycol);
```

FIG. 5.8. *Initialization of a BLACS process grid.*

	0	1	2	3
0	0	1	2	3
1	4	5	6	7

FIG. 5.9. *Eight processes mapped on a 2×4 process grid in row-major order.*

```
/* Release process grid */
Cblacs_gridexit(ctxt);

/* Shut down MPI */
MPI_Finalize();
```

FIG. 5.10. *Release of the BLACS process grid.*

on processor 1, and so on, until the pth number x_{p-1} that is stored on processor $p - 1$. The next number x_p is stored again on processor 0, etc. So,

$$x_i \text{ is stored at position } j \text{ on processor } k \quad \text{if} \quad i = j \cdot p + k, \ 0 \leq k < p. \qquad (5.1)$$

As an example, let $\mathbf{x}$ be a vector with 22 elements $x_0, x_1, \ldots, x_{21}$. If $\mathbf{x}$ is distributed cyclically, the elements are distributed over processors 0 to 4 like

$$
\begin{array}{llllll}
\mathbf{0}: & x_0 & x_5 & x_{10} & x_{15} & x_{20} \\
\mathbf{1}: & x_1 & x_6 & x_{11} & x_{16} & x_{21} \\
\mathbf{2}: & x_2 & x_7 & x_{12} & x_{17} \\
\mathbf{3}: & x_3 & x_8 & x_{13} & x_{18} \\
\mathbf{4}: & x_4 & x_9 & x_{14} & x_{19}
\end{array}
\tag{5.2}
$$

The cyclic distribution is displayed in Figure 5.11. Each of the 22 vector elements is given a "color" indicating on which processor it is stored.

FIG. 5.11. *Cyclic distrnibution of a vector.*

From the layout in (5.2) we see that two processors hold five elements while three processors hold only four elements. It is evidently not possible that all processors hold the same number of vector elements. Under these circumstances, the element distribution over the processors is optimally balanced.

5.3.2 *Block distribution of vectors*

Due to the principle of **locality of reference** (Section 1.1), it may be more efficient to distribute the vector in p big blocks of length $b = \lceil n/p \rceil$. In the example above, we could store the first $\lceil 22/5 \rceil = 5$ elements of $\mathbf{x}$ on the first processor 0, the next 5 elements on processor 1, and so on. With this block distribution, the 22-vector of before is distributed in the following way on 5 processors.

$$
\begin{array}{llllll}
\mathbf{0}: & x_0 & x_1 & x_2 & x_3 & x_4 \\
\mathbf{1}: & x_5 & x_6 & x_7 & x_8 & x_9 \\
\mathbf{2}: & x_{10} & x_{11} & x_{12} & x_{13} & x_{14} \\
\mathbf{3}: & x_{15} & x_{16} & x_{17} & x_{18} & x_{19} \\
\mathbf{4}: & x_{20} & x_{21}
\end{array}
\tag{5.3}
$$

For vectors of length n, we have

$$
\boxed{x_i \text{ is stored at position } k \text{ on processor } j \quad \text{if} \quad i = j \cdot b + k,\ 0 \le k < b.}
\tag{5.4}
$$

The block distribution is displayed in Figure 5.12. Evidently, this procedure does not distribute the elements as equally as the cyclic distribution in Figure 5.11.

FIG. 5.12. *Block distribution of a vector.*

The first $p-1$ processors all get $\lceil n/p \rceil$ elements and the last one gets the remaining elements which may be as few as one element. The difference can thus be up to $p-1$ elements. If n is much larger than p, this issue is not so important.

Nevertheless, let $n = 1000001$ and $p = 1000$. Then, $\lceil n/p \rceil = 1001$. The first 999 processors store $999 \times 1001 = 999,999$ elements, while the last processors just store 2 elements.

An advantage of the block distribution is the fast access of elements that are stored contiguously in memory of cache based computers, that is, the **locality of reference** principle of Section 1.1. Thus, the block distribution supports block algorithms. Often algorithms are implemented in blocked versions to enhance performance by improving the ration of floating point operations vs. memory accesses.

5.3.3 *Block–cyclic distribution of vectors*

A block–cyclic distribution is a compromise between the two previous distributions. It improves upon the badly balanced block distribution of Section 5.3.2, but also restores some locality of reference memory access of the cyclic distribution.

If b is a block size, usually a small integer like 2, 4, or 8, then partition the n-vector $\mathbf{x}$ into $n_b = \lceil n/b \rceil$ blocks, the first $n_b - 1$ of which consist of b elements, while the last has length $n - (n_b - 1)b = n \bmod b$. The blocks, which should be bigger than a cacheline, will now be distributed cyclically over p processors. Set $i = j \cdot b + k$, then from (5.4) we know that x_i is the kth element in block j. Let now $j = l \cdot p + m$. Then, interpreting (5.1) for blocks, we see that global block j is the lth block on processor m. Thus, we get the following distribution scheme,

$$
\boxed{
\begin{array}{l}
x_i \text{ is stored at position } l \cdot b + k \text{ on processor } m \\
\quad \text{if } \quad i = j \cdot b + k, \ 0 \le k < b \quad \text{and} \quad j = l \cdot p + m, \ 0 \le m < p.
\end{array}
} \tag{5.5}
$$

Therefore, the block–cyclic distribution generalizes both cyclic and block distributions. The cyclic distribution obtains if $b = 1$, while the block distribution is obtained when $b = \lceil n/p \rceil$.

With block size $b = 2$ and $p = 5$ processors, the 22 elements of vector $\mathbf{x}$ are stored according to

$$
\begin{array}{llllll}
\mathbf{0}: & x_0 & x_1 & x_{10} & x_{11} & x_{20} \quad x_{21} \\
\mathbf{1}: & x_2 & x_3 & x_{12} & x_{13} \\
\mathbf{2}: & x_4 & x_5 & x_{14} & x_{15} \\
\mathbf{3}: & x_6 & x_7 & x_{16} & x_{17} \\
\mathbf{4}: & x_8 & x_9 & x_{18} & x_{19}
\end{array} \tag{5.6}
$$

Figure 5.13 shows a diagram for this distribution.

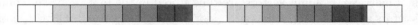

FIG. 5.13. *Block–cyclic distribution of a vector.*

The number of blocks assigned to each processor cannot differ by more than 1. Therefore, the difference in the number of elements per processor cannot exceed b, the number/block.

5.4   Distribution of matrices

Columns or rows of matrices can be distributed according to one of the three vector distributions (cyclic, block, and block–cyclic) in a straightforward manner. *Column cyclic, column block*, and *column block–cyclic* distributions are obtained if the columns of matrices are distributed in the way elements of vectors are distributed. Analogously, *row cyclic, row block*, and *row block–cyclic* distributions are obtained.

5.4.1   *Two-dimensional block–cyclic matrix distribution*

Can we distribute both rows and columns *simultaneously* according to one of the vector distributions? Let us assume that we are given a matrix A with n_r rows and n_c columns. Where, that is, at which position on which processor, should element a_{i_r,i_c} of A go? If we want to decide on this by means of the formula in (5.5) individually and independently for i_r and i_c, we need to have values for the block size and the processor number for rows and columns of A. If we have block sizes b_r and b_c and processor numbers p_r and p_c available, we can formally proceed as follows.

$$
\begin{array}{l}
a_{i_r,i_c} \text{ is stored at position } (l_r \cdot b_r + k_r, l_c \cdot b_c + k_c) \text{ on processor} \\
(m_r, m_c) \text{ if} \\
i_r = j_r b_r + k_r, \ 0 \le k_r < b_r \text{ with } \ j_r = l_r p_r + m_r, \ 0 \le m_r < p_r, \\
\text{and } i_c = j_c b_c + k_c, \ 0 \le k_c < b_c \text{ and } j_c = l_c p_c + m_c, \ 0 \le m_c < p_c.
\end{array}
\tag{5.7}
$$

How do we interpret this assignment? The $n_r \times n_c$ matrix is partitioned into small rectangular matrix blocks of size $b_r \times b_c$. These blocks are distributed over a rectangular *grid of processors* of size $p_r \times p_c$. This processor grid is a logical arrangement of the $p = p_r \cdot p_c$ processors that are available to us. Notice that some of the numbers b_r, b_c, p_r, p_c can (and sometimes must) take on the value 1.

In Figure 5.14, we show an example of a 15×20 matrix that is partitioned in a number of blocks of size 2×3. These blocks are distributed over $6 = 2 \cdot 3$ processors. Processor $(0,0)$ stores the white blocks. Notice that at the right and lower border of the matrix, the blocks may be smaller: two wide, not three; and one high, not two, respectively. Further, not all processors may get the same number of blocks. Here, processor $(0,0)$ gets 12 blocks with altogether 64 elements while processor $(0,2)$ only gets 8 blocks with 48 elements.

Such a *two-dimensional block–cyclic matrix distribution* is the method by which matrices are distributed in ScaLAPACK [12]. Vectors are treated as special cases of matrices. Column vectors are thus stored in the first processor column; row vectors are stored in the first processor row. In the ScaLAPACK convention,

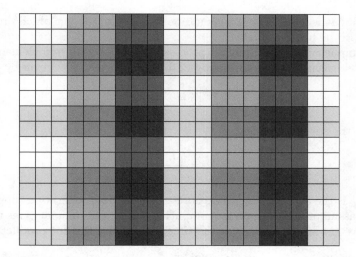

FIG. 5.14. *Block–cyclic distribution of a* 15×20 *matrix on a* 2×3 *processor grid with blocks of* 2×3 *elements.*

a grid of processors is called the *process grid*. Additionally, an assumption is made that there is just one (application) process running per processor.

5.5   Basic operations with vectors

In Sections 2.1 and 3.2.3, we discussed both the **saxpy** (2.3)

$$\mathbf{y} = \alpha \mathbf{x} + \mathbf{y},$$

and inner product operation sdot (2.4),

$$s = \mathbf{x} \cdot \mathbf{y}.$$

These operations were again reviewed in Chapter 4, particularly Section 4.7, regarding shared memory machines. In this section, we review these basic operations again in the context of distributed memory systems. What is difficult in this situation is careful management of the data distribution.

Each component of $\mathbf{y}$ can be treated independently as before, *provided* that the vectors $\mathbf{x}$ and $\mathbf{y}$ are distributed in the same layout on the processors. If vectors are not distributed in the same layout, $\mathbf{x}$ or $\mathbf{y}$ have to be *aligned*. Aligning vectors involves expensive communication. Comparing (5.2) and (5.3) we see that rearranging a cyclically distributed vector into a block distributed one corresponds to a matrix transposition. Matrix transposition is also investigated in multiple dimensional Fourier transform (FFT), Sections 5.8 and 5.9.

However, in computing sdot we have some freedom of how we implement the sum over the n products, $x_i y_i$. In a distributed memory environment, one has to think about where the sum s should be stored: That is, on which processor is the result to be made available?

For simplicity, assume that all processors hold exactly n/p elements. Then the parallel execution time for saxpy (2.3) on p processors is given by

$$T_p^{\text{saxpy}} = \frac{n}{p} T_{\text{flop}}, \qquad (5.8)$$

such that the speedup is ideal,

$$S_p^{\text{saxpy}} = \frac{T_1^{\text{saxpy}}}{T_p^{\text{saxpy}}} = p. \qquad (5.9)$$

Here, T_{flop} is the average time to execute a floating point operation (flop). Under the same assumptions as those for computing saxpy, plus a binary tree reduction schema, we get an expression for the time to compute the dot product

$$T_p^{\text{dot}} = 2\frac{n}{p} T_{\text{flop}} + T_{\text{reduce}}(p)(1) = 2\frac{n}{p} T_{\text{flop}} + \log_2(p)(T_{\text{startup}} + T_{\text{word}}). \qquad (5.10)$$

Here, $T_{\text{reduce}}(p)(1)$ means the time a reduction on p processors takes for one item. T_{startup} is the communication startup time, and T_{word} is the time to transfer a single data item. Thus, the speedup becomes

$$S_p^{\text{dot}} = \frac{T_1^{\text{dot}}}{T_p^{\text{dot}}} = \frac{p}{1 + (\log_2(p)/2n)(T_{\text{startup}} + T_{\text{word}})/T_{\text{flop}}}. \qquad (5.11)$$

In general, n would have to be much larger than $\log p$ to get a good speedup because $T_{\text{startup}} \gg T_{\text{flop}}$.

5.6 Matrix–vector multiply revisited

In Section 4.8, we discussed the matrix–vector multiply operation on shared memory machines in OpenMP. In the next two sections, we wish to revisit this operation—first in MPI, then again using the PBLAS.

5.6.1 *Matrix–vector multiplication with MPI*

To give more meat to our discussion of Sections 5.3 and 5.4 on data distribution and its importance on distributed memory machines, let us revisit our matrix–vector multiply example of Section 4.8 and give a complete example of MPI programming for the $\mathbf{y} = A\mathbf{x}$ problem. In a distributed memory environment, we first have to determine how to distribute A, $\mathbf{x}$, and $\mathbf{y}$. Assume that $\mathbf{x}$ is an N-vector and $\mathbf{y}$ is an M-vector. Hence A is $M \times N$. These two vectors will be distributed in blocks, as discussed in Section 5.3.2. Row and column block sizes are $b_r = \lceil M/p \rceil$ and $b_c = \lceil N/p \rceil$, respectively. We will call the number of elements actually used by a processor n and m. Clearly, $m = b_r$ and $n = b_c$ except perhaps on the last processor where $m = M - (p-1) \cdot b_r$ and $n = N - (p-1) \cdot b_c$.

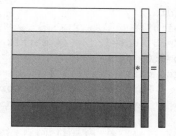

FIG. 5.15. *The data distribution in the matrix–vector product $A * \mathbf{x} = \mathbf{y}$ with five processors. Here the matrix A is square, that is, $M = N$.*

For simplicity, we allocate on each processor the same amount of memory, see the program excerpt in Figure 5.16. We distribute the matrix A in block rows, see Figure 5.15, such that each processor holds a b_r-by-N array of contiguous rows of A. This data layout is often referred to as *1-dimensional (1D) block row distribution* or *strip mining.* so, the rows of A are aligned with the elements of $\mathbf{y}$ meaning that, for all k, the k-th element $\mathbf{y}$ and the k-th row of A reside on the same processor. Again, for simplicity, we allocate an equal amount of data on each processor. Only m rows of A are accessed.

Since each processor owns complete rows of A, each processor needs all of vector $\mathbf{x}$ to form the local portion of $\mathbf{y}$. In MPI, gathering $\mathbf{x}$ on all processors is accomplished by MPI_Allgather. Process j, say, sends its portion of $\mathbf{x}$, stored in x_loc to every other process that stores it in the j-th block of x_glob.

Finally, in a local operation, the local portion of A, A_loc, is multiplied with $\mathbf{x}$ by the invocation of the level-2 BLAS dgemv.

Notice that the matrix vector multiplication changes considerably if the matrix A is distributed instead of in block rows in block *columns*. In this case the local computation precedes the communication phase which becomes a vector reduction.

5.6.2 *Matrix–vector multiply with PBLAS*

As a further and fruitful examination of the MIMD calculation, let us revisit the example of the matrix–vector product, this time using the PBLAS. We are to compute the vector $\mathbf{y} = A\mathbf{x}$ of size M. A, $\mathbf{x}$, and $\mathbf{y}$ are distributed over the two-dimensional process grid previously defined in Figure 5.8. A assumes a true two-dimensional block–cyclic distribution. $\mathbf{x}$ is stored as a $1 \times M$ matrix on the first process row; $\mathbf{y}$ is stored as an $M \times 1$ matrix on the first process column, as in Figure 5.13. Again, it is advantageous to choose block sizes as large as possible, whence the block–cyclic distributions become the simple block distributions of Figure 5.18. Blocks of A have size $\lceil M/p_r \rceil \times \lceil N/p_c \rceil$. The code fragment in Figure 5.17 shows how space is allocated for the three arrays. A has size 15×20.

```
#include <stdio.h>
#include "mpi.h"
int N=374, M=53, one=1;     /* matrix A is  M x N */
double dzero=0.0, done=1.0;
main(int argc, char* argv[]) {
/* matvec.c -- Pure MPI matrix vector product */
    int        myid, p;  /* rank, no. of procs. */
    int        m, mb, n, nb, i, i0, j, j0;
    double     *A, *x_global, *x_local, *y;
    MPI_Init(&argc, &argv);      /* Start up MPI */
    MPI_Comm_rank(MPI_COMM_WORLD, &myid); /* rank */
    MPI_Comm_size(MPI_COMM_WORLD, &p); /* number */
    /* Determine block sizes */
    mb = (M - 1)/p + 1;      /* mb = ceil(M/p)  */
    nb = (N - 1)/p + 1;      /* nb = ceil(N/p)  */
    /* Determine true local sizes */
    m = mb; n = nb;
    if (myid == p-1) m = M - myid*mb;
    if (myid == p-1) n = N - myid*nb;
    /* Allocate memory space */
    A        = (double*) malloc(mb*N*sizeof(double));
    y        = (double*) malloc(mb*sizeof(double));
    x_local  = (double*) malloc(nb*sizeof(double));
    x_global = (double*) malloc(N*sizeof(double));
    /* Initialize matrix  A  and vector  x  */
    for(j=0;j<N;j++)
        for(i = 0; i < m; i++){
            A[i+j*mb] = 0.0;
            if (j == myid*mb+i) A[i+j*mb] = 1.0;
        }
    for(j=0;j<n;j++) x_local[j] = (double)(j+myid*nb);
    /* Parallel matrix - vector multiply */
    MPI_Allgather(x_local, n, MPI_DOUBLE, x_global,
                  nb, MPI_DOUBLE, MPI_COMM_WORLD);
    dgemv_("N", &m, &N, &done, A, &mb, x_global,
          &one, &dzero, y, &one);
    for(i=0;i<m;i++)
        printf("y[%3d] = %10.2f\n", myid*mb+i,y[i]);
    MPI_Finalize();             /* Shut down MPI */
}
```

FIG. 5.16. *MPI matrix–vector multiply with row-wise block-distributed matrix.*

```
int M=15, N=20, ZERO=0, ONE=1;

/* Determine block sizes */
br = (M - 1)/pr + 1;      /* br = ceil(M/pr)  */
bc = (N - 1)/pc + 1;      /* bc = ceil(N/pc)  */
      /* Allocate memory space */
x = (double*) malloc(bc*sizeof(double));
y = (double*) malloc(br*sizeof(double));
A = (double*) malloc(br*bc*sizeof(double));
      /* Determine local matrix sizes and base indices */
i0 = myrow*br;  j0 = mycol*bc;
m = br; n = bc;
if (myrow == pr-1) m = M - i0;
if (mycol == pc-1) n = N - j0;
```

FIG. 5.17. *Block–cyclic matrix and vector allocation.*

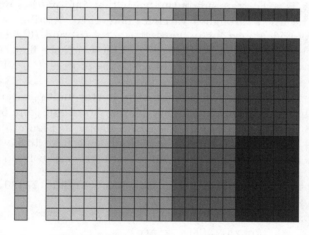

FIG. 5.18. *The* 15×20 *matrix A stored on a* 2×4 *process grid with big blocks together with the 15-vector* **y** *(left) and the 20-vector* **x** *(top).*

By consequence, $b_r = \lceil M/p_r \rceil = \lceil 15/2 \rceil = 8$ and $b_c = \lceil N/p_c \rceil = \lceil 20/4 \rceil = 5$. Thus, a 8×5 matrix is allocated on each processor. But on the last (second) process row only $m = 7$ rows of the local matrices A are used, as in Figure 5.18. On the first process row $m = b_r = 8$. On all processes $n = b_c = 5$. The code fragment is similar to the one in Figure 5.15 where the data are distributed differently. The values i_0 and j_0 hold the *global* indices of the (0,0) element of the local portion of A.

Until this point of our discussion, the processes have only had a local view of the data, matrices and vectors, although the process grid was known. Before a PBLAS or ScaLAPACK routine can be invoked, a global view of the data has to be defined. This is done by **array descriptors**. An array descriptor contains the following parameters:

(1) the number of rows in the distributed matrix (M);
(2) the number of columns in the distributed matrix (N);
(3) the row block size (b_r);
(4) the column block size (b_c);
(5) the process row over which the first row of the matrix is distributed;
(6) the process column over which the first column of the matrix is distributed;
(7) the BLACS context;
(8) the leading dimension of the local array storing the local blocks.

In Figure 5.19 we show how array descriptors are defined by a call to the ScaLAPACK descinit for the example matrix–vector multiplication. Notice that descinit is a Fortran subroutine such that information on the success of the call is returned through a variable, here info. Attributes of the array descriptors are evident, except perhaps attributes (5) and (6). These give the identifiers of those process in the process grid on which the first element of the respective array resides. This cannot always be the process $(0,0)$. This flexibility is particularly important if submatrices are accessed.

All that remains is to do the actual matrix–vector multiplication by a call to the appropriate PBLAS routine pdgemv. This is shown in Figure 5.20.

Notice the similarity to calling the BLAS dgemv in Figure 5.15. However, instead of the single reference to A, *four* arguments have to be transfered to pdgemv: These reference the local portion of A, the row and column indices of the

```
descinit_(descA, &M, &N, &br, &bc, &ZERO, &ZERO,
          &ctxt, &br, &info);
descinit_(descx, &ONE, &N, &ONE, &bc, &ZERO, &ZERO,
          &ctxt, &ONE, &info);
descinit_(descy, &M, &ONE, &br, &ONE, &ZERO, &ZERO,
          &ctxt, &br, &info);
```

FIG. 5.19. *Defining the matrix descriptors.*

```
/* Multiply  y = alpha*A*x + beta*y  */
alpha = 1.0; beta = 0.0;
pdgemv_("N", &M, &N, &alpha, A, &ONE, &ONE, descA,
        x, &ONE, &ONE, descx, &ONE, &beta, y, &ONE,
        &ONE, descy, &ONE);
```

FIG. 5.20. *General matrix–vector multiplication with PBLAS.*

"origin" of the matrix to be worked on (here twice `ONE`), and the corresponding array descriptor. Notice that according to Fortran convention, the first row and column of a matrix have index= 1. Because this is a call to a Fortran routine, this is also true even if one defined the array in **C** starting with index= 0.

5.7 ScaLAPACK

ScaLAPACK routines are parallelized versions of LAPACK routines [12]. In particular, the LAPACK block size equals the block size of the two-dimensional block–cyclic matrix distribution, $b = b_r = b_c$. We again consider the block LU factorization as discussed in Section 2.2.2.2. Three essential steps are needed:

1. The LU factorization of the actual panel. This task requires communication in one process column only for (a) determination of the pivots, and (b) for the exchange of pivot row with other rows.
2. The computation of the actual block row. This requires the broadcast of the $b \times b$ factor L_{11} of the actual pivot block, in a single collective communication step along the pivot row. The broadcast of L_{11} is combined with the broadcast of L_{21} to reduce the number of communication startups.
3. The rank-b update of the remaining matrix. This is the computationally intensive portion of the code. Before computations can start, the pivot block row (U_{12}) has to be broadcast along the process columns.

The complexity of the distributed LU factorization is considered carefully in reference [18]. Let the number of processors be p, arranged in a $p_r \times p_c$ process grid, where $p = p_r \cdot p_c$. Then the execution time for the LU factorization can be estimated by the formula

$$T_{\text{LU}}(p_r, p_c, b) \approx \left(2n \log p_r + 2\frac{n}{b} \log p_c\right) T_{\text{startup}}$$

$$+ \frac{n^2}{2p}(4p_r + p_r \log p_r + p_c \log p_c) T_{\text{word}} + \frac{2n^3}{3} T_{\text{flop}}. \quad (5.12)$$

Again, we have used the variables T_{startup}, T_{word}, and T_{flop} introduced earlier in Section 4.7. The time to send a message of length n from one process to another can be written as

$$T_{\text{startup}} + n \cdot T_{\text{word}}.$$

Formula (5.12) is derived by making simplifying assumptions. In particular, we assumed that a broadcast of n numbers to p processors costs

$$\log_2 p \, (T_{\text{startup}} + n \cdot T_{\text{word}}).$$

In fact, T_{flop} is not constant but depends on the block size b. On our Beowulf cluster, these three quantities are

1. $T_{\text{startup}} \approx 175 \cdot 10^{-6}$ s $= 175$ µs.
2. $T_{\text{word}} \approx 9.9 \cdot 10^{-8}$ s corresponding to a bandwidth of 10.5 MB/s. This means that sending a message of length 2000 takes roughly twice as long as sending only an empty message.
3. $T_{\text{flop}} \approx 2.2 \cdot 10^{-8}$ s. This means that about 8000 floating point operations could be executed at the speed of the LU factorization during T_{startup}. If we compare with the Mflop/s rate that dgemm provides, this number is even higher.

Floating point performance predicted by (5.12) is probably too good for small b because in that case, T_{word} is below average. In deriving the formula, we assumed that the load is balanced. But this not likely to be even approximately true if the block size b is big. In that case, a single process has to do a lot of work near the end of the factorization leading to a severe *load imbalance*. Thus, one must be cautious when using a formula like (5.12) to predict the execution time on a real machine.

Nevertheless, we would like to extract some information from this formula. Notice that the number of process columns p_c has a slightly smaller weight than p_r in the T_{startup} and in the T_{word} term. This is caused by the pivot search that is restricted to a process column. Therefore, it might be advisable to choose the number of process columns p_c slightly bigger than the number of process rows p_r [18]. We have investigated this on our Beowulf cluster. In Table 5.3 we show timings of the ScaLAPACK routine pdgesv that implements the solution of a linear system $A\mathbf{x} = \mathbf{b}$ by Gaussian elimination plus forward and backward substitution. The processor number was fixed to be $p = 36$ but we allowed the size of the process grid to vary. Our Beowulf has dual processor nodes, therefore only 18 nodes were used in these experiments. In fact, we only observe small differences in the timings when we used just one processor on p (dedicated) nodes. Each of the two processors have their own cache but compete for the memory access. Again, this indicates that the BLAS exploit the cache economically. The timings show that it is indeed useful to choose $p_r \leq p_c$. The smaller the problem, the smaller the ratio p_r/p_c should be. For larger problems it is advantageous to have the process grid more square shaped.

In Table 5.4 we present speedup numbers obtained on our Beowulf. These timings should be compared with those from the Hewlett-Packard Superdome, see Table 4.1. Notice that the floating point performance of a single Beowulf processor is lower than the corresponding performance of a single HP processor. This can be seen from the one-processor numbers in these two tables. Furthermore, the interprocessor communication bandwidth is lower on the Beowulf not only in an absolute sense, but also relative to the processor performance. Therefore, the speedups on the Beowulf are very low for small problem sizes. For problem sizes $n = 500$ and $n = 1000$, one may use two or four processors, respectively, for

Table 5.3 *Timings of the ScaLAPACK system solver* pdgesv *on one processor and on 36 processors with varying dimensions of the process grid.*

p_r	p_c	b	Time (s)			
			1440	2880	5760	11,520
1	1	20	27.54	347.6	2537	71,784
2	18	20	2.98	17.5	137	1052
3	12	20	3.04	12.1	103	846
4	9	20	3.49	11.2	359	653
6	6	20	5.45	14.2	293	492
1	1	80	54.60	534.4	2610	56,692
2	18	80	4.69	26.3	433	1230
3	12	80	3.43	18.7	346	1009
4	9	80	4.11	15.7	263	828
6	6	80	5.07	15.9	182	639

Table 5.4 *Times t and speedups $S(p)$ for various problem sizes n and processor numbers p for solving a random system of equations with the general solver* pdgesv *of ScaLAPACK on the Beowulf cluster. The block size for $n \le 1000$ is $b = 32$, the block size for $n > 1000$ is $b = 16$.*

p	$n = 500$		$n = 1000$		$n = 2000$		$n = 5000$	
	$t(s)$	$S(p)$	$t(s)$	$S(p)$	$t(s)$	$S(p)$	$t(s)$	$S(p)$
1	0.959	1	8.42	1.0	121	1	2220	1
2	0.686	1.4	4.92	1.7	47.3	2.7	1262	1.8
4	0.788	1.2	3.16	2.7	17.7	6.9	500	4.4
8	0.684	1.4	2.31	3.7	10.8	11	303	7.3
16	1.12	0.86	2.45	3.4	7.43	16	141	15
32	1.12	0.86	2.27	3.7	6.53	19	48	46

solving the systems of equations. The efficiency drops below 50 percent if more processors are employed. For larger problem sizes, $n \ge 2000$, we observe **superlinear speedups**. These are caused by the fact that the traffic to main memory decreases with an increasing number of processors due to the growing size of the cumulated main memory. They are real effects and can be an important reason for using a large machine.

5.8   MPI two-dimensional FFT example

We now sally forth into a more completely written out example—a two-dimensional FFT. More sophisticated versions for general n exist in packaged software form (FFTW) [55], so we restrict ourselves again to the $n = 2^m$ binary radix case for illustration. For more background, review Section 2.4. The essence of the matter is the independence of row and column transforms: we want

$$y_{p,q} = \sum_{s=0}^{n-1} \sum_{t=0}^{n-1} \omega^{ps+qt} x_{s,t},$$

which we process first by the independent rows, then the independent columns (Z represents a temporary state of x),

$$\forall s : \quad Z_{s,q} = \sum_{t=0}^{n-1} \omega^{qt} x_{s,t},$$

$$\forall q : \quad y_{p,q} = \sum_{s=0}^{n-1} \omega^{ps} Z_{s,q}.$$

In these formulae, $\omega = e^{2\pi i/n}$ is again (see Chapter 2, Section 2.4) the nth root of unity. Instead of trying to parallelize one row or column of the FFT, it is far simpler to utilize the independence of the transforms of each row, or column, respectively. Let us be quite clear about this: in computing the Z_{sq}s, each row (s) is totally independent of every other; while after the Z_{sq}s are computed, each column (q) of y ($y_{*,q}$) may be computed independently. Thus, the simplest parallelization scheme is by strip-mining (Section 5.6). Figure 5.21 illustrates the method. The number of columns in each strip is n/p, where again $p =$ NCPUs,

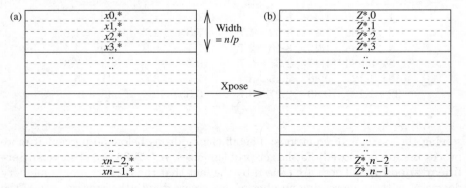

FIG. 5.21. *Strip-mining a two-dimensional FFT. (a) Transform rows of X: $xs,^*$ for $s = 0, \ldots, n-1$ and (b) transform columns of Z: Z^*,q for $q = 0, \ldots, n-1$.*

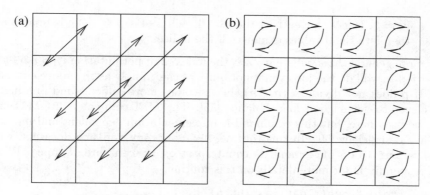

FIG. 5.22. *Two-dimensional transpose for complex data. (a) Global transpose of blocks and (b) local transposes within blocks.*

and each strip is stored on an independent processor. An observant reader will notice that this is fine to transform the columns, but what about the rows? As much as we dislike it, a transposition is required. Worse, two are required if we want the original order. A basic transposition is shown in Figure 5.22 and in the code for Xpose is shown beginning on p. 182. The transposition is first by blocks, each block contains $(n/p) \cdot (n/p)$ complex elements. Diagonal blocks are done in-place, that is on the same processor. Other blocks must be moved to corresponding transposed positions, where they are subsequently locally transposed. The following algorithm works only for $p = 2^q$ processors where $q < m = \log_2(n)$. Let r be the rank of the processor containing the block to be transposed with its corresponding other (as in Figure 5.22); to find other, where $\oplus$ is exclusive or we use a trick shown to one of the authors by Stuart Hawkinson [76] (look for "XOR trick" comment in the Xpose code),

$$
\begin{array}{l}
\text{for} \quad s = 1, \ldots, p-1\{ \\
\quad \text{other} = r \oplus s \\
\quad \text{other block} \leftrightarrow \text{current block} \\
\}.
\end{array}
$$

It is crucial that the number of processors $p = 2^q$. To show this works, two points must be made: (1) the selection other never references diagonal blocks, and (2) the other s values select all the other non-diagonal blocks. Here is a proof:

1. It can only happen that $s \oplus r = r$ if $s = 0$, but the range of s is $s \geq 1$. Therefore $s \oplus r = r$ is excluded.

2. To show that $j = s \oplus r$ exhausts the other values $0 \leq j \leq 2^q - 1$ except $j = r$, expand $s = (s_{q-1}, s_{q-2}, \ldots, s_0)$ where each s_k is a binary digit, that is, 0 or 1. If $s^{(1)} \oplus r = s^{(2)} \oplus r$, since $\oplus$ is exclusive it must be that $s_k^{(1)} = s_k^{(2)}$ for all $0 \leq k \leq q - 1$. For otherwise, by examining the 2^k term, we would need $s_k^{(1)} \oplus r_k = s_k^{(2)} \oplus r_k$ but $s_k^{(1)} \neq s_k^{(2)}$. By writing out the 1-bit $\oplus$ logic tableau, it is clear this cannot happen for either $r_k = 0$ or

$r_k = 1$. Hence, for each of the $2^q - 1$ values of s, $j = s \oplus r$ is unique and therefore the s values exhaust all the indices $j \neq r$.

For more general cases, where $p \neq 2^q$, the index digit permutation $ij = i \cdot p + j \rightarrow ji = j \cdot p + i$ will do the job even if not quite as charmingly as the above exclusive **or**. If p does not divide n $(p \nmid n)$, life becomes more difficult and one has to be clever to get a good load balance [55]. The MPI command `MPI_Alltoall` can be used here, but this command is implementation dependent and may not always be efficient [59]. In this routine, `MPI_Sendrecv_replace` does just what it says: `buf_io` on `other` and its counterpart on `rk=rank` are swapped. Please see Appendix D for more details on this routine.

```
void Xpose(float *a, int n) {
    float t0,t1;
    static float *buf_io;
    int i,ij,is,j,step,n2,nn,size,rk,other;
    static int init=-1;
    MPI_Status stat;
        MPI_Comm_size(MPI_COMM_WORLD, &size);
    MPI_Comm_rank(MPI_COMM_WORLD, &rk);
     /* number of local rows of 2D array */
    nn = n/size;
    n2 = 2*nn;
    if(init!=n){
        buf_io  = (float *)malloc(nn*n2*sizeof(float));
        init    = n;
    }
     /* local transpose of first block (in-place) */
    for(j = 0; j < nn; j ++){
        for(i = 0; i < j; i++) {
            t0 = a[rk*n2+i*2*n+j*2];
            t1 = a[rk*n2+i*2*n+j*2+1];
            a[rk*n2+i*2*n+j*2]   = a[rk*n2+j*2*n+2*i];
            a[rk*n2+i*2*n+j*2+1] = a[rk*n2+j*2*n+2*i+1];
            a[rk*n2+j*2*n+2*i]   = t0;
            a[rk*n2+j*2*n+2*i+1] = t1;
        }
    }
     /* size-1 communication steps */
    for (step = 1; step < size; step ++) {
        other = rk ^ step;           /* XOR trick */
            ij = 0;
        for(i=0;i<nn;i++){           /* fill send buffer */
            is = other*n2 + i*2*n;
            for(j=0;j<n2;j++){
```

```
            buf_io[ij++] = a[is + j];
        }
    }
/* exchange data */
    MPI_Sendrecv_replace(buf_io,2*nn*nn,MPI_FLOAT,
        other,rk,other,other,MPI_COMM_WORLD,&stat);
    /* write back recv buffer in transposed order */
    for(i = 0; i < nn; i ++){
      for(j = 0; j < nn; j ++){
        a[other*n2+j*2*n+i*2] = buf_io[i*n2+j*2];
        a[other*n2+j*2*n+i*2+1] = buf_io[i*n2+j*2+1];
      }
    }
  }
}
```

Using this two-dimensional transposition procedure, we can now write down the two-dimensional FFT itself. From Section 3.6, we use the one-dimensional FFT, cfft2, which assumes that array **w** is already filled with powers of the roots of unity: $\mathbf{w} = \{\exp(2\pi i k/n), \ k = 0, \ldots, n/2 - 1\}$.

```
void FFT2D(float *a,float *w,float sign,int ny,int n)
{
    int i,j,off;
    float *pa;
    void Xpose();
    void cfft2();
        for(i=0;i<ny;i++){
      off = 2*i*n;
      pa  = a + off;
      cfft2(n,pa,w,sign);
    }
    Xpose(a,n);
    for(i=0;i<ny;i++){
      off = 2*i*n;
      pa  = a + off;
      cfft2(n,pa,w,sign);
    }
    Xpose(a,n);
}
```

A machine readable version of this two-dimensional FFT and the following three-dimensional FFT may be downloaded from our **ftp** site [6] with all needed co-routines.

5.9   MPI three-dimensional FFT example

In higher dimensions, the independence of orthogonal directions again makes parallelization conceptually clear. Now, instead of transposing blocks, rectangular parallelepipeds (pencils) are moved. Imagine extending Figure 5.22 into the paper and making a cube of it. The three-dimensional transform is then computed in three stages (corresponding to each x_1, x_2, x_3 direction), parallelizing by indexing the other two directions (arrays $Z^{[1]}$ and $Z^{[2]}$ are temporary):

$$y_{p,q,r} = \sum_{s=0}^{n-1} \sum_{t=0}^{n-1} \sum_{u=0}^{n-1} \omega^{ps+qt+ru} x_{s,t,u},$$

$$\forall s,t: \quad Z^{[1]}_{s,t,r} = \sum_{u=0}^{n-1} \omega^{ru} x_{s,t,u},$$

$$\forall s,r: \quad Z^{[2]}_{s,q,r} = \sum_{t=0}^{n-1} \omega^{qt} Z^{[1]}_{s,t,r},$$

$$\forall q,r: \quad y_{p,q,r} = \sum_{s=0}^{n-1} \omega^{ps} Z^{[2]}_{s,q,r}.$$

Be aware that, as written, the transforms are *un-normalized*. This means that after computing first the above three-dimensional transform, then the inverse ($\omega \to \bar{\omega}$ in the above), the result will equal the input to be scaled by n^3, that is, we get $n^3 x_{s,t,u}$. First we show the transpose, then the three-dimensional code.

```
void Xpose(float *a, int nz, int nx) {
/* 3-D transpose for cubic FFT: nx = the thickness
   of the slabs, nz=dimension of the transform */
  float t0,t1;
  static float *buf_io;
  int i, ijk, j, js, k, step, n2, nb, np, off;
  static int init=-1;
  int size, rk, other;
  MPI_Status stat;

  MPI_Comm_size(MPI_COMM_WORLD, &size);
  MPI_Comm_rank(MPI_COMM_WORLD, &rk);

/* number of local planes of 3D array */
  n2 = 2*nz; np = 2*nx*nx; nb = nz*n2*nx;

  if(init!=nx){
    if(init>0) free(buf_io);
```

```
            buf_io = (float *)malloc(nb*sizeof(float));
            init   = nx;
        }
    /* local transpose of first block (in-place) */
        for(j = 0; j < nx; j++){
            off = j*2*nx + rk*n2;
            for(k = 0; k < nz; k ++){
                for(i = 0; i < k; i++) {
                    t0 = a[off + i*np + k*2];
                    t1 = a[off + i*np + k*2+1];
                    a[off+i*np+k*2]   = a[off+k*np+2*i];
                    a[off+i*np+k*2+1] = a[off+k*np+2*i+1];
                    a[off+k*np+2*i]   = t0;
                    a[off+k*np+2*i+1] = t1;
                }
            }
        }


    /* size-1 communication steps */
        for (step = 1; step < size; step ++) {
            other = rk ^ step;

    /* fill send buffer */
            ijk = 0;
            for(j=0;j<nx;j++){
                for(k=0;k<nz;k++){
                    off = j*2*nx + other*n2 + k*np;
                    for(i=0;i<n2;i++){
                        buf_io[ijk++] = a[off + i];
                    }
                }
            }
/* exchange data */
            MPI_Sendrecv_replace(buf_io,n2*nz*nx,MPI_FLOAT,
                other,rk,other,other,MPI_COMM_WORLD,&stat);

    /* write back recv buffer in transposed order */
            ijk = 0;
            for(j=0;j<nx;j++){
                off = j*2*nx + other*n2;
                for(k=0;k<nz;k++){
                    for(i=0;i<nz;i++){
                        a[off+i*np+2*k]   = buf_io[ijk];
                        a[off+i*np+2*k+1] = buf_io[ijk+1];
```

```
            ijk += 2;
        }
      }
    }
  }
}
```

Recalling `cfft2` from Section 3.5.4, we assume that array w has been initialized with $n/2$ powers of roots of unity ω, $\mathbf{w} = \{\exp(2\pi ik/n), \quad k = 0, \ldots, n/2 - 1\}$, here is the transform itself:

```
void FFT3D(float *a,float *w,float sign,int nz,int nx)
{
    int i,j,k,off,rk;
    static int nfirst=-1;
    static float *pw;
    float *pa;
    void Xpose();
    void cfft2();
        MPI_Comm_rank(MPI_COMM_WORLD,&rk);
    if(nfirst!=nx){
       if(nfirst>0) free(pw);
       pw    = (float *) malloc(2*nx*sizeof(float));
       nfirst = nx;
    }
/* X-direction */
    for(k=0;k<nz;k++){
       off = 2*k*nx*nx;
       for(j=0;j<nx;j++){
          pa = a + off + 2*nx*j;
          cfft2(nx,pa,w,sign);
       }
    }
/* Y-direction */
    for(k=0;k<nz;k++){
       for(i=0;i<nx;i++){
          off = 2*k*nx*nx+2*i;
          for(j=0;j<nx;j++){
             *(pw+2*j)   = *(a+2*j*nx+off);
             *(pw+2*j+1) = *(a+2*j*nx+1+off);
          }
          cfft2(nx,pw,w,sign);
          for(j=0;j<nx;j++){
             *(a+2*j*nx+off)   = *(pw+2*j);
```

```
            *(a+2*j*nx+1+off) = *(pw+2*j+1);
         }
      }
   }
   /* Z-direction */
   Xpose(a,nz,nx);
   for(k=0;k<nz;k++){
      off = 2*k*nx*nx;
      for(j=0;j<nx;j++){
         pa = a + off + 2*nx*j;
         cfft2(nx,pa,w,sign);
      }
   }
   Xpose(a,nz,nx);
}
```

5.10   MPI Monte Carlo (MC) integration example

In this section we illustrate the flexibility to be seen MC simulations on multiple CPUs. In Section 2.5, it was pointed out that the simplest way of distributing work across multiple CPUs in MC simulations is to split the sample into p =NCPUs pieces: $N = p \cdot (N/p)$, and each CPU computes a sample of size N/p. Another approach is a domain decomposition, where various parts of an integration domain are assigned to each processor. (See also Section 2.3.10.4 for another example of domain decomposition.) Integration is an additive procedure:

$$\int_A f(x)\, dx = \sum_i \int_{A_i} f(x)\, dx,$$

so the integration domain can be divided into $A = \cup_i A_i$ disjoint sets $\{A_i\}$, where $A_i \cap A_j = \emptyset$ when $i \neq j$. Very little communication is required. One only has to gather the final partial results (numbered i) and add them up to finish the integral. Beginning on p. 187 we show an example of integration of a more or less arbitrary function $f(x, y)$ over the star-shaped region in Figure 5.23. If f has singularities or very rapid variation in one segment of the domain, obviously these considerations would have to be considered. The star-shaped domain in Figure 5.23 can easily be divided into five pieces, which we assign to five CPUs. To effect uniform sampling on each *point* of the star, we do a little cutting and pasting. Each point has the same area as the center square, so we sample uniformly on a like-area square and rearrange these snips off this square to make the points as in Figure 5.24. Array **seeds** contains a set of initial random number **seeds** (Section 2.5) to prepare independent streams for each processor.

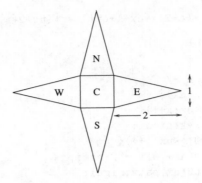

FIG. 5.23. *A domain decomposition MC integration.*

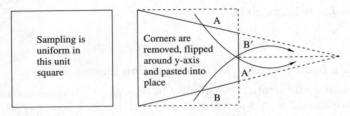

FIG. 5.24. *Cutting and pasting a uniform sample on the points.*

```
#include <stdio.h>
#include <math.h>
#include "mpi.h"
#define NP 10000
/* f(x,y) is any "reasonable" function */
#define f(x,y) exp(-x*x-0.5*y*y)*(10.0*x*x-x)*(y*y-y)
main(int argc, char **argv)
{

/* Computes integral of f() over star-shaped
   region: central square is 1 x 1, each of
   N,S,E,W points are 2 x 1 triangles of same
   area as center square */

   int i,ierr,j,size,ip,master,rank;
/* seeds for each CPU: */
   float seeds[]={331.0,557.0,907.0,1103.0,1303.0};
   float x,y,t,tot;
   static float seed;
   float buff[1];    /* buff for partial sums */
   float sum[4];     /* part sums from "points" */
```

```
    float ggl();        /* random number generator */
    MPI_Status stat;

    MPI_Init(&argc,&argv);    /* initialize MPI */
    MPI_Comm_size(MPI_COMM_WORLD,&size); /* 5 cpus */
    MPI_Comm_rank(MPI_COMM_WORLD,&rank); /* rank */
    master = 0;                          /* master */

    ip = rank;
    if(ip==master){
/* master computes integral over center square */
        tot = 0.0;
        seed   = seeds[ip];
        for(i=0;i<NP;i++){
            x = ggl(&seed)-0.5;
            y = ggl(&seed)-0.5;
            tot += f(x,y);
        }
        tot *= 1.0/((float) NP); /* center part */
    } else {
/* rank != 0 computes E,N,W,S points of star */
        seed   = seeds[ip];
        sum[ip-1] = 0.0;
        for(i=0;i<NP;i++){
            x = ggl(&seed);
            y = ggl(&seed) - 0.5;
            if(y > (0.5-0.25*x)){
                x = 2.0 - x; y = -(y-0.5);
            }
            if(y < (-0.5+0.25*x)){
                x = 2.0 - x; y = -(y+0.5);
            }
            x += 0.5;
            if(ip==2){
                t = x; x = y; y = -t;
            } else if(ip==3){
                x = -x; y = -y;
            } else if(ip==4){
                t = x; x = -y; y = t;
            }
            sum[ip-1] += f(x,y);
        }
        sum[ip-1] *= 1.0/((float) NP);
        buff[0] = sum[ip-1];
```

```
        MPI_Send(buff,1,MPI_FLOAT,0,0,MPI_COMM_WORLD);
    }
    if(ip==master){ /* get part sums of other cpus */
        for(i=1;i<5;i++){
            MPI_Recv(buff,1,MPI_FLOAT,MPI_ANY_SOURCE,
                    MPI_ANY_TAG,MPI_COMM_WORLD,
                &stat);
            tot += buff[0];
        }
        printf(" Integral = %e\n",tot);
    }
    MPI_Finalize();
}
```

5.11   PETSc

In this final section we give a brief summary of the Portable Extensible Toolkit for
Scientific computation (PETSc) [7]–[9]. PETSc is a respectably sized collection
of C routines for solving large sparse linear and nonlinear systems of equations
on parallel (and serial) computers. PETSc's building blocks (or libraries) of data
structures and routines is depicted in Figure 5.25. PETSc uses the MPI standard
for all message-passing communication. Here, we mainly want to experiment with
various preconditioners (from p. 30) that complement PETScs parallel linear
equation solvers.

Each part of the PETSc library manipulates a particular family of objects
(vectors, matrices, Krylov subspaces, preconditioners, etc.) and operations that
can be performed on them. We will first discuss how data, vectors and matrices,

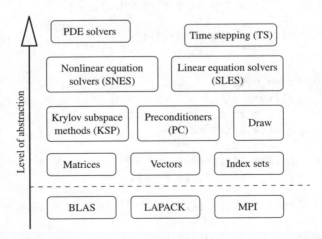

FIG. 5.25. *The PETSc software building blocks.*

are distributed by PETSc. Subsequently, we deal with the invocation of the iterative solvers, after choosing the preconditioner. We will stay close to the examples that are given in the PETSc manual [9] and the tutorial examples that come with the software [7]. The problem that we illustrate is the two-dimensional Poisson equation on a $n \times n$ grid. It is easy enough to understand how this matrix is constructed and distributed. So, we will not be so much concerned about the construction of the matrix but can concentrate on the parallel solvers and preconditioners.

5.11.1 *Matrices and vectors*

On the lowest level of abstraction, PETSc provides matrices, vectors, and index sets. The latter are used for storing permutations originating from reordering due to pivoting or reducing fill-in (e.g. [32]). We do not manipulate these explicitly.

To see how a matrix can be built, look at Figure 5.26. The building of vectors proceeds in a way similar to Figure 5.27. After defining the matrix object A, it is created by the command

MatCreate(MPI_Comm comm, int m, int n, int M, int N, Mat *A).

The default communicator is PETSC_COMM_WORLD defined in an earlier call to PetscInitialize. (Note that PetscInitialize calls MPI_Init and sets

```
Mat  A;            /* linear system matrix */
...
ierr = MatCreate(PETSC_COMM_WORLD,PETSC_DECIDE,
                 PETSC_DECIDE,n*n,n*n,&A);
ierr = MatSetFromOptions(A);

/*   Set up the system matrix  */
ierr = MatGetOwnershipRange(A,&Istart,&Iend);
for (I=Istart; I<Iend; I++) {
    v = -1.0; i = I/n; j = I - i*n;
    if (i>0) {J = I - n;
        ierr = MatSetValues(A,1,&I,1,&J,&v,
                      INSERT_VALUES);
    }
    ...
    v = 4.0;
    ierr = MatSetValues(A,1,&I,1,&I,&v,
                  INSERT_VALUES);
}
ierr = MatAssemblyBegin(A,MAT_FINAL_ASSEMBLY);
ierr = MatAssemblyEnd(A,MAT_FINAL_ASSEMBLY);
```

FIG. 5.26. *Definition and initialization of a $n \times n$ Poisson matrix.*

```
Vec  u;
...
ierr = VecCreate(PETSC_COMM_WORLD,&u);
ierr = VecSetSizes(u,PETSC_DECIDE,n*n);
ierr = VecSetFromOptions(u);
```

FIG. 5.27. *Definition and initialization of a vector.*

PETSC_COMM_WORLD to MPI_COMM_WORLD.) Parameters m and n are the number of local rows and (respectively) columns on the actual processor. Parameters M and N denote the global size of the matrix A. In our example shown in Figure 5.26, PETSc decides on how the matrix is distributed. Matrices in PETSc are always stored *block row-wise* as in Section 5.4. Internally, PETSc also blocks the rows. The usually square diagonal block plays an important role in Jacobi and domain decomposition preconditioners, p. 30. solving the examples in [132]. Two of the three authors of Eispack [133] are the principle designers of PETSc, so PETSc was used for solving the examples in [132]. The column block sizes come into play when a matrix A is multiplied with a vector $\mathbf{x}$. The PETSc function

MatMult(Mat A, Vec x, Vec y), that forms $\mathbf{y} = A\mathbf{x}$, requires that the

column blocks of A match the block distribution of vector $\mathbf{x}$. The vector that stores the matrix–vector product, here $\mathbf{y}$, has to be distributed commensurate with A, that is, their block row distributions have to match.

The invocation of MatSetFromOptions in Figure 5.26 sets the actual matrix format. This format can be altered by runtime options. Otherwise, the default matrix format MPIAIJ is set which denotes a "parallel" matrix which is distributed block row-wise and stored in the CSR format (Section 2.3.9) on the processors.

After the formal definition of A, matrix elements are assigned values. Our example shows the initialization of an $n \times n$ Poisson matrix, that is, by the 5-point stencil [135]. We give the portion of the code that defines the leftmost nonzero off-diagonal and the diagonal. This is done element × element with a call to

MatSetValues(Mat A, int m, int *idxm, int n,
    int *idxn, PetscScalar *vals, InsertMode insmod).

Here vals is an m × n array of values to be inserted into A at the rows and column given by the index vectors idxm and idxn. The InsertMode parameter can either be INSERT_VALUES or ADD_VALUES.

The numbers of the rows that will go on a particular processor are obtained through

MatGetOwnershipRange(Mat A, int *is, int *ie)

It is more economical if the elements are inserted into the matrix by those processors the elements are assigned to. Otherwise, these values have to be transferred to the correct processor. This is done by the pair of commands MatAssemblyBegin and MatAssemblyEnd. These routines bring the matrix into the final format which is designed for matrix operations. The reason for having two functions for assembling matrices is that during the assembly which may involve communication, other matrices can be constructed or computation can take place. This is latency hiding which we have encountered several times, beginning with Chapter 1, Section 1.2.2.

The definition and initialization of the distributed matrix A does not explicitly refer to the number of processors involved. This makes it easier to investigate the behavior of algorithms when the number of processors is varied.

The definition of vectors follows a similar line as the definition of matrices shown in Figure 5.27.

5.11.2 *Krylov subspace methods and preconditioners*

PETSc provides a number of Krylov subspace (Section 2.3.5) procedures for solving linear systems of equations. The default solver is **restarted** GMRES [11]. Here we are solving a symmetric positive definite system, so the preconditioned conjugate gradient algorithm, see Figure 2.6, is more appropriate [129]. In PETSc, a pointer (called a context, Section 5.2) has to be defined in order to access the linear system solver object. The Krylov subspace method [129] and the preconditioner will then be properties of the solver as in Figure 5.28. After the definition of the pointer, sles, the system matrix and the matrix that defines the preconditioner are set. These matrices can be equal if the preconditioner can be extracted from the system matrix, for example, using Jacobi (Section 2.3.2), Gauss–Seidel (GS) (Section 2.3.3), or similar preconditioners, or if the preconditioner is obtained by an incomplete factorization of the system matrix. In this case, PETSc allocates the memory needed to store the preconditioner. The application programmer can help PETSc by providing information on the amount of additional memory needed. This information will enhance performance in the setup phase.

```
/*  Create linear solver context  */
ierr = SLESCreate(PETSC_COMM_WORLD,&sles);

/*   Set operator  */
ierr = SLESSetOperators(sles,A,A,
                        DIFFERENT_NONZERO_PATTERN);

/*   Set Krylov subspace method   */
ierr = SLESGetKSP(sles,&ksp);
ierr = KSPSetType(ksp,KSPCG);
ierr = KSPSetTolerances(ksp,1.e-6,PETSC_DEFAULT,
                        PETSC_DEFAULT,PETSC_DEFAULT);
```

FIG. 5.28. *Definition of the linear solver context and of the Krylov subspace method.*

```
ierr = SLESGetPC(sles,&pc);
ierr = PCSetType(pc,PCJACOBI);
```

FIG. 5.29. *Definition of the preconditioner, Jacobi in this case.*

```
ierr = SLESSolve(sles,b,x,&its);
```

FIG. 5.30. *Calling the PETSc solver.*

If the preconditioner is the simple Jacobi preconditioner, then its definition only requires getting a pointer to the preconditioner and setting its type, as shown in Figure 5.29.

Finally, the PETSc solver is invoked by calling SLESSolve with two input parameters: the solver context, and the right-hand side vector; and two output parameters: the solution vector and the number of iterations (see Figure 5.30). Most of the properties of the linear system solver can be chosen by options [7]–[9].

5.12   Some numerical experiments with a PETSc code

In this section, we discuss a few experiments that we executed on our Beowulf PC cluster for solving the Poisson equation $-\Delta u = f$ on a square domain by using a 5-point finite difference scheme [136]. This equation is simple and we encountered it when discussing the red–black reordering to enhance parallelism when using the GS preconditioner in Chapter 2, Section 2.3.10.3.

In Table 5.5, we list solution times and in parentheses the number of iteration steps to reduce the initial residual by a factor 10^{-16}. Data are listed for three problem sizes. The number of grid points in one axis direction is n, so the number of linear systems is n^2. In consequence, we are solving problems of order 16,129, 65,025, and 261,121 corresponding to $n = 127$, 255, and 511, respectively. In the left-hand column of Table 5.5 is given the data for the conjugate gradient method solution when using a Jacobi preconditioner.

The second column, indicated by "Block Jacobi (1)," the data are obtained using a tridiagonal matrix preconditioner gotten by dropping the outermost two diagonals of the Poisson matrix shown in Figure 2.10. To that end, we assemble this tridiagonal matrix, say M, the same way as in Figure 5.26. However, we now assign the rows to each processor (rank). Here, procs denotes the number of processors involved and myid is the rank of the actual processor (Figure 5.31). These numbers can be obtained by calling MPI functions or the corresponding functions of PETSc. Parameter nlocal is a multiple of n and is equal to blksize on all but possibly the last processor. The function that sets the involved operators, cf. Figure 5.28, then reads

```
ierr = SLESSetOperators(sles,A,M,
                  DIFFERENT_NONZERO_PATTERN);
```

The third column in Table 5.5, indicated by "Block Jacobi (2)," is obtained by replacing M again by A. In this way the whole Poisson matrix is taken

Table 5.5 *Execution times in seconds (iteration steps) for solving an $n^2 \times n^2$ linear system from the two-dimensional Poisson problem using a preconditioned conjugate gradient method.*

n	p	Jacobi	Block Jacobi (1)	Block Jacobi (2)	IC (0)
127	1	2.95 (217)	4.25 (168)	0.11 (1)	5.29 (101)
	2	2.07 (217)	2.76 (168)	0.69 (22)	4.68 (147)
	4	1.38 (217)	1.66 (168)	0.61 (38)	3.32 (139)
	8	1.32 (217)	1.53 (168)	0.49 (30)	3.12 (137)
	16	1.51 (217)	1.09 (168)	0.50 (65)	2.02 (128)
255	1	29.0 (426)	34.6 (284)	0.50 (1)	42.0 (197)
	2	17.0 (426)	22.3 (284)	4.01 (29)	31.6 (263)
	4	10.8 (426)	12.5 (284)	3.05 (46)	20.5 (258)
	8	6.55 (426)	6.91 (284)	2.34 (66)	14.6 (243)
	16	4.81 (426)	4.12 (284)	16.0 (82)	10.9 (245)
	32	4.23 (426)	80.9 (284)	2.09 (113)	21.7 (241)
511	1	230.0 (836)	244.9 (547)	4.1 (1)	320.6 (384)
	2	152.2 (836)	157.3 (547)	36.2 (43)	253.1 (517)
	4	87.0 (836)	86.2 (547)	25.7 (64)	127.4 (480)
	8	54.1 (836)	53.3 (547)	15.1 (85)	66.5 (436)
	16	24.5 (836)	24.1 (547)	21.9 (110)	36.6 (422)
	32	256.8 (836)	17.7 (547)	34.5 (135)	107.9 (427)

```
blksize = (1 + (n-1)/procs)*n;
nlocal = min((myid+1)*blksize,n*n) - myid*blksize;
ierr = MatCreate(PETSC_COMM_WORLD,nlocal,nlocal,
                 n*n,n*n,&A);
```

FIG. 5.31. *Defining PETSc block sizes that coincide with the blocks of the Poisson matrix.*

into account when the diagonal blocks are determined. Thus, the preconditioner changes as the processor number changes. For $p = 1$ we have $M = A$ such that the iteration converges in one iteration step. This shows how much time a direct solution would take. The last column in Table 5.5, indicated by "IC (0)" is from an incomplete Cholesky factorization preconditioner with zero fill-in as discussed in Section 2.3.10.5. To use this preconditioner, the matrices have to be stored in the MPIRowbs format,

```
ierr = MatCreateMPIRowbs(PETSC_COMM_WORLD,
             PETSC_DECIDE, n*n, PETSC_DEFAULT,
             PETSC_NULL, &A);
```

The `MPIRowbs` matrix format is the format that BlockSolve95 [82] uses to store matrices. PETSc can compute incomplete Cholesky factorizations, but only the diagonal blocks. In contrast, BlockSolve95 provides a global ICC factorization that we want to exploit here. PETSc provides an interface to BlockSolve95 that is accessible just through the above command. To run the code, we have to indicate to BlockSolve95 that our system is a *scalar system*, meaning that there is one degree of freedom per grid point. This can be done by the option `-mat_rowbs_no_inode` which can also be set by

```
PetscOptionsSetValue("-mat_rowbs_no_inode",0);
```

This statement has to appear after `PetscInitialize()` but before any other PETSc command.

Now let us look more closely at the numbers in Table 5.5. The first two columns show preconditioners that do not depend on the processor number. Therefore the iteration counts are constant for a problem size. With both Jacobi and Block Jacobi (1), the iteration count increases in proportion to the number of grid points n in each space dimension. Notice that $1/n$ is the mesh width. In the cases Block Jacobi (2) and IC (0), the preconditioners depend on the processor number, so the iteration count also changes with p. Clearly, with Block Jacobi (2), the preconditioner gets weaker as p grows, so the iteration count increases. With IC (0) the iteration count stays relatively constant for one problem size. The incomplete factorization is determined not only by matrix A but also by p. Communication issues must also be taken into account.

As with dense systems, the speedups are little with small problem sizes. While a problem size 16,129 may be considered large in the dense case, this is not so for sparse matrices. For example, the matrix A for $n = 127$ only has about $5 \cdot 127^2 = 80{,}645$ nonzero elements, while in the smallest problem size one might justify the use of up to 4 processors, but for the larger problems up to 16 processors still give increasing speedups. Recall that we used only one processor of the dual processor nodes of our Beowulf. The execution times for $p \leq 16$ were obtained on processors from one frame of 24 processors. Conversely, the times with 32 processors involved the interframe network with lower (aggregated) bandwidth. At some places the loss in performance when going from 16 to 32 processors is huge while at others it is hardly noticeable.

The execution times indicate that on our Beowulf the Block Jacobi (2) preconditioner worked best. It takes all of the local information into account and does the most it can with it, that is, does a direct solve. This clearly gave the lowest iteration counts. IC (0) is not as efficient in reducing the iteration counts, but of course it requires much less memory than Block Jacobi (2). On the other hand, IC (0) does not reduce the iteration numbers so much that it can compete with the very simple Jacobi and Block Jacobi (1) preconditioners.

In summary, on a machine with a weak network, it is important to reduce communications as much as possible. This implies that the number of iterations needed to solve a problem should be small. Of the four preconditioners that we illustrate here, the one that consumes the most memory but makes the most out of the local information performed best.

Exercise 5.1 Effective bandwidth test   From Pallas,

http://www.pallas.com/e/products/pmb/download.htm,

download the EFF_BW benchmark test. See Section 4.2 for a brief description of EFF_BW, in particular, Figures 4.3 and 4.4. Those figures are given for the HP9000 cluster, a shared memory machine. However, the EFF_BW test uses MPI, so is completely appropriate for a distributed memory system. *What is to be done?* Unpack the Pallas EFF_BW test, edit the makefile for your machine, and construct the benchmark. Run the test for various message lengths, different numbers of CPUs, and determine: (1) the bandwidth for various message sizes, and (2) the latency just to do the handshake, that is, extrapolate to zero message length to get the latency.

Exercise 5.2 Parallel MC integration   In Section 5.10 is described a parallel MC numerical integration of an arbitrary function $f(x, y)$ for five CPUs. Namely, for the star-shaped region, each contribution—the central square and four points of the star—is computed on a different processor. A copy of the code can be downloaded from our website, the filename is Chapter5/uebung5.c:

www.inf.ethz.ch/~arbenz/book

What is to be done? In this exercise, we would like you to modify this code in several ways:

1. To test the importance of independent random number streams:

   (a) noting the commented seeds for each cpu line in the code, you can see five random number seeds, 331, 557, etc. This is crude and the numbers are primes. Change these to almost anything other than zero, however, and look for effects on the resulting integration.

   (b) In fact, try the same seed on each processor and see if there are any noticeable effects on the integration result.

   (c) What can you conclude about the importance of independent streams for a numerical integration? Integration is an additive process, so there is little communication.

2. By closer examination of Figure 5.24, find a modification to further subdivide each independent region. There are some hints below on how to do this. Modify the code to run on 20 processors. Our Beowulf machine is a perfect platform for these tests.

3. Again run the integration on 20 CPUs and compare your results with the 5-CPU version. Also, repeat the test for dependence on the random number streams.

Hint: To modify the code for 20 CPUs, refer to Figure 5.24. The points of the star, labeled N,S,E,W, were done with cut and paste. We used the following initial sampling for these points:

$$x = \text{ran3} - \tfrac{1}{2}, \qquad y = \text{ran3} - \tfrac{1}{2}.$$

The corners of the distribution were cut, rotated around the y-axis, and shifted up or down and inserted into place to make the triangles. The **N,W,** and **S** points are simply rotations of the **E**-like sample in Figure 5.24:

$$\left(\begin{array}{c} x' \\ y' \end{array} \right) = \left(\begin{array}{cc} \cos(\theta) & \sin(\theta) \\ -\sin(\theta) & \cos(\theta) \end{array} \right) \left(\begin{array}{c} x \\ y \end{array} \right),$$

where $\theta = \pi/2, \pi, 3\pi/2$ respectively. The **points** of the star-shaped region were indexed by **rank**$= 1, 2, 3, 4$ in counterclockwise order. The central region can be simply subdivided into four equal squares, each sampled analogous to the (x, y) sampling above. To do the *points*, dividing the base $= 1$, length $= 2$ triangles into four similar ones is an exercise in plane geometry. However, you may find the algebra of shifts and rotations a little messy. Checking your result against the 5-CPU version is but one way to test your resulting code. Reference: P. Pacheco [115].

Exercise 5.3   Solving partial differential equations by MC: Part II In Chapter 2, Exercise 2.1, was given a solution method for solving elliptic partial differential equations by an MC procedure. Using your solution to that exercise, the current task is to parallelize the method using MPI. *What is to be done?*

1. Starting with your solution from Chapter 2, the simplest parallelization procedure is to compute multiple initial **x** values in parallel. That is, given **x** to start the random walk, a solution $u(\mathbf{x})$ is computed. Since each **x** is totally independent of any other, you should be able to run several different **x** values each on a separate processor.

2. Likewise, either as a Gedanken experiment or by writing a PBS script, you should be able to imagine that several batch jobs each computing a different $u(\mathbf{x})$ value is also a perfectly sensible way to do this in parallel. After all, no **x** value computation communicates with any other.

Exercise 5.4   Matrix–vector multiplication with the PBLAS The purpose of this exercise is to initialize distributed data, a matrix and two vectors, and to actually use one of the routines of the parallel BLAS. We have indicated in Section 5.6 how the matrix–vector product is implemented in PBLAS, more information can be found in the ScaLAPACK users guide [12] which is available on-line, too.

What is to be done?

Initialize a $pr \times pc$ process grid as square as possible, cf. Figure 5.8, such that $pr \cdot pc = p$, the number of processors that you want to use. Distribute a 50×100

matrix, say A, in a cyclic blockwise fashion with 5×5 blocks over the process grid. Initialize the matrix such that

$$a_{i,j} = |i - j|.$$

Distribute the vector $\mathbf{x}$ over the first row of the process grid, and initialize it such that $x_i = (-1)^i$. The result shall be put in vector $\mathbf{y}$ that is distributed over the first column of the process grid. You do not need to initialize it.

Then call the PBLAS matrix–vector multiply, pdgemv, to compute $\mathbf{y} = A\mathbf{x}$. If all went well, the elements in $\mathbf{y}$ have all equal value.

Hints

- Use the tar file Chapter 5/uebung6a.tar as a starting point for your work. It contains a skeleton and a make file which is necessary for correct compilation. We included a *new* qsub_mpich which you should use for submission. Check out the parameter list by just calling qsub_mpich (without parameters) before you start. Note that your C code is supposed to read and use those parameters.

Exercise 5.5   Solving $A\mathbf{x} = \mathbf{b}$ using ScaLAPACK   This exercise continues the previous Exercise 5.4, but now we want to solve a system of equation whose right hand side is from the matrix–vector product. So, the matrix A must be square $(n \times n)$ and nonsingular and the two vectors $\mathbf{x}$ and $\mathbf{y}$ have the same length n. To make things simple initialize the elements of A by randomly (e.g. by rand) except the diagonal elements that you set to n. Set all elements of $\mathbf{x}$ equal to one.

What is to be done?

Proceed as in the previous Exercise 5.4 to get $\mathbf{y} = A\mathbf{x}$. Then call the ScaLAPACK subroutine pdgesv to solve $A\mathbf{x} = \mathbf{y}$. Of course, this should give back the vector $\mathbf{x}$ you started from. Check this by an appropriate function that you find in Table 5.2.

Exercise 5.6   Distribute a matrix by a master–slave procedure   In the examples before, each processor computed precisely those entries of the matrix A that it needs to store for the succeeding computation. Now, we assume that the matrix is read by the "master" process 0 from a file and distributed to the other processes 1 to p, the "slaves."

What is to be done?

Write a function (using MPI primitives) that distributes the data from process rank zero to all involved processes. You are given the numbers pr, pc, br, bc, and N, a two-dimensional array Aglob[N][N] and finally an array bglob[N] containing the data to be spread.

Try not to waste much memory on the different processes for the local storage. ScaLAPACK requires that all the local memory blocks are of the same size. Consult the manual and the example.

Hints

(a) Use the tar file `Chapter5/uebung6.tar` as a starting point for your work. It contains a skeleton and a make file which is necessary for correct compilation. We included a *new* `qsub_mpich` which you should use for submission. Check out the parameter list by just calling `qsub_mpich` (without parameters) before you start. Note that your **C** code is supposed to read and use those parameters.

(b) The manuals, reference cards and source code needed for this assignment (`uebung6.tar`) can be downloaded from our website [6].

Exercise 5.7   More of ScaLAPACK   This is a follow-up of Exercise 5.5. The subroutine `pdgesv` for solving the systems of equations calls the subroutine `pdgetrf` for the factorization and the subroutine `pdgetrs` for forward and backward substitution. Measure the execution times and speedups of `pdgetrf` and `pdgetrs` separately. Why are they so different?

APPENDIX A

SSE INTRINSICS FOR FLOATING POINT

A.1 Conventions and notation

Intel **icc** Compiler version 4.0 names reflect the following naming conventions: an "_mm" prefix indicates an SSE2 vector operation, and is followed by a plain spelling of the operation or the actual instruction's mnemonic. Suffixes indicating datatype are: **s** = scalar, **p** = packed (means full vector), **i** = integer with **u** indicating "unsigned." Datatypes are _m128, a vector of four 32-bit floating point words or two 64-bit double precision words, and _m64 is a vector of four 16-bit integers or two 32-bit integers. The set below is not a complete set of the intrinsics: only those relevant to single precision floating point operations are listed. The complete set of intrinsics is given in the primary reference [27], in particular volume 3. The other two volumes contain more detailed information on the intrinsic to hardware mappings.

Compilation of **C** code using these intrinsics requires the Intel **icc** compiler, available from their web-site [24]. This compiler does some automatic vectorization and users are advised to turn on the diagnostics via the -vec_report switch:

$$\text{icc -O3 -axK -vec\_report3 yourjob.c -lm.}$$

Very important: On Intel Pentium III, 4, and Itanium chips, bit ordering is **little endian**. This means that bits (and bytes, and words in vectors) in a datum are numbered from right to left: the least significant bit is numbered 0 and the numbering increases as the bit significance increases toward higher order.

A.2 Boolean and logical intrinsics

- _m128 _mm_andnot_ps(_m128, _m128)
  Synopsis: Computes the bitwise AND–NOT of four operand pairs. d = _mm_andnot_ps(a,b) computes, for $i = 0, \ldots, 3$, the **and** of the complement of a_i and b_i: $d_i \leftarrow \neg \, a_i$ **and** b_i. That is, where $\mathbf{a} = (a_3, a_2, a_1, a_0)$ and $\mathbf{b} = (b_3, b_2, b_1, b_0)$, the result is

  $$\mathbf{d} \leftarrow (\neg \, a_3 \text{ and } b_3, \neg \, a_2 \text{ and } b_2, a_1 \text{ and } b_1, \neg \, a_0 \text{ and } b_0).$$

- _m128 _mm_or_ps(_m128, _m128)

Synopsis: Vector bitwise **or** of four operand pairs. d = _mm_or_ps(a,b) computes, for $i = 0, \ldots, 3$, the **or** of a_i and b_i: $d_i \leftarrow a_i$ **or** b_i. That is,

$$\mathbf{d} \leftarrow \mathbf{a} \textbf{ or } \mathbf{b}.$$

- _m128 _mm_shuffle_ps(_m128, _m128, unsigned int)
  Synopsis: Vector shuffle of operand pairs. d = _mm_shuffle_ps(a,b,c) selects any two of the elements of **a** to set the lower two words of **d**; likewise, any two words of **b** may be selected and stored into the upper two words of **d**. The selection mechanism is encoded into c. The first bit pair sets d_0 from **a**, the second bit pair sets d_1 from **a**, the third bit pair sets d_2 from **b**, and the fourth bit pair sets d_3 from **b**. For example, c = _MM_SHUFFLE(2,3,0,1) = 0xb1 = 10 11 00 01 selects (remember little endian goes right to left):

  element 01 of **a** for d_0: $d_0 \leftarrow a_1$
  element 00 of **a** for d_1: $d_1 \leftarrow a_0$
  element 11 of **b** for d_2: $d_2 \leftarrow b_3$
  element 10 of **b** for d_3: $d_3 \leftarrow b_2$

with the result that $\mathbf{d} \leftarrow (b_2, b_3, a_0, a_1)$, where $\mathbf{d} = (d_3, d_2, d_1, d_0)$. As a second example, using the same shuffle encoding as above ($c = 0xb1$), z = _mm_shuffle_ps(y,y,c) gives $\mathbf{z} \leftarrow (y_2, y_3, y_0, y_1)$, the gimmick we used to turn the real and imaginary parts around in Figure 3.22.

A final set of comparisons return integers and test only low order pairs. The general form for these is as follows.

- int _mm_ucomi**br**_ss(_m128, _m128)
  Synopsis: Vector binary relation (**br**) comparison of low order operand pairs. d = _mm_**br**_ps(a,b) tests a_0 **br** b_0. If the binary relation **br** is satisfied, one (1) is returned; otherwise zero (0).

The set of possible binary relations (**br**) is shown in Table A.1.

- _m128 _mm_xor_ps(_m128, _m128)
  Synopsis: Vector bitwise exclusive or (**xor**). d = _mm_xor_ps(a,b) computes, for $i = 0, \ldots, 3$, $d_i \leftarrow a_i \oplus b_i$. That is,

$$\mathbf{d} \leftarrow \mathbf{a} \oplus \mathbf{b}.$$

A.3   Load/store operation intrinsics

- _m128 _mm_load_ps(float*)
  Synopsis: Load Aligned Vector Single Precision, d = _mm_load_ps(a) loads, for $i = 0, \ldots, 3$, a_i into d_i: $d_i \leftarrow a_i$. Pointer a must be 16-byte aligned. See Section 1.2, and particularly Section 3.19: this alignment is very important.

Table A.1 *Available binary relations for the* _mm_comp**br**_ps *and* _mm_comp**br**_ss *intrinsics. Comparisons 1 through 6,* **eq**, **lt**, **le**, **gt**, **ge**, *and* **neq** *are the only ones available for* _mm_comi**br** *collective comparisons. It should be noted that* **eq** *is nearly the same as* **unord** *except that the results are different if one operand is NaN [114].*

Binary relation **br**	Description	Mathematical expression	Result if operand NaN
eq	Equality	$\mathbf{a} = \mathbf{b}$	False
lt	Less than	$\mathbf{a} < \mathbf{b}$	False
le	Less than or equal	$\mathbf{a} \leq \mathbf{b}$	False
gt	Greater than	$\mathbf{a} > \mathbf{b}$	False
ge	Greater than or equal	$\mathbf{a} \geq \mathbf{b}$	False
neq	Not equal	$\mathbf{a} \neq \mathbf{b}$	True
nge	Not greater than or equal	$\mathbf{a} < \mathbf{b}$	True
ngt	Not greater than	$\mathbf{a} \leq \mathbf{b}$	True
nlt	Not less than	$\mathbf{a} \geq \mathbf{b}$	True
nle	Not less than or equal	$\mathbf{a} > \mathbf{b}$	True
ord	One is larger	$\mathbf{a} \lessgtr \mathbf{b}$	False
unord	Unordered	$\neg\,(\mathbf{a} \lessgtr \mathbf{b})$	True

- `void _mm_store_ps(float*, _m128)`
  Synopsis: Store Vector of Single Precision Data to Aligned Location, `_mm_store_ps(a,b)` stores, for $i = 0, \ldots, 3$, b_i into a_i: $a_i \leftarrow b_i$. Pointer a must be 16-byte aligned. See Section 1.2, and particularly Section 3.19: this alignment is very important.
- `_m128 _mm_movehl_ps(_m128, _m128)`
  Synopsis: Move High to Low Packed Single Precision, `d = _mm_movehl_ps (a,b)` moves the two low order words of **b** into the high order position of **d** and extends the two low order words of **a** into low order positions of **d**. That is, where $\mathbf{a} = (a_3, a_2, a_1, a_0)$ and $\mathbf{b} = (b_3, b_2, b_1, b_0)$, `_mm_movehl_ps(a,b)` sets $\mathbf{d} \leftarrow (a_3, a_2, b_3, b_3)$.
- `_m128 _mm_loadh_pi(_m128, _m64*)`
  Synopsis: Load High Packed Single Precision, `d = _mm_loadh_ps(a,p)` sets the two upper words of **d** with the 64 bits of data loaded from address p and passes the two low order words of **a** to the low order positions of **d**. That is, where the contents of the two words beginning at the memory location pointed to by p are (b_1, b_0) and $\mathbf{a} = (a_3, a_2, a_1, a_0)$, then `_mm_loadh_ps(a,p)` sets $\mathbf{d} \leftarrow (b_1, b_0, a_1, a_0)$.
- `void _mm_storeh_pi(_m64*, _m128)`
  Synopsis: Store High Packed Single Precision, `_mm_storeh_ps(p,b)` stores the two upper words of **b** into memory beginning at the address p. That is, if $\mathbf{b} = (b_3, b_2, b_1, b_0)$, then `_mm_storeh_ps(p,b)` stores (b_3, b_2) into the memory locations pointed to by p.

- _m128 _mm_loadl_pi(_m128, _m64*)

  Synopsis: Load Low Packed Single Precision, d = _mm_loadl_ps(a,p) sets the two lower words of **d** with the 64 bits of data loaded from address p and passes the two high order words of **a** to the high order positions of **d**. That is, where the contents of the two words beginning at the memory location pointed to by p are (b_1, b_0) and $\mathbf{a} = (a_3, a_2, a_1, a_0)$, then _mm_loadl_ps(a,p) sets $\mathbf{d} \leftarrow (a_3, a_2, b_1, b_0)$.

- void _mm_storel_pi(_m64*, _m128)

  Synopsis: Store Low Packed Single Precision, _mm_storel_ps(p,b) stores the two lower words of **b** into memory beginning at the address p. That is, if $\mathbf{b} = (b_3, b_2, b_1, b_0)$, then _mm_storel_ps(p,b) stores (b_1, b_0) into the memory locations pointed to by p.

- _m128 _mm_load_ss(float*)

  Synopsis: Load Low Scalar Single Precision, d = _mm_load_ss(p) loads the lower word of **d** with the 32 bits of data from address p and zeros the three high order words of **d**. That is, if the content of the memory location at p is b, then _mm_load_ss(p) sets $\mathbf{d} \leftarrow (0, 0, 0, b)$.

- void _mm_store_ss(float*, _m128)

  Synopsis: Store Low Scalar Single Precision, _mm_store_ss(p,b) stores the low order word of **b** into memory at the address p. That is, if $\mathbf{b} = (b_3, b_2, b_1, b_0)$, then _mm_store_ss(p,b) stores b_0 into the memory location pointed to by p.

- _m128 _mm_move_ss(_m128, _m128)

  Synopsis: Move Scalar Single Precision, d = _mm_move_ss(a,b) moves the low order word of **b** into the low order position of **d** and extends the three high order words of **a** into **d**. That is, where $\mathbf{a} = (a_3, a_2, a_1, a_0)$ and $\mathbf{b} = (b_3, b_2, b_1, b_0)$, _mm_move_ss(a,b) sets $\mathbf{d} \leftarrow (a_3, a_2, a_1, b_0)$.

- _m128 _mm_loadu_ps(float*)

  Synopsis: Load Unaligned Vector Single Precision, d = _mm_loadu_ps(a) loads, for $i = 0, \ldots, 3$, a_i into d_i: $d_i \leftarrow a_i$. Pointer a need not be 16-byte aligned. See Section 1.2, and particularly Section 3.19.

- void _mm_storeu_ps(float*, _m128)

  Synopsis: Store Vector of Single Precision Data to Unaligned Location, _mm_storeu_ps(a,b) stores, for $i = 0, \ldots, 3$, b_i into a_i: $a_i \leftarrow b_i$. Pointer a need not be 16-byte aligned. See Section 1.2, and particularly Section 3.19.

- _m128 _mm_unpackhi_ps(_m128, _m128)

  Synopsis: Interleaves two upper words, d = _mm_unpackhi_ps(a,b) selects (a_3, a_2) from **a** and (b_3, b_2) from **b** and interleaves them. That is d = _mm_unpackhi_ps(a,b) sets $\mathbf{d} \leftarrow (b_3, a_3, b_2, a_2)$.

- _m128 _mm_unpacklo_ps(_m128, _m128)

  Synopsis: Interleaves the two lower words, d = _mm_unpacklo_ps(a,b) selects (a_1, a_0) from **a** and (b_1, b_0) from **b** and interleaves them. That is d = _mm_unpacklo_ps(a,b) sets $\mathbf{d} \leftarrow (b_1, a_1, b_0, a_0)$.

There is a final set of load/store intrinsics which are said to be **composite**, which says that they cannot be mapped onto single hardware instructions. They are, however extremely useful and we have used them in Figure 3.22.

- `__m128 __mm_set_ps1(float)`
  Synopsis: Sets the four floating point elements to the same scalar input, d = `__mm_set_ps1(a)` sets $\mathbf{d} \leftarrow (a, a, a, a)$.
- `__m128 __mm_set_ps(float,float,float,float)`
  Synopsis: Sets the four floating point elements to the array specified, d = `__mm_set_ps(a3,a2,a1,a0)` sets $\mathbf{d} \leftarrow (a3, a2, a1, a0)$.
- `__m128 __mm_setr_ps(float,float,float,float)`
  Synopsis: Sets the four floating point elements to the array specified, but in reverse order: d = `__mm_set_ps(a3,a2,a1,a0)` sets $\mathbf{d} \leftarrow (a0, a1, a2, a3)$.
- `__m128 __mm_setzero_ps(void)`
  Synopsis: Sets four elements to zero, d = `__mm_setzero_ps()` sets $\mathbf{d} \leftarrow (0, 0, 0, 0)$.
- `__m128 __mm_load_ps1(float*)`
  Synopsis: Sets the four floating point elements to a scalar taken from memory, d = `__mm_load_ps1(p)` sets $\mathbf{d} \leftarrow (*p, *p, *p, *p)$.
- `__m128 __mm_loadr_ps(float*)`
  Synopsis: Sets the four floating point elements to a vector of elements taken from memory, but in reverse order. d = `__mm_loadr_ps1(p)` sets $\mathbf{d} \leftarrow (*p, *(p + 1), *(p + 2), *(p + 3))$.
- `void __mm_store_ps1(float*, __m128)`
  Synopsis: Stores low order word into four locations, `__mm_store_ps1(p,a)` stores a_0 into locations p+3,p+2,p+1,p. That is, p[3] = a[0], p[2] = a[0], p[1] = a[0], p[0] = a[0].
- `void __mm_storer_ps(float*, __m128)`
  Synopsis: Stores four floating point elements into memory, but in reverse order: `__mm_storer_ps(p,b)` sets p[3] = a[0], p[2] = a[1], p[1] = a[2], p[0] = a[3].

A.4 Vector comparisons

The general form for comparison operations using binary relations is as follows.

- `__m128 __mm_cmpbr_ps(__m128, __m128)`
  Synopsis: Test Binary Relation **br**, d = `__mm_cmpbr_ps(a, b)` tests, for $i = 0, \ldots, 3$, a_i **br** b_i, and if the **br** relation is satisfied $d_i = $ **all 1s**; $d_i = \mathbf{0}$ otherwise.

The binary relation **br** must be one of those listed in Table A.1.
  For example, if **br** is **lt** (less than),

- `__m128 __mm_cmplt_ps(__m128, __m128)`

Synopsis: Compare for Less Than, d = _mm_cmplt_ps(a,b) compares, for each $i = 0, \ldots, 3$, the pairs (a_i, b_i), and sets $d_i = $ **all 1s** if $a_i < b_i$; otherwise $d_i = \mathbf{0}$.

A.5   Low order scalar in vector comparisons

Other comparisons, with suffix **ss** compare low order scalar elements within a vector. Table A.1 indicates which **br** binary relations are available for **ss** suffix comparisons.As an example of an **ss** comparison, if **br** is less than ($<$),

- _m128 _mm_cmplt_ss(_m128, _m128)
  Synopsis: Compare Scalar Less Than, d = _mm_cmplt_ss(a,b) computes a mask of 32-bits in d_0: if low order pair $a_0 < b_0$, the $d_0 = $ **all 1s**; otherwise $d_0 = \mathbf{0}$. That is, if $\mathbf{a} = (a_3, a_2, a_1, a_0)$ and $\mathbf{b} = (b_3, b_2, b_1, b_0)$, then _mm_cmplt_ss(a,b) only compares the (a_0, b_0) pair for less than, and sets only d_0 accordingly. The other elements of **a** and **b** are not compared and the corresponding elements of **d** are not reset.

The general form for these **ss** comparisons is as follows.

- _m128 _mm_cmp**br**_ss(_m128, _m128)
  Synopsis: Compare Scalar binary relation, d = _mm_cmp**br**_ss(a,b) computes a mask of 32-bits in d_0: if the low order pair a_0 **br** b_0, then $d_0 = $ **all 1s**; otherwise $d_0 = \mathbf{0}$. The remaining elements of **a** and **b** are not compared and the higher order elements of **d** are not reset.

A.6   Integer valued low order scalar in vector comparisons

Comparisons labeled comi, with suffix **ss** also only compare low order scalar elements within a vector. The first six entries in Table A.1 indicate which **br** binary relations are available for comi **ss** suffix comparisons.

The general form for these comi **ss** comparisons is as follows.

- int int_mm_comi**br**_ss(_m128, _m128)
  Synopsis: Scalar binary relation (**br**), d = int_mm_comi**br**_ss(a,b) compares the low order pair with binary relation **br** and if a_0 **br** b_0, then $d = 1$; otherwise $d = 0$.

For example, if **br** is **ge** (greater than or equal), then d = int_mm_comige_ss(a,b) compares the low order pair (a_0, b_0) and if $a_0 \geq b_0$ then $d = 1$; otherwise $d = 0$ is returned.

A.7   Integer/floating point vector conversions

- _m128 _mm_cvt_pi2ps(_m128, _m64)
  Synopsis: Packed Signed Integer to Packed Floating Point Conversion, d = _mm_cvt_pi2ps(a,b) converts the two 32-bit integers in **b** into two 32-bit

floating point words and returns the result in **d**. The high order words of **a** are passed to **d**. That is, if __m64 vector **b** = (b_1, b_0) and __m128 vector **a** = (a_3, a_2, a_1, a_0), then **d** = $(a_3, a_2, (float)b_1, (float)b_0)$.

- __m64 _mm_cvt_ps2pi(__m128)
  Synopsis: Packed Floating Point to Signed Integer Conversion, d = _mm_cvt_ps2pi_ss(a) converts the two low order 32-bit floating point words in **a** into two 32-bit integer words in the current rounding mode and returns the result in **d**. The two high order words of **a** are ignored. That is, if the __m128 vector is **a** = (a_3, a_2, a_1, a_0), then __m64 vector **d** = $((int)a_1, (int)a_0)$.

- __m128 _mm_cvt_si2ss(__m128, int)
  Synopsis: Scalar Signed Integer to Single Floating Point Conversion, d = _mm_cvt_si2ss(a,b) converts the 32-bit signed integer b to a single precision floating point entry which is stored in the low order word d_0. The three high order elements of **a**, (a_3, a_2, a_1) are passed through into **d**. That is, if the __m128 vector **a** = (a_3, a_2, a_1, a_0), then **d** $\leftarrow$ $(a_3, a_2, a_1, (float)b)$.

- int _mm_cvt_ss2si(__m128)
  Synopsis: Scalar Single Floating Point to Signed Integer Conversion, d = _mm_cvt_ss2si(a) converts the low order 32-bit floating point element a_0 to a signed integer result d with truncation. If **a** = (a_3, a_2, a_1, a_0), then $d \leftarrow (int)a_0$.

- __m64 _mm_cvt_ps2pi(__m128)
  Synopsis: Packed Single Precision to Packed Integer Conversion, d = _mm_cvt_ps2pi(a) converts the two lower order single precision floating point elements of **a** into two integer 32-bit integers with truncation. These are stored in **d**. That is, if the __m128 vector **a** = (a_3, a_2, a_1, a_0), then (d_1, d_0) = **d** $\leftarrow$ $((int)a_1, (int)a_0)$.

- int _mm_cvt_ss2si(__m128)
  Synopsis: Scalar Single Floating Point to Signed Integer Conversion, d = _mm_cvt_ss2si(a) converts the low order 32-bit floating point element a_0 to a signed integer result d using the current rounding mode. If **a** = (a_3, a_2, a_1, a_0), then $d \leftarrow (int)a_0$.

A.8 Arithmetic function intrinsics

- __m128 _mm_add_ps(__m128, __m128)
  Synopsis: Add Four Floating Point Values, d = _mm_add_ps(a,b) computes, for $i = 0, \ldots, 3$, the sums $d_i = a_i + b_i$.

- __m128 _mm_add_ss(__m128, __m128)
  Synopsis: Add lowest numbered floating point elements, pass remaining from the first operand. d = _mm_add_ss(a,b) computes $a_0 + b_0$ and passes remaining a_is to **d**. That is, where **a** = (a_3, a_2, a_1, a_0) and **b** = (b_3, b_2, b_1, b_0), the result is **d** $\leftarrow$ $(a_3, a_2, a_1, a_0 + b_0)$.

- _m128 _mm_div_ps(_m128, _m128)
  Synopsis: Vector Single Precision Divide, d = _mm_div_ps(a,b) computes
  $\mathbf{d} \leftarrow (a_3/b_3, a_2/b_2, a_1/b_1, a_0/b_0)$.
- _m128 _mm_div_ss(_m128, _m128)
  Synopsis: Scalar Single Precision Divide, d = _mm_div_ss(a,b) computes
  the division of the low order floating point pair a_0/b_0 and passes the
  remaining elements of **a** to **d**. That is, $\mathbf{d} \leftarrow (a_3, a_2, a_1, a_0/b_0)$.
- _m128 _mm_max_ps(_m128, _m128)
  Synopsis: Vector Single Precision Maximum, d = _mm_max_ps(a,b) com-
  putes, for $i = 0, \ldots, 3$, the respective maxima $d_i \leftarrow a_i \vee b_i$. That is,

$$\mathbf{d} \leftarrow (a_3 \vee b_3, a_2 \vee b_2, a_1 \vee b_1, a_0 \vee b_0).$$

- _m128 _mm_max_ss(_m128, _m128)
  Synopsis: Scalar Single Precision Maximum, d = _mm_max_ss(a,b) computes $a_0 \vee b_0$ and passes the remaining elements of **a** to **d**. That is,

$$\mathbf{d} \leftarrow (a_3, a_2, a_1, a_0 \vee b_0).$$

- _m128 _mm_min_ps(_m128, _m128)
  Synopsis: Vector Single Precision Minimum, d = _mm_min_ps(a,b) com-
  putes, for $i = 0, \ldots, 3$, the respective minima $d_i \leftarrow a_i \wedge b_i$. That is,

$$\mathbf{d} \leftarrow (a_3 \wedge b_3, a_2 \wedge b_2, a_1 \wedge b_1, a_0 \wedge b_0).$$

- _m128 _mm_min_ss(_m128, _m128)
  Synopsis: Scalar Single Precision Minimum, d = _mm_min_ss(a,b) computes $a_0 \wedge b_0$ and passes the remaining elements of **a** to **d**. That is,

$$\mathbf{d} \leftarrow (a_3, a_2, a_1, a_0 \wedge b_0).$$

- _m128 _mm_mul_ps(_m128, _m128)
  Synopsis: Vector Single Precision Multiply, d = _mm_mul_ps(a,b) com-
  putes, for $i = 0, \ldots, 3$, $a_i \cdot b_i$ single precision floating point products.
  That is,

$$\mathbf{d} \leftarrow (a_3 \cdot b_3, a_2 \cdot b_2, a_1 \cdot b_1, a_0 \cdot b_0).$$

- _m128 _mm_mul_ss(_m128, _m128)
  Synopsis: Scalar Single Precision Multiply, d = _mm_mul_ss(a,b) computes single precision floating point product $a_0 \cdot b_0$ and stores this in d_0;
  the remaining elements of **d** are set with the high order elements of **a**.
  That is,

$$\mathbf{d} \leftarrow (a_3, a_2, a_1, a_0 \cdot b_0).$$

- $\_\_m128\ \_mm\_rcp\_ps(\_\_m128)$
  Synopsis: Vector Reciprocal Approximation, d = $\_mm\_rcp\_ps(a,b)$ computes approximations to the single precision reciprocals $1.0/a_i$. That is,

$$\mathbf{d} \leftarrow (1.0/a_3, 1.0/a_2, 1.0/a_1, 1.0/a_0).$$

The maximum error is

$$|d_i \cdot a_i - 1.0| \leq 1.5 \times 2^{-12}.$$

- $\_\_m128\ \_mm\_rcp\_ss(\_\_m128)$
  Synopsis: Scalar Reciprocal Approximation, d = $\_mm\_rcp\_ss(a,b)$ computes approximations to the single precision reciprocal $1.0/a_0$ which is stored in d_0; the remaining elements of $\mathbf{a}$ are passed through. That is,

$$\mathbf{d} \leftarrow (a_3, a_2, a_1, 1.0/a_0).$$

The maximum error is

$$|d_0 \cdot a_0 - 1.0| \leq 1.5 \times 2^{-12}.$$

- $\_\_m128\ \_mm\_rsqrt\_ps(\_\_m128)$
  Synopsis: Approximation of Vector Reciprocal Square Root, d = $\_mm\_rsqrt\_ps(a)$ computes approximations to the single precision reciprocal square roots $1.0/\sqrt{a_i}$. That is,

$$\mathbf{d} \leftarrow \left(\frac{1}{\sqrt{a_3}}, \frac{1}{\sqrt{a_2}}, \frac{1}{\sqrt{a_1}}, \frac{1}{\sqrt{a_0}} \right)$$

The maximum error is

$$|d_i \cdot \sqrt{a_i} - 1.0| \leq 1.5 \times 2^{-12}.$$

- $\_\_m128\ \_mm\_rsqrt\_ss(\_\_m128)$
  Synopsis: Approximation of Scalar Reciprocal Square Root, d = $\_mm\_rsqrt\_ps(a)$ computes approximation to the single precision reciprocal square root $1.0/\sqrt{a_0}$, and remaining values of $\mathbf{a}$ are passed through. That is,

$$\mathbf{d} \leftarrow \left(a_3, a_2, a_1, \frac{1}{\sqrt{a_0}} \right)$$

The maximum error is

$$|d_0 \cdot \sqrt{a_0} - 1.0| \leq 1.5 \times 2^{-12}.$$

- $\_$m128 $\_$mm$\_$sqrt$\_$ps($\_$m128)
  Synopsis: Vector Square Root, d = $\_$mm$\_$sqrt$\_$ps(a) computes, for $i = 0, \ldots, 3$, the square roots $d_i = \sqrt{a_i}$. That is,

  $$\mathbf{d} \leftarrow (\sqrt{a_3}, \sqrt{a_2}, \sqrt{a_1}, \sqrt{a_0}).$$

- $\_$m128 $\_$mm$\_$sqrt$\_$ss($\_$m128)
  Synopsis: Scalar Square Root, d = $\_$mm$\_$sqrt$\_$ss(a) computes the square root $d_0 = \sqrt{a_0}$; the remaining elements of **a** are passed through. That is,

  $$\mathbf{d} \leftarrow (a_3, a_2, a_1, \sqrt{a_0}).$$

- $\_$m128 $\_$mm$\_$sub$\_$ps($\_$m128, $\_$m128)
  Synopsis: Vector Subtract, d = $\_$mm$\_$sub$\_$ps(a,b) computes, for $i = 0, \ldots, 3$, the differences $a_i - b_i$. That is,

  $$\mathbf{d} \leftarrow (a_3 - b_3, a_2 - a_2, a_1 - b_1, a_0 - b_0).$$

- $\_$m128 $\_$mm$\_$add$\_$ss($\_$m128, $\_$m128)
  Synopsis: Scalar Subtract, d = $\_$mm$\_$sub$\_$ss(a,b) computes the difference $d_0 = a_0 + b_0$, and the remaining values of **a** are passed through. That is,

  $$\mathbf{d} \leftarrow (a_3, a_2, a_1, a_0 - b_0).$$

APPENDIX B

ALTIVEC INTRINSICS FOR FLOATING POINT

The Apple/Motorola Altivec intrinsics are invoked using the Apple developers' kit **C** compiler [22]. This version of gcc has been extensively modified by Apple within the Darwin program and now effects some automatic vectorization. The use of Altivec intrinsics requires the -faltivec switch:

$$\text{gcc -O3 -faltivec yourcode.c -lm.}$$

Very important: On the Motorola/IBM/Apple G-4 chips, the bit ordering (also byte, and word for vector data) convention is **big endian**. This means the highest order (most significant) bit is numbered 0 and the numbering increases toward less significant bits—numbering is left to right. The set of intrinsics given below is not complete: only those intrinsics relevant to single precision floating point operations are given. A more detailed and complete set is given in the Motorola manual [22].

B.1 Mask generating vector comparisons

- vector signed int vec_cmpb (vector float, vector float)
  Synopsis: Vector Compare Bounds Floating Point, d = vec_cmpb(a,b) computes $d_i[0,1] = [a_i > b_i, a_i < -b_i]$, for $i = 0, \ldots, 3$. For example, if $a_i \le b_i$, bit 0 of d_i will be set to 0, otherwise bit 0 of d_i will be set to 1; and if $a_i \ge -b_i$, bit 1 of d_i will be set to 0, otherwise bit 1 will be set to 1.

Other comparisons are based on simple **binary** relations of the following form. See Table B.1 for a list of available **br**s.

- vector bool int vec_cmp**br** (vector float, vector float)
  Synopsis: Vector Compare binary relation, d = vec_cmp**br**(a,b) sets $d_i =$ **all 1s** if respective floating point element a_i **br** b_i, but $d_i = \mathbf{0}$ otherwise. For example, if **br** is equality ($=$), then when $a_i = b_i$, the corresponding d_i of vector **d** will be set to a mask of all 1s, otherwise $d_i = 0$.

There are other comparison functions which represent collective comparisons with binary relations, **br**, vec_all**br** (collective **all**) and vec_any**br** (collective **any**). These are described in Section B.6 on Collective Comparisons.

Table B.1 *Available binary relations for comparison functions. For additional relations applicable to* Collective Operations, *see Table B.2.*

All comparison functions		
Binary relation br	Description	Mathematical expression
eq	Equality	$\mathbf{a} = \mathbf{b}$
ge	Greater than or equal	$\mathbf{a} \geq \mathbf{b}$
gt	Greater than	$\mathbf{a} > \mathbf{b}$
le	Less than or equal	$\mathbf{a} \leq \mathbf{b}$
lt	Less than	$\mathbf{a} < \mathbf{b}$

The *mask* (results **d** above) is used with the following selection functions.

- `vector float vec_sel(vector float, vector float, vector bool int)`
  Synopsis: Vector Select, `d = vec_sel(a,b,c)` sets successive bits of **d** either to the corresponding bit of **b** or to that of **a** according to whether the indexing bit of **c** is set. Perhaps more precisely, if $i = 0, \ldots, 127$ indexes the bits of $\mathbf{d}, \mathbf{a}, \mathbf{b}$, then `d[i] = (c[i] == 1)?b[i]:a[i]`, see [84], Section 2.11.

- `vector float vec_splat(vector float, unsigned literal)`
  Synopsis: Vector Splat, `d = vec_splat(a,b)` selects element $b \bmod 4$ from **a** and distributes it to each element of **d**. For example, `d = vec_splat(a,7)` chooses element a_3 from **a** because $3 = 7 \bmod 4$, so $\mathbf{d} \leftarrow (a_3, a_3, a_3, a_3)$. If **d** and **a** are not `vector float`, then the index is $b \bmod n$, where n is the number of elements of **a** and **d**. If these were byte vectors, the index will be $k = b \bmod 16$ and the corresponding byte k of **a** will be distributed to **d**.

B.2   Conversion, utility, and approximation functions

- `vector float vec_ctf(vector int, unsigned literal)`
  Synopsis: Vector Convert from Fixed Point Word, `d = vec_ctf(a,b)` computes $d_i = (\texttt{float})a_i \cdot 2^b$, where b is a 5-bit unsigned literal. For example, if $a_i = 7.1$ and $b = 3$, then `d = vec_ctf(a,3)` gives element $d_i = 56.8 = 7.1 \cdot 2^3$.

- `vector float vec_expte(vector float)`
  Synopsis: Vector is 2 raised to the Exponent Estimate Floating Point, `d = vec_expte(a)` computes $d_i = 2^{a_i}$ to a 3-bit accurate result. For example, if $a_i = 0.5$, then $\sqrt{2} \approx d_i = 1.5 = 2^1 \cdot (1 \cdot 2^{-1} + 1 \cdot 2^{-2} + 0 \cdot 2^{-3})$.

- `vector float vec_floor(vector float)`
  Synopsis: Vector Floor, `d = vec_floor(a)` computes $d_i = \lfloor a_i \rfloor$, for $i = 0, \ldots, 3$, where a_i is the floating point representation of the largest less than or equal to a_i. For example, in the case $a_2 = 37.3$, then $d_2 \leftarrow 37.0$.

- `vector float vec_loge(vector float)`
  Synopsis: Vector $\log 2$ Estimate Floating Point `d = vec_loge(a)` computes $d_i = \log_2 a_i$ to a 3-bit accurate result. For example, if $a_i = e$, then $\log_2(a_i) = 1/\log(2) \approx d_i = 1.5 = 2^1 \cdot (1 \cdot 2^{-1} + 1 \cdot 2^{-2} + 0 \cdot 2^{-3})$.
- `vector float vec_mergeh(vector float, vector float)`
  Synopsis: Vector Merge High, `d = vec_mergeh(a,b)` merges **a** and **b** according to $\mathbf{d} = (d_0, d_1, d_2, d_3) = (a_0, b_0, a_1, b_1)$.
- `vector float vec_mergel(vector float, vector float)`
  Synopsis: Vector Merge Low, `d = vec_mergel(a,b)` merges **a** and **b** according to $\mathbf{d} = (d_0, d_1, d_2, d_3) = (a_2, b_2, a_3, b_3)$.
- `vector float vec_trunc(vector float)`
  Synopsis: Vector Truncate, `d = vec_trunc(a)` computes, for $i = 0, \ldots, 3$, $d_i = \lfloor a_i \rfloor$ if $a_i \geq 0.0$, or $d_i = \lceil a_i \rceil$ if $a_i < 0.0$. That is, each a_i is rounded to an integer (floating point representation) toward zero in the IEEE round-to-zero mode.
- `vector float vec_re(vector float, vector float)`
  Synopsis: Vector Reciprocal Estimate, `d = vec_re(a)` computes a reciprocal approximation $d_i \approx 1./a_i$ for $i = 0, \ldots, 3$. This approximation is accurate to 12 bits: that is, the maximum error of the estimate d_i satisfies

$$|d_i \cdot a_i - 1| \leq 2^{-12}.$$

- `vector float vec_round(vector float)`
  Synopsis: Vector Round, `d = vec_round(a)` computes, for each $i = 0, \ldots, 3$, d_i as the nearest integer (in floating point representation) to a_i in IEEE round-to-nearest mode. For example, $a_i = 1.499$ yields $d_i = 1.0$. If $\lfloor a_i \rfloor$ and $\lceil a_i \rceil$ are equally near, rounding is to the even integer: $a_i = 1.5$ yields $d_i = 2.0$.
- `vector float vec_rsqrte(vector float)`
  Synopsis: Vector Reciprocal Square Root Estimate, `d = vec_rsqrte(a)` computes, for $i = 0, \ldots, 3$, an approximation to each reciprocal square root $1/\sqrt{a_i}$ to 12 bits of accuracy. That is, for each a_i, $i = 0, \ldots, 3$,

$$|d_i \cdot \sqrt{a_i} - 1| \leq 2^{-12}.$$

B.3 Vector logical operations and permutations

- `vector float vec_and(vector float, vector float)`
  Synopsis: Vector Logical AND, `d = vec_and(a,b)` computes, for $i = 0, \ldots, 3$, $d_i = a_i$ **and** b_i bitwise.
- `vector float vec_andc(vector float, vector float)`
  Synopsis: Vector Logical AND with 1s Complement, `d = vec_andc(a,b)` computes $d_i = a_i$ **and** $\neg\, b_i$ for $i = 0, \ldots, 3$ bitwise.

- `vector float vec_ceil(vector float)`
  Synopsis: Vector Ceiling, `d = vec_ceil(a)` computes $d_i = \lceil a_i \rceil$, for $i = 0, \ldots, 3$, where d_i is the floating point representation of the smallest integer greater than or equal to a_i. For example, if $a_2 = 37.3$, then $d_2 \leftarrow 38.0$.

- `vector float vec_nor(vector float, vector float)`
  Synopsis: Vector Logical NOR, `d = vec_nor(a,b)` computes the bitwise **or** of each pair of element a_i **or** b_i, then takes the 1s complement of that result: $d_i = \neg (a_i \text{ or } b_i)$. In other words, `vec_nor(a,b)` computes $\mathbf{d} = \neg (\mathbf{a} \text{ or } \mathbf{b})$ considered as the negation of the 128-bit **or** of boolean operands $\mathbf{a}$ and $\mathbf{b}$.

- `vector float vec_or(vector float, vector float)`
  Synopsis: Vector Logical OR, `d = vec_or(a,b)` computes the bitwise **or** of each pair (a_i, b_i) and stores the results into the corresponding d_i for $i = 0, \ldots, 3$. That is, $\mathbf{d} = \mathbf{a} \text{ or } \mathbf{b}$ as a 128-bit boolean operation.

- `vector float vec_perm(vector float, vector float, vector unsigned char)`
  Synopsis: Vector Permute, `d = vec_perm(a,b,c)` permutes bytes of vectors $\mathbf{a}, \mathbf{b}$ according to permutation vector $\mathbf{c}$. Here is the schema: for bytes of $\mathbf{c}$, call these $\{c_i : i = 0, \ldots, 15\}$, low order bits 4–7 of c_i index a byte of either $\mathbf{a}$ or $\mathbf{b}$ for selecting d_i: $j = c_i[4 : 7]$. Selection bit 3 of c_i, that is, $c_i[3]$, picks either a_j or b_j according to $c_i[3] = 0$ (sets $d_i \leftarrow a_j$), or $c_i[3] = 1$ (sets $d_i \leftarrow b_j$). For example, if byte $c_2 = 00011001$, then $j = 1001 = 9$, so $d_2 = b_9$ because bit 3 of c_2 is 1, whereas if $c_2 = 00001001$, then $d_2 = a_9$ because bit 3 of c_2, that is, $c_2[3] = 0$ in that case. Examine variable `pv3201` in the Altivec FFT of Section 3.6 for a more extensive example.

- `vector float vec_xor(vector float, vector float)`
  Synopsis: Vector Logical XOR, `d = vec_xor(a,b)` computes $\mathbf{d} = \mathbf{a} \oplus \mathbf{b}$. That is, the exclusive or (**xor**) of 128-bit quantities $\mathbf{a}$ and $\mathbf{b}$ is taken and the result stored in $\mathbf{d}$.

B.4   Load and store operations

- `vector float vec_ld(int, float*)`
  Synopsis: Vector Load Indexed, `d = vec_ld(a,b)` loads vector $\mathbf{d}$ with four elements beginning at the memory location computed as the largest 16-byte aligned location less than or equal to $a + b$, where b is a `float*` pointer.

- `vector float vec_lde(int, float*)`
  Synopsis: Vector Load Element Indexed, `d = vec_lde(a,b)` loads an element d_k from the location computed as the largest 16-byte aligned location less than or equal to $a + b$ which is a multiple of 4. Again, b is a `float*` pointer. Index k is computed from the aligned address `mod` 16 then divided by 4. All other d_i values for $i \neq k$ are undefined.

- `vector float vec_ldl(int, float*)`
  Synopsis: Vector Load Indexed least recently used (LRU), `d = vec_ld(a,b)` loads vector $\mathbf{d}$ with four elements beginning at the memory location

computed as the largest 16-byte aligned location less than or equal to $a + b$, where b is a float* pointer. vec_ldl is the same as vec_ld except the load marks the cache line as least recently used: see Section 1.2.1.

- void vec_st(vector float, int, float*)
  Synopsis: Vector Store Indexed, vec_st(a,b,c) stores 4-word a beginning at the first 16-byte aligned address less than or equal to $c + b$. For example, vec_store(a,4,c) will store a 16-byte aligned vector (a_0, a_1, a_2, a_3) into locations c_4, c_5, c_6, c_7, that is, at location c + 4.

- void vec_ste(vector float, int, float*)
  Synopsis: Vector Store Element Indexed, vec_ste(a,b,c) stores a single floating point element a_k of a at largest 16-byte aligned location effective address (EA) less than or equal to $b + c$ which is a multiple of 4. Indexed element a_k chosen by $k = (\text{EA } \textbf{mod } 16)/4$.

- void vec_stl(vector float, int, float*)
  Synopsis: Vector Store Indexed LRU, vec_stl(a,b,c) stores a at largest 16-byte aligned location less than or equal to $b + c$. The cache line stored into is marked LRU.

B.5 Full precision arithmetic functions on vector operands

- vector float vec_abs(vector float)
  Synopsis: Vector Absolute Value, d = vec_abs(a) computes $d_i \leftarrow |a_i|$ for $i = 0, \ldots, 3$.

- vector float vec_add(vector float, vector float)
  Synopsis: Vector Add, d = vec_add(a,b) computes $d_i \leftarrow a_i + b_i$ for $i = 0, \ldots, 3$.

- vector float vec_madd(vector float, vector float, vector float)
  Synopsis: Vector Multiply Add, d = vec_madd(a,b,c) computes, for $i = 0, \ldots, 3$, $d_i = a_i \cdot b_i + c_i$. For example, if a scalar $a \rightarrow (a, a, a, a)$ (scalar propagated to a vector), the y = vec_madd(a,x,y) is a saxpy operation, see Section 2.1.

- vector float vec_max(vector float, vector float)
  Synopsis: Vector Maximum, d = vec_max(a,b) computes, for $i = 0, \ldots, 3$, $d_i = a_i \vee b_i$, so each d_i is set to the larger of the pair (a_i, b_i).

- vector float vec_min(vector float, vector float)
  Synopsis: Vector Maximum, d = vec_max(a,b) computes, for $i = 0, \ldots, 3$, $d_i = a_i \wedge b_i$. So each d_i is set to the smaller of the pair (a_i, b_i).

- vector float vec_nmsub(vector float, vector float, vector float)
  Synopsis: Vector Multiply Subtract, d = vec_nmsub(a,b,c) computes, for $i = 0, \ldots, 3$, $d_i = a_i \cdot b_i - c_i$. This intrinsic is similar to vec_madd except $d \leftarrow a \cdot b - c$ with a minus sign.

- vector float vec_sub(vector float, vector float)
  Synopsis: Vector Subtract, d = vec_sub(a,b) computes for $i = 0, \ldots, 3$, the elements of d by $d_i = a_i - b_i$.

B.6   Collective comparisons

The following comparison functions return a single integer result depending upon whether either (1) **all** pairwise comparisons between two operand vectors satisfy a binary relation, or (2) if **any** corresponding pair satisfy a binary relation or bound when comparing two operand vectors. Tables B.1 and B.2 show the available binary relations.

The general form for the `vec_all_br` integer functions is as follows.

- `int vec_all_br(vector float, vector float)`
  Synopsis: Elements Satisfy a binary relation, `d = vec_all_br(a,b)` returns one (1) if a_i **br** b_i for every $i = 0, \ldots, 3$, but zero (0) otherwise. For example, if **br** is equality (=), then if each $a_i = b_i$, then $d = 1$; otherwise $d = 0$.

In addition to the available binary relations given in Table B.1, there are additional functions shown in Table B.2. There are also collective *unary* **all** operations shown below.

- `int vec_all_nan(vector float)`
  Synopsis: All Elements Not a Number, `d = vec_all_nan(a)` returns one (1) if for every $i = 0, \ldots, 3$, a_i is not a number (NaN) (see [114]); but zero (0) otherwise.

Table B.2   *Additional available binary relations for collective comparison functions. All binary relations shown in Table B.1 are also applicable. The distinction between, for example, `vec_any_nge` and `vec_any_lt` is in the way NaN operands are handled. Otherwise, for valid IEEE floating point representations apparently similar functions are equivalent.*

Collective comparison functions			
Binary relation br	Description	Mathematical expression	Result if operand NaN
ne	Not equal	$\mathbf{a} \neq \mathbf{b}$	
nge	Not greater than or equal	$\mathbf{a} < \mathbf{b}$	True
ngt	Not greater than	$\mathbf{a} \leq \mathbf{b}$	True
nle	Not less than or equal	$\mathbf{a} > \mathbf{b}$	True
nlt	Not less than	$\mathbf{a} \geq \mathbf{b}$	True
*Collective **all** comparisons only*			
in	Within bounds	$\forall i, |a_i| \leq |b_i|$	
*Collective **any** comparisons only*			
out	Out of bounds	$\exists i, |a_i| > |b_i|$	

- `int vec_all_numeric(vector float)`
  Synopsis: All Elements Numeric, `d = vec_all_numeric(a)` returns one (1) if every a_i, for $i = 0, \ldots, 3$, is a valid floating point numerical value; but returns zero (0) otherwise.

Additionally, there are vector comparisons which return an integer one (1) if any (a_i, b_i) pair satisfies a **binary** relation; or a zero (0) otherwise. Available collective binary relations are shown in Table B.2. The general form for the **any** functions is as follows.

- `int vec_any_`**br**`(vector float, vector float)`
  Synopsis: Any Element Satisfies **br**, `d = vec_any_`**br**`(a,b)` returns one (1) if any a_i **br** b_i for $i = 0, \ldots, 3$, but returns zero (0) otherwise. For example, if **br** is equality (=), then for $i = 0, \ldots, 3$ if any $a_i = b_i$, then `d = vec_any_eq(a,b)` returns one (1); if no pair (a_i, b_i) are equal, `d = vec_any_eq(a,b)` returns zero (0).

Finally, there are *unary* **any** operations. These are as follows.

- `int vec_any_nan(vector float)`
  Synopsis: Any Element Not a Number, `d = vec_any_nan(a)` returns one (1) if any a_i is not a number (NaN) for $i = 0, \ldots, 3$, but returns zero (0) otherwise [114].
- `int vec_any_numeric(vector float)`
  Synopsis: Any Element Numeric, `d = vec_any_numeric(a)` returns one (1) if any a_i for $i = 0, \ldots, 3$ is a valid floating point numerical value, but returns zero (0) otherwise.

APPENDIX C

OPENMP COMMANDS

A detailed descriptions of OpenMP commands can be found in Chandra *et al.* [17]. On our HP9000, we used the following **guidec** compiler switches [77]:

```
guidec +O3 +Oopenmp filename.c -lm -lguide.
```

Library `/usr/local/KAI/guide/lib/32/libguide.a` was specified by `-lguide`. A maximum of eight CPUs (Section 4.8.2) is requested (C-shell) by

```
setenv OMP_NUM_THREADS 8.
```

C/C++ Open MP syntax
Define parallel region
#pragma omp parallel [clause] ... structured block
Work-sharing
#pragma omp for [clause] ... for loop

#pragma omp sections [clause] ...
{
[**#pragma omp section**
structured block]
}

#pragma omp single [clause] ... structured block
Combination parallel/work-sharing
#pragma omp parallel for [clause] ... for loop

#pragma omp parallel sections [clause] ...
{
[**#pragma omp section**
structured block]
}

C/C++ Open MP syntax (cont.)
Synchronization
#pragma omp master structured block
#pragma omp critical [(name)] structured block
#pragma omp barrier
#pragma omp atomic expression
#pragma omp flush [(list)]
#pragma omp ordered structured block
Data environment
#pragma omp threadprivate (vbl1, vbl2, ...)

C/C++ Clause	Parallel region	for	Sections	Single	Parallel for	Parallel sections
shared(list)	y				y	y
private(list)	y	y	y	y	y	y
firstprivate(list)	y	y	y	y	y	y
lastprivate(list)		y	y		y	y
default(private | shared | none)						
default(shared | none)	y				y	y
reduction (operator | intrinsic : list)	y	y	y		y	y
copyin (list)	y				y	y
if (expression)	y				y	y
ordered		y			y	
schedule(type[,chunk])		y			y	
nowait		y	y	y		

APPENDIX D

SUMMARY OF MPI COMMANDS

A complete description for the MPI commands can be found on the Argonne National Laboratory website [110] and most are listed, with some examples, in Pacheco [115]. Our list is not complete: only those relevent to our discussion and examples are described. See Chapter 5.

D.1 Point to point commands

Blocking sends and receives

MPI_Get_count: This function returns the number of elements received by the operation which initialized **status**, in particular **MPI_Recv**.

```
int MPI_Get_count(
    MPI_Status   *status,     /* input */
    MPI_Datatype datatype,    /* input */
    int          *count)      /* output */
```

MPI_Recv: This function begins receiving data sent by rank **source** and stores this into memory locations beginning at the location pointed to by **message**.

```
int MPI_Recv(
    void         *message,    /* output */
    int          count,       /* input */
    MPI_Datatype datatype,    /* input */
    int          source,      /* input */
    int          tag,         /* input */
    MPI_Comm     comm,        /* input */
    MPI_Status   *status)     /* output */
```

MPI_Send: This function initiates transmission of data **message** to process **dest**.

```
int MPI_Send(
    void         *message,    /* input */
    int          count,       /* input */
    MPI_Datatype datatype,    /* input */
    int          dest,        /* input */
    int          tag,         /* input */
    MPI_Comm     comm)        /* input */
```

Buffered point to point communications

MPI_Bsend is a buffered send. Buffer allocation is done by **MPI_Buffer_attach** and de-allocated by **MPI_Buffer_detach**. Again, **message** is the starting location for the contents of the send message and **count** is the number of **datatype** items to be sent to **dest**.

```
int MPI_Bsend(
    void        *message,   /* input */
    int         count,      /* input */
    MPI_Datatype datatype,  /* input */
    int         dest,       /* input */
    int         tag,        /* input */
    MPI_Comm    comm)       /* input */
```

MPI_Bsend is usually received by **MPI_Recv**.

Buffer allocation/de-allocation functions

MPI_Buffer_attach indicates that memory space beginning at **buffer** should be used as buffer space for outgoing messages.

```
int MPI_Buffer_attach(
    void        *buffer,   /* input */
    int         size)      /* input */
```

MPI_Buffer_detach indicates that previously attached memory locations should be de-allocated for buffer use. This function returns the address of the pointer to previously allocated space and location of the integer containing its size. This is useful for nested library replace/restore.

```
int MPI_Buffer_detach(
    void        *buffer,   /* output */
    int         *size)     /* output */
```

Non-blocking communication routines

MPI_Ibsend is a non-blocking buffered send.

```
int MPI_Ibsend(
    void        *message,   /* input */
    int         count,      /* input */
    MPI_Datatype datatype,  /* input */
    int         dest,       /* input */
    int         tag,        /* input */
    MPI_Comm    comm,       /* input */
    MPI_Request *request)   /* output */
```

MPI_Irecv is a non-blocking receive. Just because the function has returned does not mean the message (buffer) information is available. **MPI_Wait** (page 223) may be used with the **request** argument to assure completion. **MPI_Test** may be used to determine the status of completion.

```
int MPI_Irecv(
        void          *message,   /* output */
        int           count,      /* input */
        MPI_Datatype  datatype,   /* input */
        int           source,     /* input */
        int           tag,        /* input */
        MPI_Comm      comm,        /* input */
        MPI_Request   *request)   /* output */
```

MPI_Isend is a non-blocking normal send.

```
int MPI_Isend(
        void          *message,   /* input */
        int           count,      /* input */
        MPI_Datatype  datatype,   /* input */
        int           dest,       /* input */
        int           tag,        /* input */
        MPI_Comm      comm,        /* input */
        MPI_Request   *request)   /* output */
```

MPI_Request_free functions somewhat like **dealloc**: the memory referenced by **request** is marked for de-allocation and **request** is set to **MPI_REQUEST_NULL**.

```
int MPI_Request_free(
        MPI_Request  *request)   /* input/output */
```

MPI_Test Tests the completion of a non-blocking operation associated with **request**.

```
int MPI_Test(
        MPI_Request  *request,   /* input/output */
        int          *flag,      /* output */
        MPI_Status   *status)    /* output */
```

MPI_Testall This is similar to **MPI_Test** except that it tests whether all the operations associated with a whole array of **requests** are finished.

```
int MPI_Testall(
        int           array_size, /* input */
        MPI_Request   *requests,  /* input/output */
        int           *flag,      /* output */
        MPI_Status    *statii)    /* output array */
```

MPI_Testany This is similar to **MPI_Testall** except that it only tests if at least one of the **requests** has finished.

```
int MPI_Testany(
    int            array_size, /* input */
    MPI_Request   *requests,   /* input/output */
    int           *done_index, /* output */
    int           *flag,       /* output */
    MPI_Status    *status)     /* output array */
```

MPI_Testsome This is similar to **MPI_Testany** except that it determines how many of the **requests** have finished. This count is returned in **done_count** and the indices of which of the **requests** have been completed is returned in **done_ones**.

```
int MPI_Testsome(
    int            array_size, /* input */
    MPI_Request   *requests,   /* input/output */
    int           *done_count, /* output */
    int           *done_ones,  /* output array */
    MPI_Status    *statii)     /* output array */
```

MPI_Wait This function only returns when **request** has completed.

```
int MPI_Wait(
    MPI_Request   *request,    /* input/output */
    MPI_Status    *status)     /* output */
```

MPI_Waitall This function only returns when all the **requests** have been completed. Some may be null.

```
int MPI_Waitall(
    int            array_size, /* input  */
    MPI_Request   *requests,   /* input/output */
    MPI_Status    *statii)     /* output array */
```

MPI_Waitany This function blocks until at least one of the **requests**, **done_one**, has been completed.

```
int MPI_Waitany(
    int            array_size, /* input  */
    MPI_Request   *requests,   /* input/output */
    int           *done_one,   /* output */
    MPI_Status    *status)     /* output */
```

MPI_Waitsome This function only returns when at least one of the **requests** has completed. The number of **requests** finished is returned in **done_count** and the indices of these are returned in array **done_ones**.

```
int MPI_Waitsome(
    int           array_size,  /* input  */
    MPI_Request   *requests,   /* input/output */
    int           *done_count, /* output */
    int           *done_ones,  /* output array */
    MPI_Status    *statii)      /* output array */
```

Test and delete operations

MPI_Cancel assigns a cancellation request for an operation.

```
int MPI_Cancel(
    MPI_request   request)     /* input */
```

MPI_Iprobe Determine whether a message matching the arguments specified in **source**, **tag**, and **comm** can be received.

```
int MPI_Iprobe(
    int           source,   /* input */
    int           tag,      /* input */
    MPI_Comm      comm,      /* input */
    int           *flag,     /* output */
    MPI_Status    *status)    /* output struct */
```

MPI_Probe Block a **request** until a message matching the arguments specified in **source**, **tag**, and **comm** is available.

```
int MPI_Probe(
    int           source,   /* input */
    int           tag,      /* input */
    MPI_Comm      comm,      /* input */
    MPI_Status    *status)    /* output struct */
```

MPI_Test_canceled determines whether an operation associated with **status** was successfully canceled.

```
int MPI_Test_canceled(
    MPI_Status    *status,   /* input struct */
    int           *flag)     /* input */
```

Persistent communication requests

MPI_Bsend_init creates send request for persistent and buffered message.

```
int MPI_Bsend_init(
    void          *message,   /* input */
    int           count,      /* input */
    MPI_Datatype  datatype,   /* input */
    int           dest,       /* input */
```

```
        int           tag,        /* input */
        MPI_Comm      comm,       /* input */
        MPI_Request  *request)    /* output struct */
```

MPI_Recv_init creates a request for a persistent buffered receive.

```
    int MPI_Recv_init(
        void          *message,   /* output */
        int           count,      /* input */
        MPI_Datatype  datatype,   /* input */
        int           source,     /* input */
        int           tag,        /* input */
        MPI_Comm      comm,       /* input */
        MPI_Request  *request)    /* output struct */
```

MPI_Send_init creates a persistent standard send request.

```
    int MPI_Send_init(
        void          *message,   /* output */
        int           count,      /* input */
        MPI_Datatype  datatype,   /* input */
        int           dest,       /* input */
        int           tag,        /* input */
        MPI_Comm      comm,       /* input */
        MPI_Request  *request)    /* output struct */
```

MPI_Start initiates the non-blocking operation associated with **request**.

```
    int MPI_Start(
        MPI_Request  *request)    /* input/output */
```

MPI_Startall initiates a set of non-blocking operations associated with **requests**.

```
    int MPI_Startall(
        int           array_size,  /* input */
        MPI_Request  *requests)   /* input/output */
```

Combined send and receive routines

MPI_Sendrecv sends the contents of **send_data** to **dest** and gets data from **source** and stores these in **recv_data**.

```
    int MPI_Sendrecv(
        void          *send_data, /* input */
        int           sendcount,  /* input */
        MPI_Datatype  sendtype,   /* input */
        int           dest,       /* input */
        int           sendtag,    /* input */
```

```
void          *recv_data,  /* output */
int           recvcount,   /* input */
MPI_Datatype  recvtype,    /* input */
int           source,      /* input */
int           recvtag,     /* input */
MPI_Comm      comm,        /* input */
MPI_status    *status)     /* output */
```

MPI_Sendrecv_replace sends the contents of **buffer** to **dest** and replaces these data from **source**.

```
int MPI_Sendrecv_replace(
    void          *message,   /* input/output */
    int           count,      /* input */
    MPI_Datatype  datatype,   /* input */
    int           dest,       /* input */
    int           sendtag,    /* input */
    int           source,     /* input */
    int           recvtag,    /* input */
    MPI_Comm      comm,        /* input */
    MPI_status    *status)     /* output */
```

D.2   Collective communications

Broadcasts and barriers

MPI_Barrier blocks all processes in **comm** until each process has called it (**MPI_Barrier**).

```
int MPI_Barrier(
    MPI_Comm      comm)       /* input */
```

MPI_Bcast sends the contents of **send_data** with rank **root** to every process in **comm**, including **root**.

```
int MPI_Bcast(
    void          *send_data, /* input/output */
    int           count,      /* input */
    MPI_Datatype  datatype,   /* input */
    int           root,       /* input */
    MPI_Comm      comm)        /* input */
```

Scatter and gather operations (see Section 3.2.2)

MPI_Gather gathers all the data **send_data** sent from each process in the communicator group **comm** into **recv_data** of processor **root**.

```
int MPI_Gather(
    void          *send_data,  /* input */
```

```
int            sendcount,  /* input */
MPI_datatype   sendtype,   /* input */
void           *recv_data, /* output */
int            recvcount,  /* input */
MPI_datatype   recvtype,   /* input */
int            root,       /* input */
MPI_Comm       comm)       /* input */
```

MPI_Gatherv gathers all the sent data **send_data** from each process in the communicator group **comm** into **recv_data** of processor **root**, but with the additional capability of different type signatures.

```
int MPI_Gatherv(
    void           *send_data,    /* input */
    int            sendcount,     /* input */
    MPI_datatype   sendtype,      /* input */
    void           *recv_data,    /* output */
    int            *recvcounts,   /* input array */
    int            *recvoffsets,  /* input array */
    MPI_datatype   recvtype,      /* input */
    int            root,          /* input */
    MPI_Comm       comm)          /* input */
```

MPI_Scatter scatters the data **send_data** from process **root** to each of the processes in the communicator group **comm**.

```
int MPI_Scatter(
    void           *send_data,    /* input */
    int            sendcount,     /* input array */
    MPI_datatype   sendtype,      /* input */
    void           *recv_data,    /* output */
    int            recvcount,     /* input */
    MPI_datatype   recvtype,      /* input */
    int            root,          /* input */
    MPI_Comm       comm)          /* input */
```

MPI_Scatterv scatters the data **send_data** from process **root** to each of the processes in the communicator group **comm**, but with the additional capability of different type signatures.

```
int MPI_Scatterv(
    void           *send_data,    /* input */
    int            *sendcounts,   /* input array */
    int            *sendoffsets,  /* input array */
    MPI_datatype   sendtype,      /* input */
    void           *recv_data,    /* output */
```

```
int           recvcount,   /* input */
MPI_datatype  recvtype,    /* input */
int           root,        /* input */
MPI_Comm      comm)        /* input */
```

MPI_Allgather collects all the processes' **send_data** messages from all the processors in **comm** communicator group.

```
int MPI_Allgather(
    void          *send_data, /* input */
    int           sendcount,  /* input */
    MPI_Datatype  sendtype,   /* input */
    void          *recv_data, /* output */
    int           recvcount,  /* input */
    MPI_Datatype  recvtype,   /* input */
    MPI_Comm      comm)       /* input */
```

MPI_Allgatherv collects all the processes' **send_data** messages from all the processors in **comm** communicator group as in **MPI_Allgather**, but permits different type signatures.

```
int MPI_Allgatherv(
    void          *send_data,  /* input */
    int           sendcount,   /* input */
    MPI_datatype  sendtype,    /* input */
    void          *recv_data,  /* output */
    int           *recvcounts, /* input array */
    int           *offsets,    /* input array */
    MPI_datatype  recvtype,    /* input */
    MPI_Comm      comm)        /* input */
```

MPI_Alltoall is an all-to-all scatter/gather operation. All the processors in **comm** communicator group share each others' **send_data**.

```
int MPI_Alltoall(
    void          *send_data, /* input */
    int           sendcount,  /* input */
    MPI_datatype  sendtype,   /* input */
    void          *recv_data, /* output */
    int           recvcount,  /* input */
    MPI_datatype  recvtype,   /* input */
    MPI_Comm      comm)       /* input */
```

MPI_Alltoallv is an all-to-all scatter/gather operation with the additional facility of allowing different type signatures. All the processors in **comm** communicator group share each others' **send_data**.

```
int MPI_Alltoallv(
    void         *send_data,    /* input */
    int          *sendcounts,   /* input array */
    int          *sendoffsets,  /* input array */
    MPI_datatype sendtype,      /* input */
    void         *recv_data,    /* output */
    int          *recvcounts,   /* input array */
    int          *recvoffsets,  /* input array */
    MPI_datatype recvtype,      /* input */
    MPI_Comm     comm)          /* input */
```

Reduction operations (see Section 3.3)

MPI_Reduce is a generic reduction operation. Each data **segment** from each of the processes in the communicator group **comm** is combined according to the rules of **operator** (see Table D.1). The result of this reduction is stored in the process **root**.

```
int MPI_Reduce(
    void         *segment,      /* input */
    void         *result,       /* output */
    int          count,         /* input */
    MPI_datatype datatype,      /* input */
    MPI_op       operator,      /* input */
    int          root,          /* input */
    MPI_Comm     comm)          /* input */
```

MPI_Allreduce is a generic reduction operation. Each data segment **segment** from each of the processes in the communicator group **comm** is combined according to the rules of operator **operator** (see Table D.1). The result of this reduction is stored on each process of the **comm** group in **result**.

```
int MPI_Allreduce(
    void         *segment,      /* input */
    void         *result,       /* output */
    int          count,         /* input */
    MPI_datatype datatype,      /* input */
    MPI_op       operator,      /* input */
    MPI_Comm     comm)          /* input */
```

MPI_Op_create creates an operation for **MPI_Allreduce**. **fcn** is a pointer to a function which returns void and its template is given in Section D.3 on p. 234. Integer variable **commute** should be 1 (true) if the operands commute, but 0 (false) otherwise.

Table D.1   *MPI datatypes available for collective reduction operations.*

Pre-defined reduction operations	
MPI operations	Operation
MPI_MAX	Maximum ($\vee$)
MPI_MIN	Minimum ($\wedge$)
MPI_SUM	Summation (Σ)
MPI_PROD	Product ($\prod$)
MPI_BAND	Boolean AND (**and**)
MPI_LAND	Logical AND (**&&**)
MPI_BOR	Boolean OR (**or**)
MPI_LOR	Logical OR (**||**)
MPI_BXOR	Boolean exclusive OR ($\otimes$)
MPI_LXOR	Logical exclusive OR
MPI_MAXLOC	Maximum and its location
MPI_MINLOC	Minimum and its location
MPI datatypes for reductions	
MPI datatype	Equiv. **C** datatype
MPI_CHAR	Signed char
MPI_SHORT	Signed short int
MPI_INT	Signed int
MPI_LONG	Signed long int
MPI_FLOAT	Float
MPI_DOUBLE	Double
MPI_LONG_DOUBLE	Long double

```
int MPI_Op_create(
    MPI_User_function*  fcn,        /* input */
    int                 commute,    /* input */
    MPI_Op*             operator)   /* output */
```

MPI_Op_free frees the operator definition defined by **MPI_Op_create**.

```
int MPI_Op_free(
    MPI_Op*        operator)    /* input/output */
```

MPI_Reduce_scatter is a generic reduction operation which scatters its results to each processor in the communication group **comm**. Each data segment **segment** from each of the processes in the communicator group **comm** is combined according to the rules of operator **operator** (see Table D.1). The result of this reduction is scattered to each process in **comm**.

```
int MPI_Reduce_scatter(
    void       *segment,    /* input */
    void       *recv_data,  /* output */
```

```
int            *recvcounts,  /* input */
MPI_datatype   datatype,     /* input */
MPI_op         operator,     /* input */
MPI_Comm       comm)         /* input */
```

MPI_Scan computes a partial reduction operation on a collection of processes in **comm**. On each process k in **comm**, **MPI_Scan** combines the results of the reduction of all the segments of processes of **comm** with rank less than or equal to k and stores those results on k.

```
int MPI_Scan(
    void           *segment,   /* input */
    void           *result,    /* output */
    int            count,      /* input */
    MPI_datatype   datatype,   /* input */
    MPI_op         operator,   /* input */
    MPI_Comm       comm)       /* input */
```

Communicators and groups of communicators

MPI_Comm_group accesses the group associated with a given communicator. If **comm** is an inter-communicator, **MPI_Comm_group** returns (in **group**) the local group.

```
int MPI_Comm_group(
    MPI_comm    comm,      /* input */
    MPI_Group*  group)     /* output */
```

MPI_Group_compare compares **group1** with **group2**: the result of the comparison indicates that the two groups are same (both order and members), similar (only members the same), or not equal. See Table D.2 for **result** definitions.

Table D.2 *MPI pre-defined constants.*

Pre-defined MPI constants (in `mpi.h`)	
MPI constants	Usage
MPI_ANY_SOURCE	Wildcard source for receives
MPI_ANY_TAG	Wildcard tag for receives
MPI_UNDEFINED	Any MPI constant undefined
MPI_COMM_WORLD	Any MPI communicator wildcard
MPI_COMM_SELF	MPI communicator for self
MPI_IDENT	Groups/communicators identical
MPI_CONGRUENT	Groups congruent
MPI_SIMILAR	Groups similar
MPI_UNEQUAL	Groups/communicators not equal

```
int MPI_Group_compare(
    MPI_Group      group1,        /* input */
    MPI_Group      group2,        /* input */
    int            *result)       /* output */
```

MPI_Group_difference compares **group1** with **group2** and forms a new group which consists of the elements of **group1** which are not in **group2**. That is, **group3 = group1 \ group2**.

```
int MPI_Group_difference(
    MPI_Group      group1,        /* input */
    MPI_Group      group2,        /* input */
    MPI_Group*     group3)        /* output */
```

MPI_Group_excl forms a new group **group_out** which consists of the elements of **group** by excluding those whose ranks are listed in **ranks** (the size of **ranks** is **nr**).

```
int MPI_Group_excl(
    MPI_Group      group,         /* input */
    int            nr,            /* input */
    int            *ranks,        /* input array */
    MPI_Group      *group_out)    /* output */
```

MPI_Group_free frees (releases) group **group**. Group handle **group** is reset to **MPI_GROUP_NULL**.

```
int MPI_Group_free(
    MPI_Group      group)         /* input */
```

MPI_Group_incl examines **group** and forms a new group **group_out** whose members have ranks listed in array **ranks**. The size of **ranks** is **nr**.

```
int MPI_Group_incl(
    MPI_Group      group,         /* input */
    int            nr,            /* input */
    int            *ranks,        /* input */
    MPI_Group      *group_out)    /* output */
```

MPI_Group_intersection forms the intersection of **group1** and **group2**. That is, **MPI_Comm_intersection** forms a new group **group_out** whose members consist of processes of both input groups but ordered the same way as **group1**.

```
int MPI_Group_intersection(
    MPI_Group      group1,        /* input */
    MPI_Group      group2,        /* input */
    MPI_Group      *group_out)    /* output */
```

MPI_Group_rank returns the rank of the calling processes in a group. See also **MPI_Comm_rank**.

```
int MPI_Group_rank(
    MPI_Group      group,       /* input */
    int            *rank)       /* output */
```

MPI_Group_size returns the number of elements (processes) in a group.

```
int MPI_Group_size(
    MPI_Group      group,       /* input */
    int            *size)       /* output */
```

MPI_Group_union forms the union of of **group1** and **group2**. That is, **group_out** consists of **group1** followed by the processes of **group2** which do not belong to **group1**.

```
int MPI_Group_union(
    MPI_Group      group1,      /* input */
    MPI_Group      group2,      /* input */
    MPI_Group      *group_out)  /* output */
```

Managing communicators

MPI_Comm_compare compares the communicators **comm1** and **comm2** and returns **result** which is indentical if the contexts and groups are the same; congruent, if the groups are the same but different contexts; similar, if the groups are similar but the contexts are different; and unequal, otherwise. The values for these results are given in Table D.2.

```
int MPI_Comm_compare(
    MPI_Comm       comm1,       /* input */
    MPI_Comm       comm2,       /* input */
    int            *result)     /* output */
```

MPI_Comm_create creates a new communicator **comm_out** from the input **comm** and **group**.

```
int MPI_Comm_create(
    MPI_Comm       comm,        /* input */
    MPI_Group      group,       /* input */
    MPI_Comm       *comm_out)   /* output */
```

MPI_Comm_free frees (releases) a communicator.

```
int MPI_Comm_free(
    MPI_Comm       *comm)       /* input/output */
```

Communication status struc

```
typedef struct {
    int count;
    int MPI_SOURCE;
```

```
                    int MPI_TAG;
                    int MPI_ERROR;
                    int private_count;
               } MPI_Status;
```

D.3   Timers, initialization, and miscellaneous

Timers

MPI_Wtick returns the resolution (precision) of **MPI_Wtime** in seconds.

```
              double MPI_Wtick(void)
```

MPI_Wtime returns the wallclock time in seconds since the last (local) call to it. This is a local, not global, timer: a previous call to this function by another process does not interfere with a local timing.

```
              double MPI_Wtime(void)
```

Startup and finish

MPI_Abort terminates all the processes in **comm** and returns an error code to the process(es) which invoked **comm**

```
         int MPI_Abort(
            MPI_Comm     *comm,        /* input */
            int          error_code)   /* input */
```

MPI_Finalize terminates the current **MPI** threads and cleans up memory allocated by **MPI**.

```
              int MPI_Finalize(void)
```

MPI_Init starts up **MPI**. This procedure must be called before any other **MPI** function may be used. The arguments mimmick those of **C** main() except **argc** is a pointer since it is both an input and output.

```
         int MPI_Init(
            int          *argc,        /* input/output */
            char         **arv)        /* input/output */
```

Prototypes for user-defined functions

MPI_User_function defines the basic template of an operation to be created by **MPI_Op_create**.

```
         typedef MPI_User_function(
            void         *invec,     /* input vector */
            void         *inoutvec,  /* input/output vector */
            int          length,     /* length of vecs. */
            MPI_Datatype datatype)   /* type of vec elements */
```

APPENDIX E

FORTRAN AND C COMMUNICATION

In this book, essentially all code examples are written in ANSI Standard **C**. There are two important reasons for this: (1) **C** is a low level language that lends itself well to bit and byte manipulations, but at the same time has powerful macro and pointer facilities and (2) **C** support on Intel Pentium and Motorola G-4 machines is superior to Fortran, and we spend considerable time discussing these chips and their instruction level parallelism. In brief, the most important characteristics of Fortran and **C** are these:

1. Fortran passes scalar information to procedures (subroutines and functions) by **address** (often called by **reference**), while **C** passes scalars by **value**.

2. Fortran arrays have contiguous storage on the first index (e.g. a(2,j) immediately follows a(1,j)), while **C** has the second index as the "fast" one (e.g. a[i][2] is stored immediately after a[i][1]). Furthermore, indexing is normally numbered from 0 in **C**, but from 1 in Fortran.

3. Fortran permits dynamically dimensioned arrays, while in **C** this is not automatic but must be done by hand.

4. Fortran supports complex datatype: complex z is actually a two-dimensional array $(\Re z, \Im z)$. **C** in most flavors does not support complex type. Cray **C** and some versions of the Apple developers kit gcc do support complex type, but they do not use a consistent standard.

5. **C** has extensive support for pointers. Cray-like pointers in Fortran are now fairly common, but g77, for example, does not support Fortran pointers. Fortran 90 supports a complicated construction for pointers [105], but is not available on many Linux machines.

Now let us examine these issues in more detail. Item 1 is illustrated by the following snippets of code showing that procedure subr has its reference to variable x passed by address, so the set value (π) of x will be returned to the program.

1. Fortran passes all arguments to procedures by **address**

```
program address
real x
call subr(x)
print *," x=",x
stop
end
```

```
subroutine subr(y)
real y
y = 3.14159
return
end
```

Conversely, **C** passes information to procedures by **value**, except arrays which are passed by **address**.

```
#include <stdio.h>
main()
{
    float x,*z;
    float y[1];
    void subrNOK(float),subrOK(float*,float*);
    subrNOK(x);       /* x will not be set */
    printf(" x= %e\n",x);
    subrOK(y,z);      /* y[0],z[0] are set */
    printf(" y[0] = %e, z = %e\n",y[0],*z);
}
```

This one is incorrect and x in `main` is not set.

```
void subrNOK(x)
float x;
{ x = 3.14159; }
```

but `*y,*z` are properly set here

```
void subrOK(float *x,float *y)
{ *x   = 3.14159; y[0] = 2.71828; }
```

2. A 3×3 matrix A given by

$$A = \begin{pmatrix} a_{00} & a_{01} & a_{02} \\ a_{10} & a_{11} & a_{12} \\ a_{20} & a_{21} & a_{22} \end{pmatrix}$$

is stored in **C** according to the scheme $a_{ij} = $ `a[j][i]`, whereas the analogous scheme for the $1 \le i, j \le 3$ numbered array in Fortran

$$A = \begin{pmatrix} a_{11} & a_{12} & a_{13} \\ a_{21} & a_{22} & a_{23} \\ a_{31} & a_{32} & a_{33} \end{pmatrix}$$

is $a_{ij} = $ `a(i,j)`.

3. Fortran allows dynamically dimensioned arrays.

```
            program dims
c   x is a linear array when declared
            real x(9)
            call subr(x)
            print *,x
            stop
            end
            subroutine subr(x)
c   but x is two dimensional here
            real x(3,3)
            do i=1,3
              do j=1,3
                x(j,i) = float(i+j)
              enddo
            enddo
            return
            end
```

C does not allow dynamically dimensioned arrays. Often by using define, certain macros can be employed to work around this restriction. We do this on page 108, for example, with the am macro. For example,

```
define am(i,j) *(a+i+lda*j)
oid proc(int lda, float *a)
                float seed=331.0, ggl(float*);
    int i,j;
    for(j=0;j<lda;j++){
       for(i=0;i<lda;i++){
          am(i,j) = ggl(&seed); /* Fortran order */
       }
    }
    undef am
```

will treat array a in proc just as its Fortran counterpart—with the leading index i of a(i,j) being the "fast" one.

4. In this book, we adhere to the Fortran storage convention for complex datatype. Namely, if an array complex z(m), declared in Fortran, is accessed in a C procedure in an array float z[m][2], then $\Re z_k =$ real(z(k)) = z[k-1][0], and $\Im z_k =$ aimag(z(k)) = z[k-1][1] for each $1 \le k \le m$.

Although it is convenient and promotes consistency with Fortran, use of this complex convention may exact a performance penalty. Since storage in memory between two successive elements z(k),z(k+1) is two floating point words apart, special tricks are needed to do complex arithmetic (see Figure 3.22). These are unnecessary if all the arithmetic is on float data.

5. **C** uses &x to indicate the **address** of x. By this device, x can be set within a procedure by *px = 3.0, for example, where the location or address of x is indicated by px → x. Thus,

```
px  = &x;
*px = y;
/* is the same as */
x   = y;
```

Now let us give some examples of **C** ↔ Fortran communication. Using rules 1 and 5, we get the following for calling a Fortran routine from **C**. This is the most common case for our needs since so many high performance numerical libraries are written in Fortran.

1. To call a Fortran procedure from **C**, one usually uses an **underscore** for the Fortran named routine. Cray platforms do not use this convention. The following example shows how scalar and array arguments are usually communicated.

```
int n=2;
unsigned char c1='C',c2;
float x[2];
/* NOTE underscore */
void subr_(int*,char*,char*,float*);
subr_(&n,&c1,&c2,x);
printf("n=%d,c1=%c,c2=%c,x=%e,%e\n",
       n,c1,c2,x[0],x[1]);
        ...
          subroutine subr(n,c1,c2,x)
integer n
character*1 c1,c2
real x(n)
print *,"in subr: c1=",c1
c2='F'
do i=1,n
   x(i) = float(i)
enddo
return
end
```

For **C** calling Fortran procedures, you will likely need some libraries libf2c.a (or libf2c.so), on some systems libftn.a (or libftn.so), or some variant. For example, on Linux platforms, you may need libg2c.a: g2c instead of f2c. To determine if an **unsatisfied external** is in one of these libraries, "ar t libf2c.a" lists all compiled modules in archive libf2c.a. In the shared object case, "nm libftn.so" will list all the named modules in the .so object. Be aware that both ar t and nm may produce voluminous output, so judicious use of grep is advised.

2. Conversely, to call a C procedure from Fortran:

```
      program foo
      integer n
      real x(2)
      character*1 c1,c2
      c1 = 'F'
      n  = 2
      call subr(c1,c2,n,x)
      print *,"c1=",c1,", c2=",c2,", n=",n,
     *          ", x=",x(1),x(2)
      ...
```

```
/* NOTE underscore in Fortran called module */
void subr_(char *c1,char *c2,int *n,float *x)
{
    int i;
    printf("in subr: c1=%c\n",*c1);
    *c2 = 'C';
    for(i=0;i<*n;i++) x[i] = (float)i;
}
```

If you have Fortran calling C procedures, you may need libraries libc.a, libm.a, or their .so shared object variants. Again, to determine if an unsatisfied external is in one of these libraries, ar or nm may be helpful. See the description for C calling Fortran item above. In this case, it is generally best to link the C modules to Fortran using the Fortran compiler/linker, to wit:

```
g77 -o try foo.o subr.o
```

APPENDIX F

GLOSSARY OF TERMS

This glossary includes some specific terms and acronyms used to describe parallel computing systems. Some of these are to be found in [27] and [22], others in Computer Dictionary.

- **Align** refers to data placement in memory wherein block addresses are exactly equal to their block addresses modulo block size.
- **Architecture** is a detailed specification for a processor or computer system.
- **Bandwidth** is a somewhat erroneously applied term which means a data transfer rate, in bits/second, for example. Previously, the term meant the range of frequencies available for analog data.
- **Biased exponent** is a binary exponent whose positive and negative range of values is shifted by a constant (bias). This bias is designed to avoid two sign bits in a floating point word—one for the overall sign and one for the exponent. Instead, a floating point word takes the form (ex is the exponent, and $1/2 \le x_0 < 1$ is the mantissa),

$$x = \pm \, 2^{\text{ex}} \cdot x_0,$$

where ex is represented as $\mathsf{exponent} = \mathsf{ex} + \mathsf{bias}$, so the data are stored

Sign bit	Exponent	Mantissa

- **Big endian** is a bit numbering convention wherein the bits (also bytes) are numbered from left to right—the high order bit is numbered 0, and the numbering increases toward the lowest order.
- **Block** refers to data of fixed size and often aligned (see cache block).
- **Branch prediction** at a data dependent decision point in code is a combination of hardware and software arrangements of instructions constructed to make a speculative prediction about which branch will be taken.
- **Burst** is a segment of data transferred, usually a cache block.
- **Cache block** at the lowest level (L1), is often called a cache line (16 bytes), whereas in higher levels of cache, the size can be as large as a **page** of 4 KB. See Table 1.1.
- **Cache coherency** means providing a memory system with a common view of the data. Namely, modified data can appear only in the local cache in

which it was stored so fetching data from memory might not get the most up-to-date version. A hardware mechanism presents the whole system with the most recent version.

- **Cache flush** of data means they are written back to memory and the cache lines are removed or marked invalid.
- **Cache** is a locally accessible high speed memory for instructions or data. See Section 1.2.
- **Cache line** is a cache block at the lowest level L1.
- **CMOS** refers to complementary metal oxide semiconductor. Today, most memory which requires power for viability is CMOS.
- **Communication** for our purposes means transferring data from one location to another, usually from one processor's memory to others'.
- **Cross-sectional bandwidth** refers to a maximum data rate possible between halves of a machine.
- **Direct mapped cache** is a system where a datum may be written only into one cache block location and no other. See Section 1.2.1.
- **Dynamic random access memory (DRAM)** Voltage applied to the base of a transistor turns on the current which charges a capacitor. This charge represents one storage bit. The capacitor charge must be refreshed regularly (every few milliseconds). Reading the data bit destroys it.
- **ECL** refers to emitter coupled logic, a type of bipolar transistor with very high switching speeds but also high power requirements.
- **Effective address (EA)** of a memory datum is the cache address plus offset within the block.
- **Exponent** means the binary exponent of a floating point number $x = 2^{ex} \cdot x_0$ where ex is the exponent. The mantissa is $1/2 \leq x_0 < 1$. In IEEE arithmetic, the high order bit of x_0 is not stored and is assumed to be 1, see [114].
- **Fast Fourier Transform (FFT)** is an algorithm for computing $\mathbf{y} = W\mathbf{x}$, where $W_{jk} = \omega^{jk}$ is the jkth power of the nth root of unity ω, and $\mathbf{x}, \mathbf{y}$ are complex $n$vectors.
- **Fetch** means getting data from memory to be used as an instruction or for an operand. If the data are already in cache, the process can be foreshortened.
- **Floating-point register (FPR)** refers to one register within a set used for floating point data.
- **Floating-point unit** refers to the hardware for arithmetic operations on floating point data.
- **Flush** means that when data are to be modified, the old data may have to be stored to memory to prepare for the new. Cache flushes store local copies back to memory (if already modified) and mark the blocks invalid.
- **Fully associative** cache designs permit data from memory to be stored in any available cache block.
- **Gaussian elimination** is an algorithm for solving a system of linear equations $A\mathbf{x} = \mathbf{b}$ by using row or column reductions.

- **General purpose register (GPR)** usually refers to a register used for immediate storage and retrieval of integer operations.
- **Harvard architecture** is distinct from the original von Neumann design, which had no clear distinction between instruction data and arithmetic data. The Harvard architecture keeps distinct memory resources (like caches) for these two types of data.
- **IEEE 754** specifications for floating point storage and operations were inspired and encouraged by W. Kahan. The IEEE refined and adopted this standard, see Overton [114].
- **In-order** means instructions are issued and executed in the order in which they were coded, without any re-ordering or rearrangement.
- **Instruction latency** is the total number of clock cycles necessary to execute an instruction and make ready the results of that instruction.
- **Instruction parallelism** refers to concurrent execution of hardware machine instructions.
- **Latency** is the amount of time from the initiation of an action until the first results begin to arrive. For example, the number of clock cycles a multiple data instruction takes from the time of issue until the first result is available is the instruction's latency.
- **Little endian** is a numbering scheme for binary data in which the lowest order bit is numbered 0 and the numbering increases as the significance increases.
- **Loop unrolling** hides pipeline latencies by processing segments of data rather than one/time. Vector processing represents one hardware mode for this unrolling, see Section 3.2, while template alignment is more a software method, see Section 3.2.4.
- **Mantissa** means the x_0 portion of a floating point number $x = 2^{\mathrm{ex}} \cdot x_0$, where $1/2 \leq x_0 < 1$.
- **Monte Carlo (MC)** simulations are mathematical experiments which use random numbers to generate possible configurations of a model system.
- **Multiple instruction, multiple data (MIMD)** mode of parallelism means that more than one CPU is used, each working on independent parts of the data to be processed and further that the machine instruction sequence on each CPU may differ from every other.
- **NaN** in the IEEE floating point standard is an abbreviation for a particular unrepresentable datum. Often there are more than one such NaN. For example, some cause exceptions and others are tagged but ignored.
- **No-op** is an old concept wherein cycles are wasted for synchronization purposes. The "no operation" neither modifies any data nor generates bus activity, but a clock cycle of time is taken.
- **Normalization** in our discussions means two separate things. (1) In numerical floating point representations, normalization means that the highest order bit in a mantissa is set (in fact, or implied as in IEEE), and the exponent is adjusted accordingly. (2) In our MC discussions,

normalization means that a probability density distribution $p(x)$ is multiplied by a positive constant such that $\int p(x)\,\mathrm{d}x = 1$, that is, the total probability for x having some value is unity.

- **Out of order execution** refers to hardware rearrangement of instructions from computer codes which are written in-order.
- **Page** is a 4 KB aligned segment of data in memory.
- **Persistent data** are those that are expected to be loaded frequently.
- **Pipelining** is a familiar idea from childhood rules for arithmetic. Each arithmetic operation requires multiple stages (steps) to complete, so modern computing machines allow multiple operands sets to be computed simultaneously by pushing new operands into the lowest stages as soon as those stages are available from previous operations.
- **Pivot** in our discussion means the element of maximum absolute size in a matrix row or column which is used in Gaussian elimination. Pivoting usually improves the stability of this algorithm.
- **Quad pumped** refers to a clocking mechanism in computers which involves two overlapping signals both of whose leading and trailing edges turn switches on or off.
- **Quad word** is a group of four 32-bit floating point words.
- **Reduced instruction set computer (RISC)** means one with fixed instruction length (usually short) operations and typically relatively few data access modes. Complex operations are made up from these.
- **Redundancy** in this book means the extra work that ensues as a result of using a parallel algorithm. For example, a simple Gaussian elimination tridiagonal system solver requires fewer floating point operations than a cyclic reduction method, although the latter may be much faster. The extra operations represent a redundancy. In the context of branch prediction, instructions which issue and start to execute but whose results are subsequently discarded due to a missed prediction are redundant.
- **Rename** registers are those whose conventional numbering sequence is reordered to match the numbered label of an instruction. See Figures 3.13 and 3.14 and attendant discussion.
- **Set associative** cache design means that storage is segmented into sets. A datum from memory is assigned to its associated set according to its address.
- **Shared memory** modes of parallelism mean that each CPU (processor) has access to data stored in a common memory system. In fact, the memory system may be distributed but read/write conflicts are resolved by the intercommunication network.
- **Single instruction stream, multiple data streams (SIMD)** usually means vector computing. See Chapter 3.
- **Slave** typically means an arbitrarily ranked processor assigned a task by an equally arbitrarily chosen master.
- **Snooping** monitors addresses by a bus master to assure data coherency.

- **Speedup** refers to the ratio of program execution time on a pre-parallelization version to the execution time of a parallelized version—on the same type of processors. Or perhaps conversely: it is the ratio of processing rate of a parallel version to the processing rate for a serial version of the same code on the same machine.

- **Splat** operations take a scalar value and store it in all elements of a vector register. For example, the `saxpy` operation ($\mathbf{y} \leftarrow a \cdot \mathbf{x} + \mathbf{y}$) on SSE and Altivec hardware is done by *splatting* the constant a into all the elements of a vector register and doing the $a \cdot \mathbf{x}$ multiplications as Hadamard products $a_i \cdot x_i$, where each $a_i = a$. See Equation (2.3).

- **Stage** in our discussion means a step in a sequence of arithmetic operations which may subsequently be used concurrently with successive steps of an operation which has not yet finished. This stage will be used for new operands while the subsequent stages work on preceding operands. For example, in multiplication, the lowest order digit stage may be used for the next operand pair while higher order multiply/carry operations on previous operands are still going on.

- **Startup** for our purposes refers to the amount of time required to establish a communications link before any actual data are transferred.

- **Static random access memory (SRAM)** does not need to be refreshed like DRAM and reading the data is not destructive. However, the storage mechanism is *flip-flops* and requires either four transistors and two resistors, or six transistors. Either way, SRAMs cells are more complicated and expensive than DRAM.

- **Superscalar machine** means one which permits multiple instructions to run concurrently with earlier instruction issues.

- **Synchronization** in parallel execution forces unfinished operations to finish before the program can continue.

- **Throughput** is the number of concurrent instructions which are running per clock cycle.

- **Vector length (VL)** is the number of elements in a vector register, or more generally the number in the register to be processed. For example, $\mathbf{VL} \leq 64$ on Cray SV-1 machines, $\mathbf{VL} = 4$ for single precision data on SSE hardware (Pentium III or 4) and Altivec hardware (Macintosh G-4).

- **Vector register** is a set of registers whose multiple data may be processed by invoking a single instruction.

- **Word** is a floating point datum, either 32-bit or 64-bit for our examples.

- **Write back** is a cache write strategy in which data to be stored in memory are written only to cache until the corresponding cache lines are again to be modified, at which time they are written to memory.

- **Write through** is a cache write strategy in which modified data are immediately written into memory as they are stored into cache.

APPENDIX G

NOTATIONS AND SYMBOLS

and   Boolean and: i **and** $j = 1$ if $i = j = 1$, 0 otherwise.

$a \vee b$ means the maximum of a, b: $a \vee b = \mathtt{max(a,b)}$.

$a \wedge b$ means the minimum of a, b: $a \wedge b = \mathtt{min(a,b)}$.

$\forall x_i$ means for **all** x_i.

A^{-1} is the inverse of matrix A.

$A^{-\mathrm{T}}$ is a matrix transpose: $[A^{\mathrm{T}}]_{ij} = A_{ji}$.

$\mathbf{E}x$ is the expectation value of x: for a discrete sample of x, $\mathbf{E}x = \frac{1}{N} \sum_{i=1}^{N} x_i$. For continuous x, $\mathbf{E}x = \int p(x)\, x \, \mathrm{d}x$.

$\langle x \rangle$ is the average value of x, that is, physicists' notation $\langle x \rangle = \mathbf{E}x$.

$\exists x_i$ means there exists an x_i.

$\Im z$ is the imaginary part of z: if $z = x + iy$, then $\Im z = y$.

(x, y) is the usual vector inner product: $(x, y) = \sum_i x_i y_i$.

$m|n$ says integer m divides integer n exactly.

$\neg a$ is the Boolean complement of a: bitwise, $\neg 1 = 0$ and $\neg 0 = 1$.

$||x||$ is some vector norm: for example, $||x|| = (x, x)^{1/2}$ is an L_2 norm.

$\oplus$ **When** applied to **binary data**, this is a Boolean exclusive OR: for each independent bit, $i \oplus j = 1$ if only one of $i = 1$ or $j = 1$ is true, but is zero otherwise.
     When applied to **matrices**, this is a direct sum: $A \oplus B$ is a block diagonal matrix with A, then B, along the diagonal.

or   Boolean OR operation.

$\otimes$ Kronecker product of matrices: when A is $p \times p$, B is $q \times q$, $A \otimes B$ is a $pq \times pq$ matrix whose i, jth $q \times q$ block is $a_{i,j}B$.

$p(x)$ is a probability density: $P\{x \le X\} = \int_{x \le X} p(x)\, \mathrm{d}x$.

$p(x|y)$ is a conditional probability density: $\int p(x|y)\, \mathrm{d}x = 1$.

$\Re z$ is the real part of z: if $z = x + iy$, then $\Re z = x$.

$x \leftarrow y$ means that the current value of x (if any) is replaced by y.

$U(0, 1)$ means a uniformly distributed random number between 0 and 1.

VL   the vector length: number of elements processed in SIMD mode.

VM   is a vector mask: a set of flags (bits) within a register, each corresponding to a test condition on words in a vector register.

$\mathbf{w}(t)$ is a vector of independent Brownian motions: see Section 2.5.3.2.

REFERENCES

1. 3DNow: Technology Manual, No. 21928G/0, March 2000. *Advanced Micro Devices Version of XMM*. Available from URL http://www.amd.com/ gb-uk/Processors/SellAMDProducts/ 0,, 30_177_5274_5284% 5E992% 5E1144, 00.html.
2. M. Abramowitz and I. Stegun (eds). *Handbook of Mathematical Functions*. US National Bureau of Standards, Washington, DC, 1964.
3. J. C. Agüí and J. Jiménez. A binary tree implementation of a parallel distributed tridiagonal solver. *Parallel Comput.* 21:233–241, 1995.
4. E. Anderson, Z. Bai, C. Bischof, J. Demmel, J. Dongarra, J. Du Croz *et al.* *LAPACK Users' Guide—Release 2.0*. Society for Industrial and Applied Mathematics, Philadelphia, PA, 1994. (Software and guide are available from Netlib at URL: http://www.netlib.org/lapack/.)
5. P. Arbenz and M. Hegland. On the stable parallel solution of general narrow banded linear systems. In P. Arbenz, M. Paprzycki, A. Sameh, and V. Sarin (eds), *High Performance Algorithms for Structured Matrix Problems*, pp. 47–73. Nova Science Publishers, Commack, NY, 1998.
6. P. Arbenz and W. Petersen. http://www.inf.ethz.ch/~arbenz/book.
7. S. Balay, K. Buschelman, W. D. Gropp, D. Kaushik, L. C. McInnes, and B. F. Smith. PETSc home page. http://www.mcs.anl.gov/petsc, 2001.
8. Satish Balay, W. D. Gropp, L. C. McInnes, and B. F. Smith. Efficient management of parallelism in object oriented numerical software libraries. In E. Arge, A. M. Bruaset, and H. P. Langtangen (eds), *Modern Software Tools in Scientific Computing*, pp. 163–202. Birkhäuser Press, Basel, 1997.
9. S. Balay, W. D. Gropp, L. C. McInnes, and B. F. Smith. *PETSc Users Manual*. Technical Report ANL-95/11 - Revision 2.1.5, Argonne National Laboratory, 2003.
10. R. Balescu. *Equilibrium and NonEquilibrium Statistical Mechanics*. Wiley-Interscience, New York, 1975.
11. R. Barret, M. Berry, T. F. Chan, J. Demmel, J. Donato, J. Dongarra, V. Eijkhout, R. Pozo, Ch. Romine, and H. van der Vorst. *Templates for the Solution of Linear Systems: Building Blocks for Iterative Methods*. Society for Industrial and Applied Mathematics, Philadelphia, PA, 1994. Available from Netlib at URL http://www.netlib.org/templates/index.html.
12. L. S. Blackford, J. Choi, A. Cleary, E. D'Azevedo, J. Demmel, I. Dhillon, J. Dongarra, S. Hammarling, G. Henry, A. Petitet, K. Stanley, D. Walker, and R. C. Whaley. *ScaLAPACK Users' Guide*. Society for Industrial and Applied Mathematics, Philadelphia, PA, 1997. (Software and guide are available from Netlib at URL http://www.netlib.org/scalapack/.)
13. S. Bondeli. Divide and conquer: A parallel algorithm for the solution of a tridiagonal linear system of equations. *Parallel Comput.*, 17:419–434, 1991.

14. R. P. Brent. Random number generation and simulation on vector and parallel computers. In D. Pritchard and J. Reeve (eds), *Euro-Par '98 Parallel Processing*, pp. 1–20. Springer, Berlin, 1998. (Lecture Notes in Computer Science, 1470.)

15. E. O. Brigham. *The Fast Fourier Transform*. Prentice Hall, Englewood Cliffs, NJ, 1974.

16. E. O. Brigham. *The Fast Fourier Transform and its Applications*. Prentice Hall, Englewood Cliffs, NJ, 1988.

17. R. Chandra, R. Menon, L. Dagum, D. Kohr, and D. Maydan. *Parallel Programming in OpenMP*. Morgan Kaufmann, San Francisco, CA, 2001.

18. J. Choi, J. Demmel, I. Dhillon, J. J. Dongarra, S. Ostrouchov, A. P. Petitet, K. Stanley, D. W. Walker, and R. C. Whaley. ScaLAPACK: A portable linear algebra library for distribute memory computers—design issues and performance. LAPACK Working Note 95, University of Tennessee, Knoxville, TN, March 1995. Available from http://www.netlib.org/lapack/lawns/.

19. J. Choi, J. J. Dongarra, S. Ostrouchov, A. P. Petitet, D. W. Walker, and R. C. Whaley. A proposal for a set of parallel basic linear algebra subprograms. LAPACK Working Note 100, University of Tennessee, Knoxville, TN, May 1995. Available from the Netlib software repository.

20. Apple Computer Company. Altivec Address Alignment. http://developer.apple.com/ hardware/ve/ alignment.html.

21. J. W. Cooley and J. W. Tukey. An algorithm for the machine calculations of complex Fourier series. *Math. Comp.*, 19:297–301, 1965.

22. Apple Computer Corp. *Power PC Numerics*. Addison Wesley Publication Co., Reading, MA, 1994.

23. Intel Corporation. Intel Developers' Group. http://developer.intel.com.

24. Intel Corporation. Integer minimum or maximum element search using streaming SIMD extensions. Technical Report, Intel Corporation, 1 Jan. 1999. AP-804, Order No. 243638-002.

25. Intel Corporation. *Intel Architecture Software Developer's Manual: Vol 2 Instruction Set Reference*. Intel Corporation, 1999. Order No. 243191. http://developer.intel.com.

26. Intel Corporation. *Intel Math Kernel Library, Reference Manual*. Intel Corporation, 2001. Order No. 630813-011. http://www.intel.com/software/products/mkl/mkl52/, go to *Technical Information*, and download User Guide/Reference Manual.

27. Intel Corporation. *Intel Pentium 4 and Intel Xeon Processor Optimization Manual*. Intel Corporation, 2001. Order No. 248966-04, http://developer.intel.com.

28. Intel Corporation. Split radix fast Fourier transform using streaming SIMD extensions, version 2.1. Technical Report, Intel Corporation, 28 Jan. 1999. AP-808, Order No. 243642-002.

29. Motorola Corporation. MPC7455 RISC Microprocessor hardware specifications. http://e-www.motorola.com/brdata/PDFDB/docs/MPC7455EC.pdf.

30. Motorola Corporation. *Altivec Technology Programming Environments Manual, Rev. 0.1*. Motorola Corporation, 1998. Available as ALTIVECPIM.pdf, document ALTIVECPEM/D, http://www.motorla.com.

31. R. Crandall and J. Klivington. Supercomputer-style FFT library for Apple G-4. Technical Report, Adv. Computation Group, Apple Computer Company, 6 Jan. 2000.

32. E. Cuthill. Several strategies for reducing the bandwidth of matrices. In D. J. Rose and R. Willoughby (eds), *Sparse Matrices and their Applications*. Plenum Press, New York, 1972.

33. P. J. Davis and P. Rabinowitz. *Methods of Numerical Integration*. Academic Press, Orlando, FL, 1984.

34. L. Devroye. *Non-Uniform Random Variate Generation*. Springer, New York, 1986.

35. Diehard rng tests. George Marsaglia's diehard random number test suite. Available at URL http://stat.fsu.edu/pub/diehard.

36. J. J. Dongarra. Performance of various computers using standard linear equations software. Technical Report, NETLIB, Sept. 8, 2002. http://netlib.org/benchmark/performance.ps.

37. J. J. Dongarra, J. R. Bunch, C. B. Moler, and G. W. Stewart. *LINPACK Users' Guide*. Society for Industrial and Applied Mathematics, Philadelphia, PA, 1979.

38. J. J. Dongarra, J. Du Croz, I. Duff, and S. Hammarling. A proposal for a set of level 3 basic linear algebra subprograms. *ACM SIGNUM Newslett.*, 22(3):2–14, 1987.

39. J. J. Dongarra, J. Du Croz, I. Duff, and S. Hammarling. A proposal for a set of level 3 basic linear algebra subprograms. *ACM Trans. Math. Software*, 16:1–17, 1990.

40. J. J. Dongarra, J. Du Croz, S. Hammarling, and R. J. Hanson. An extended set of fortran basic linear algebra subprograms. *ACM Trans. Math. Software*, 14:1–17, 1988.

41. J. J. Dongarra, J. Du Croz, S. Hammarling, and R. J. Hanson. An extended set of fortran basic linear algebra subprograms: Model implementation and test programs. *ACM Trans Math Software*, 14:18–32, 1988.

42. J. J. Dongarra, I. S. Duff, D. C. Sorensen, and H. A. van der Vorst. *Numerical Linear Algebra for High-Performance Computers*. Society for Industrial and Applied Mathematics, Philadelphia, PA, 1998.

43. I. S. Duff, M. A. Heroux, and R. Pozo. An overview of the sparse basic linear algebra subprograms: The new standard from the BLAS technical forum. *ACM Trans. Math. Software*, 28(2):239–267, 2002.

44. P. Duhamel and H. Hollmann. Split-radix fft algorithm. *Electr. Lett.*, 1:14–16, 1984.

45. C. Dun, M. Hegland, and M. Osborne. Parallel stable solution methods for tridiagonal linear systems of equations. In R. L. May and A. K. Easton (eds), *Computational Techniques and Applications: CTAC-95*, pp. 267–274. World Scientific, Singapore, 1996.

46. A. Erdélyi, *et al. Higher Transcendental Functions, the Bateman Manuscript Project, 3 vols*. Robert E. Krieger Publ., Malabar, FL, 1981.

47. B. W. Chars, *et al*. Maple, version 8. Symbolic computation. http://www.maplesoft.com/.

48. C. May, *et al*, (ed.). *Power PC Architecture*. Morgan Kaufmann, San Fracisco, CA, 1998.

49. J. F. Hart, *et al. Computer Approximations*. Robert E. Krieger Publ. Co., Huntington, New York, 1978.

50. R. P. Feynman and A. R. Hibbs. *Quantum Mechanics and Path Integrals*. McGraw-Hill, New York, 1965.

51. R. J. Fisher and H. G. Dietz. Compiling for SIMD within a register. In S. Chatterjee (ed.), *Workshop on Languages and Compilers for Parallel Computing, Univ. of North Carolina, August 7–9, 1998*, pp. 290–304. Springer, Berlin, 1999. http://www.shay.ecn.purdue.edu/\~swar/.

52. Nancy Forbes and Mike Foster. The end of moore's law? *Comput. Sci. Eng.*, 5(1):18–19, 2003.

53. G. E. Forsythe, M. A. Malcom, and C. B. Moler. *Computer Methods for Mathematical Computations*. Prentice-Hall, Englewood Cliffs, NJ, 1977.

54. G. E. Forsythe and C. B. Moler. *Computer Solution of Linear Algebraic Systems*. Prentice-Hall, Englewood Cliffs, NJ, 1967.

55. M. Frigo and S. G. Johnson. FFTW: An adaptive software architecture for the FFT. In *Proceedings of the 1998 IEEE International Conference on Acoustics, Speech and Signal Processing (ICASSP '98)*, Vol. 3, pp. 1381–1384. IEEE Service Center, Piscataway, NJ, 1998. Available at URL http://www.fftw.org.

56. J. E. Gentle. *Random Number Generation and Monte Carlo Methods*. Springer Verlag, New York, 1998.

57. R. Gerber. *The Software Optimization Cookbook*. Intel Press, 2002. http://developer.intel.com/intelpress.

58. R. Geus and S. Röllin. Towards a fast parallel sparse matrix-vector multiplication. *Parallel Comput.*, 27(7):883–896, 2001.

59. S. Goedecker and A. Hoisie. *Performance Optimization of Numerically Intensive Codes*. Software, Environments, Tools. SIAM Books, Philadelphia, 2001.

60. G. H. Golub and C. F. van Loan. *Matrix Computations*, 3rd edn. The Johns Hopkins University Press, Baltimore, MD, 1996.

61. G. H. Gonnet. Private communication.

62. D. Graf. Pseudo random randoms—generators and tests. Technical Report, ETHZ, 2002. Semesterarbeit.

63. A. Greenbaum. *Iterative Methods for Solving Linear Systems*. SIAM, Philadelphia, PA, 1997.

64. W. Gropp, E. Lusk, and A. Skjellum. *Using MPI: Portable Parallel Programming with the Message-Passing Interface*. MIT Press, Cambridge, MA, 1995.

65. M. J. Grote and Th. Huckle. Parallel preconditioning with sparse approximate inverses. *SIAM J. Sci. Comput.*, 18(3):838–853, 1997.

66. H. Grothe. Matrix generators for pseudo-random vector generation. *Statistical Lett.*, 28:233–238, 1987.

67. H. Grothe. Matrixgeneratoren zur Erzeugung gleichverteilter Pseudozufallsvektoren. PhD Thesis, Technische Hochschule Darmstadt, 1988.

68. Numerical Algorithms Group. G05CAF, 59-bit random number generator. Technical Report, Numerical Algorithms Group, 1985. NAG Library Mark 18.

69. M. Hegland. On the parallel solution of tridiagonal systems by wrap-around partitioning and incomplete LU factorizattion. *Numer. Math.*, 59:453–472, 1991.

70. D. Heller. Some aspects of the cyclic reduction algorithm for block tridiagonal linear systems. *SIAM J. Numer. Anal.*, 13:484–496, 1976.

71. J. L. Hennessy and D. A. Patterson. *Computer Architecture A Quantitative Approach*, 2nd edn. Morgan Kaufmann, San Francisco, CA, 1996.

72. M. R. Hestenes and E. Stiefel. Methods of conjugent gradients for solving linear systems. *J. Res. Nat. Bur. Standards*, 49:409–436, 1952.

73. Hewlett-Packard Company. *HP MLIB User's Guide. VECLIB, LAPACK, ScaLAPACK, and SuperLU*, 5th edn., September 2002. Document number B6061-96020. Available at URL http://www.hp.com/.

74. R. W. Hockney. A fast direct solution of Poisson's equation using Fourier analysis. *J. ACM*, 12:95–113, 1965.

75. Kai Hwang. *Advanced Computer Architecture: Parallelism, Scalability, Programmability*. McGraw-Hill, New York, 1993.

76. Intel Corporation, Beaverton, OR. *Paragon XP/S Supercomputer*, Intel Corporation Publishing, June 1992.

77. Intel Corporation, Beaverton, OR. *Guide Reference Manual (C/C++ Edition)*, March 2000. http://developer.intel.com/software/products/trans/kai/.

78. The Berkeley Intelligent RAM Project: A study project about integration of memory and processors. See http://iram.cs.berkeley.edu/.

79. F. James. RANLUX: A Fortran implementation of the high-quality pseudo-random number generator of Lüscher. *Comput. Phys. Commun.*, 79(1):111–114, 1994.

80. P. M. Johnson. Introduction to vector processing. *Comput. Design*, 1978.

81. S. L. Johnsson. Solving tridiagonal systems on ensemble architectures. *SIAM J. Sci. Stat. Comput.*, 8:354–392, 1987.

82. M. T. Jones and P. E. Plassmann. *BlockSolve95 Users Manual: Scalable library software for the parallel solution of sparse linear systems*. Technical Report ANL-95/48, Argonne National Laboratory, December 1995.

83. K. Kankaala, T. Ala-Nissala, and I. Vattulainen. Bit level correlations in some pseudorandom number generators. *Phys. Rev. E*, 48:4211–4216, 1993.

84. B. W. Kernighan and D. M. Richie. *The C Programming Language: ANSI C Version*, 2nd edn. Prentice Hall Software Series. Prentice-Hall, Englewood Cliffs, NJ, 1988.

85. Ch. Kim. RDRAM Project, development status and plan. RAMBUS developer forum, Japan, July 2–3, http://www.rambus.co.jp/forum/downloads/MB/2samsung_chkim.pdf, also information about RDRAM development http://www.rdram.com/, another reference about the CPU-Memory gap is http://www.acuid.com/memory_io.html.

86. P. E. Kloeden and E. Platen. *Numerical Solution of Stochastic Differential Equations*. Springer, New York, 1999.

87. D. Knuth. *The Art of Computer Programming, vol 2: Seminumerical Algorithms*. Addison Wesley, New York, 1969.

88. L. Yu. Kolotilina and A. Yu. Yeremin. Factorized sparse approximate inverse preconditionings I. Theory. *SIAM J. Matrix Anal. Appl.*, 14:45–58, 1993.

89. E. Kreyszig. *Advanced Engineering Mathematics*, John Wiley, New York, 7th edn, 1993.

90. LAM: An open cluster environment for MPI. http://www.lam-mpi.org.

91. S. Lavington. *A History of Manchester Computers.* British Computer Society, Swindon, Wiltshire, SN1 1BR, UK, 1998.

92. C. Lawson, R. Hanson, D. Kincaid, and F. Krogh. Basic linear algebra subprograms for Fortran usage. Technical Report SAND 77-0898, Sandia National Laboratory, Albuquerque, NM, 1977.

93. C. Lawson, R. Hanson, D. Kincaid, and F. Krogh. Basic linear algebra subprograms for Fortran usage. *ACM Trans. Math. Software*, 5:308–325, 1979.

94. A. K. Lenstra, H. W. Lenstra, and L. Lovacz. Factoring polynomials with rational coefficients. *Math. Ann.*, 261:515–534, 1982.

95. A. Liegmann. Efficient solution of large sparse linear systems. PhD Thesis No. 11105, ETH Zurich, 1995.

96. Ch. van Loan. *Computational Frameworks for the Fast Fourier Transform.* Society for Industrial and Applied Mathematics, Philadelphia, PA, 1992. (Frontiers in Applied Mathematics, 10.)

97. Y. L. Luke. *Mathematical Functions and their Approximations.* Academic Press, New York, 1975.

98. M. Lüscher. A portable high-quality random number generator for lattice field theory simulations. *Comput. Phys. Commun.*, 79(1):100–110, 1994.

99. Neal Madras. *Lectures on Monte Carlo Methods.* Fields Institute Monographs, FIM/16. American Mathematical Society books, Providence, RI, 2002.

100. George Marsaglia. Generating a variable from the tail of the normal distribution. *Technometrics*, 6:101–102, 1964.

101. George Marsaglia and Wai Wan Tsang. The ziggurat method for generating random variables. *J. Statis. Software*, 5, 2000. Available at URL http://www.jstatoft.org/v05/i08/ziggurat.pdf.

102. N. Matsuda and F. Zimmerman. PRNGlib: A parallel random number generator library. Technical Report, Centro Svizzero Calculo Scientifico, 1996. Technical Report TR-96-08, http://www.cscs.ch/pubs/tr96abs.html#TR-96-08-ABS/.

103. M. Matsumoto and Y. Kurita. Twisted GFSR generators. *ACM Trans. Model. Comput. Simulation*, pages part I: 179–194, part II: 254–266, 1992 (part I), 1994 (part II). http://www.math.keio.ac.jp/~matumoto/emt.html.

104. J. Mauer and M. Troyer. A proposal to add an extensible random number facility to the standard library. ISO 14882:1998 C++ Standard.

105. M. Metcalf and J. Reid. *Fortran 90/95 Explained.* Oxford Science Publications, Oxford, 1996.

106. G. N. Milstein. *Numerical Integration of Stochastic Differential Equations.* Kluwer Academic Publishers, Dordrecht, 1995.

107. G. E. Moore, Cramming more components into integrated circuits. *Electronics*, 38(8):114–117, 1965. Available at URL: ftp://download.intel.com/research/silicon/moorsepaper.pdf.

108. Motorola. Complex floating point fast Fourier transform for altivec. Technical Report, Motorola Inc., Jan. 2002. AN21150, Rev. 2.

109. MPI routines. http://www-unix.mcs.anl.gov/mpi/www/www3/.

110. MPICH—A portable implementation of MPI. http://www-unix.mcs.anl.gov/mpi/mpich/.

111. Netlib. A repository of mathematical software, data, documents, address lists, and other useful items. Available at URL http://www.netlib.org.

112. Numerical Algorithms Group, Wilkinson House, Jordon Hill, Oxford. *NAG Fortran Library Manual*. BLAS usage began with Mark 6, the Fortran 77 version is currently Mark 20, http://www.nag.co.uk/.

113. J. Ortega. *Introduction to Parallel and Vector Solution of Linear Systems*. Plenum Press, New York, 1998.

114. M. L. Overton. *Numerical Computing with IEEE Floating Point Arithmetic*. SIAM Books, Philadelphia, PA, 2001.

115. P. S. Pacheco. *Parallel Programming with MPI*. Morgan Kaufmann, San Francisco, CA, 1997.

116. Mpi effective bandwidth test. Available at URL http://www.pallas.de/pages/pmbd.htm.

117. G. Parisi. *Statistical Field Theory*. Addison-Wesley, New York, 1988.

118. O. E. Percus and M. H. Kalos. Random number generators for mimd processors. *J. Parallel distribut. Comput.*, 6:477–497, 1989.

119. W. Petersen. Basic linear algebra subprograms for CFT usage. Technical Note 2240208, Cray Research, 1979.

120. W. Petersen. Lagged fibonacci series random number generators for the NEC SX-3. *Int. J. High Speed Comput.*, 6(3):387–398, 1994. Software available at http://www.netlib.org/random.

121. W. P. Petersen. Vector Fortran for numerical problems on Cray-1. *Comm. ACM*, 26(11):1008–1021, 1983.

122. W. P. Petersen. Some evaluations of random number generators in REAL*8 format. Technical Report, TR-96-06, Centro Svizzero Calculo Scientifico, 1996.

123. W. P. Petersen. General implicit splitting for numerical simulation of stochastic differential equations. *SIAM J. Num. Anal.*, 35(4):1439–1451, 1998.

124. W. P. Petersen, W. Fichtner, and E. H. Grosse. Vectorized Monte Carlo calculation for ion transport in amorphous solids. *IEEE Trans. Electr. Dev.*, ED-30:1011, 1983.

125. A. Ralston, E. D. Reilly, and D. Hemmendinger (eds). *Encyclopedia of Computer Science*. Nature Publishing Group, London, 4th edn, 2000.

126. S. Röllin and W. Fichtner. Parallel incomplete lu-factorisation on shared memory multiprocessors in semiconductor device simulation. Technical Report 2003/1, ETH Zürich, Inst. für Integrierte Systeme, Feb 2003. Parallel Matrix Algorithms and Applications (PMAA'02), Neuchatel, Nov. 2002, to appear in special issue on parallel computing.

127. Y. Saad. Krylov subspace methods on supercomputers. *SIAM J. Sci. Stat. Comput.*, 10:1200–1232, 1989.

128. Y. Saad. SPARSKIT: A basic tool kit for sparse matrix computations. Technical Report 90-20, Research Institute for Advanced Computer Science, NASA Ames Research Center, Moffet Field, CA, 1990.

129. Y. Saad. *Iterative Methods for Sparse Linear Systems*. PWS Publishing Company, Boston, MA, 1996.

130. H. A. Schwarz. Ueber einen Grenzübergang durch alternirendes Verfahren. *Vierteljahrsschrift Naturforsch. Ges. Zürich*, 15:272–286, 1870. Reprinted in: Gesammelte Mathematische Abhandlungen, vol. 2, pp. 133-143, Springer, Berlin, 1890.

131. D. Sima. The design space of register renaming techniques. *IEEE Micro.*, 20(5):70–83, 2000.

132. B. F. Smith, P. E. Bjørstad, and W. D. Gropp. *Domain Decomposition: Parallel Multilevel Methods for Elliptic Partial Differential Equations.* Cambridge University Press, Cambridge, 1996.

133. B. T. Smith, J. M. Boyle, J. J. Dongarra, B. S. Garbow, Y. Ikebe, V. C. Klema et al. *Matrix Eigensystem Routines—EISPACK Guide.* Lecture Notes in Computer Science 6. Springer, Berlin, 2nd edn, 1976.

134. SPRNG: The scalable parallel random number generators library for ASCI Monte Carlo computations. See http://sprng.cs.fsu.edu/.

135. J. Stoer and R. Bulirsch. *Einführung in die Numerische Mathematik II.* Springer, Berlin, 2nd edn, 1978.

136. J. Stoer and R. Bulirsch. *Introduction to Numerical Analysis.* Springer, New York, 2nd edn, 1993.

137. H. Stone. Parallel tridiagonal equation solvers. *ACM Trans. Math. Software,* 1:289–307, 1975.

138. P. N. Swarztrauber. Symmetric FFTs. *Math. Comp.,* 47:323–346, 1986.

139. Nec sx-6 system specifications. Available at URL http://www.sw.nec.co.jp/hpc/sx-e/sx6.

140. C. Temperton. Self-sorting fast Fourier transform. Technical Report, No. 3, European Centre for Medium Range Weather Forcasting (ECMWF), 1977.

141. C. Temperton. Self-sorting mixed radix fast Fourier transforms. *J. Comp. Phys.,* 52:1–23, 1983.

142. Top 500 supercomputer sites. A University of Tennessee, University of Mannheim, and NERSC/LBNL frequently updated list of the world's fastest computers. Available at URL http://www.top500.org.

143. B. Toy. The LINPACK benchmark program done in C, May 1988. Available from URL http://netlib.org/benchmark/.

144. H. A. van der Vorst. Analysis of a parallel solution method for tridiagonal linear systems. *Parallel Comput.,* 5:303–311, 1987.

145. Visual Numerics, Houston, TX. *International Mathematics and Statistics Library.* http://www.vni.com/.

146. K. R. Wadleigh and I. L. Crawford. *Software Optimization for High Performance Computing.* Hewlett-Packard Professional Books, Upper Saddle River, NJ, 2000.

147. H. H. Wang. A parallel method for tridiagonal equations. *ACM Trans. Math. Software,* 7:170–183, 1981.

148. R. C. Whaley. Basic linear algebra communication subprograms: Analysis and implementation across multiple parallel architectures. LAPACK Working Note 73, University of Tennessee, Knoxville, TN, June 1994. Available at URL http://www.netlib.org/lapack/lawns/.

149. R. C. Whaley and J. Dongarra. Automatically tuned linear algebra software. LAPACK Working Note 131, University of Tennessee, Knoxville, TN, December 1997. Available at URL http://www.netlib.org/lapack/lawns/.

150. R. C. Whaley, A. Petitet, and J. Dongarra. Automated empirical optimization of software and the ATLAS project. LAPACK Working Note 147, University of Tennessee, Knoxville, TN, September 2000. Available at URL http://www.netlib.org/lapack/lawns/.

151. J. H. Wilkinson and C. Reinsch (eds). *Linear Algebra.* Springer, Berlin, 1971.

INDEX